PERSPECTIVES ON ABORTION

Edited by
PAUL SACHDEV

The Scarecrow Press, Inc.
Metuchen, N.J., and London
1985

363.460973
P467

Library of Congress Cataloging in Publication Data
Main entry under title:

Perspectives on abortion.

 Bibliography: p.
 Includes index.
 1. Abortion--United States--Addresses, essays,
lectures. 2. Abortion--Canada--Addresses, essays,
lectures. 3. Abortion--United States--Public opinion--
Addresses, essays, lectures. 4. Public opinion--
United States--Addresses, essays, lectures. 5. Abortion
--Addresses, essays, lectures. I. Sachdev, Paul.
HQ767.5.U5P47 1985   363.4'6'0973   84-10573
ISBN 0-8108-1708-X

To My Mother and Late Father
Whom I Revere for Their
Nobility and Ideals

CONTENTS

PREFACE

Few social practices have been as ancient and, culturally and geographically, as universal as abortion. For centuries, medical procedures as a means of abortion or euphemism for extracting a menstrual period have existed as solutions for unwanted pregnancies. Abortion, however, has rarely been treated like other surgical procedures. It generally has been available under certain conditions that vary from highly restrictive to less restrictive, depending on cultural, economic, and religious forces, sexual and marital values, and political lobbying. The abortion debate is centered on two opposing and irreconcilable positions: advocating the right of the women to reproductive freedom (pro-choice), and the right of the state to protect the fetus as developing life (pro-life).

The scientific evidence of the fetus being a person and alive from conception has reinforced the position of opponents of legalized abortion (Verny and Kelly, 1981). Aided by the conservatism of the 1980s, they made some political gains as reflected in the Helms-Hyde Amendments to restrict abortions through withdrawal of government funding or requiring of mandatory third party consent (Henshaw, et al., 1982; Time, April 6, 1981), actions viewed by the pro-choice forces as repressive and punitive. The pro-life group contends that unregulated abortions encourage irresponsible sex, weaken the resolve of unmarried women about contraception, and pose threats to traditional family values. The protagonists countercharge that sex is here to stay and, given the unreliability of modern contraceptive techniques, restricted abortions will only result in illegal and unsafe abortions or compulsory parenthood and unwanted children who are prone to developmental handicaps (Davis & Matejcek, 1981; Matejcek, et al., 1978; 1979; 1980; Simon, 1981). The most recent U.S. Supreme Court ruling (Akron Clinic vs. The State), which reaffirmed the constitutional rights of women to obtain an abortion without undue state interference, resulted in a stiffening of the resolve of pro-life and pro-choice advocates to refute each other's goal.

In this sense, abortion is more than a moral issue eluding a satisfactory resolution. It is also an emotional issue that involves the core of femininity, the woman's sexuality and her family, and symbolizes the rejection of her conventional role as childbearer. Despite the assurance offered by more recent studies on the psychological sequelae of abortion, the willful loss of the fetus remains a potential major trauma for many women because of the social significance of motherhood and the normative value regarding the sanctity of life. Since a woman's cultural and familial values greatly influence her emotional and psychological reactions, public attitudes that reflect increasing disapproval of abortion for eugenic reasons render her more vulnerable to potentially stressful abortion experience (Davis, 1980). The media with its provocative and passionate rhetoric further ignites emotional fervor, thus inhibiting prudent reflection on the issue.

The significant increase in unprotected sex that has resulted in an epidemic proportion of unintended pregnancies among teenagers seems to confirm the anti-abortionists' apprehensions about the effect of abortion on young unmarried women's sexual and contraceptive behavior (Westoff, et al., 1981; Zelnik & Kantner, 1980). The pro-choice group discounts this argument and places the onus on the absence of contraceptive instruction and sex education.

It appears that, given the complex mix of moral, political, social, economic, and medical factors, the problem of abortion is not an issue susceptible to permanent resolution. It can only be coped with, suggests Callahan (1970).

As the public debate rages on unabated, with no sign of resolution in sight, the demand for abortions continues steadily. There were 1.5 million abortions, or 42.8 per 100 live births, performed on women in the United States in 1980, up from 23.9 percent in 1973. For Canada, the abortion rates (per 100 live births) rose from 3 percent (11,200 abortions) in 1970 to 17.7 percent (65,053 abortions) in 1981 (Tietze, 1983).

Changes in social and political contexts as well as the increasing demand for abortion have provided a stimulus for examination of both traditional and newly emerging issues, ethical and scientific, which present new challenges for professionals in their roles as researchers, service providers, and teachers in the field. This volume provides, in one sourcebook, nineteen original essays contributed by distinguished scholars in the field who address the shifting public attitudes as they affect legislative dilemmas, policy decisions, research concerns, and abortion practice.

As American society continues to face heated battles between pro-choice and pro-life forces over conflicting rights and moralities, the book examines in Part I the abortion debate in its historical context, and the respective roles of Western Christian theology, human embryology, and cultural forces in the phenomenon of the anti-abortion movement. It offers insights for a more rational abortion policy that is balanced, morally acceptable, and sanguine in character. Since public policies and legislative trends are largely influenced by the way the dominant views on an issue prevail in society, Part III examines two national-opinion surveys of the 1960s and 1970s, to determine the contributory factors and the trends over time in the attitudes of the United States public and the service providers toward abortion, and their impact on the availability and utilization of abortion services.

Two issues of focal concern to professionals (and primary targets of anti-abortion activists) are the increasing number of abortions among young single women and the high incidence of repeat abortions. Since abortion is the most frequently performed operation in the United States, another focus of public health attention is the morbidity and mortality rates from legal abortions. Nevertheless, professional and public interest in the long-standing issue of the effect of abortion on women's psychological health and on the economic and emotional well-being of their families has not waned. These issues are the target of inquiry in Part II.

In Part IV, of particular relevance to clinical practitioners are two essays on abortion counseling that critically review empirical studies on this highly significant yet neglected component of abortion service, offering an organized presentation of counseling contents, processes, techniques, and potential benefits. The final chapter provides a synthesized overview of the issues discussed and their implications for abortion policy and practice.

Thus, covering the spectrum of the most salient of abortion issues, Perspectives on Abortion pertains to the interests of a wide variety of professionals and paraprofessionals, including physicians, social workers, psychiatrists, nurses, sociologists, psychologists, demographers, and hos-

pital administrators, as well as others whose professional
pursuits involve contact with women. The book may also
serve as a current reference text for courses in human sexuality, population, demography, counseling, women's studies,
and social-welfare policy. Nor need its benefit be limited to
a North American audience, easily extending to other countries where politicians and academics face the same public
debate and polarization in society regarding the rights of the
unborn versus the rights of women to reproductive freedom.
To further broaden the relevance of the book, data from
Canada, England, Scotland, Denmark, Yugoslavia, and Czech-
oslovakia have been included.

    This book was made possible only by the generous sup-
port and contributions of the most prominent investigators in
the field. I owe them a debt of gratitude for the diligence,
promptness, and intellectual humility with which they responded to my chevying and editorial comments. Special appreciation goes to Dr. Christopher Tietze who not only contributed a scholarly paper but also provided valuable assistance
overall.

                                    Paul Sachdev
                                    June 1983

References

Callahan, Daniel J. Abortion: Law, Choice and Morality.
    New York: Collier-Macmillan, 1970, p. 486.

Davis, H. P. , and Matejcek, Z. "Children Born to Women
    Denied Abortion: An Update. " Family Planning Perspec-
    tives, 1981, 13: 32-34.

Davis, J. A. General Social Surveys, 1972-1980: Cumula-
    tive Data. Chicago: National Opinion Research Center,
    1980.

Henshaw, S. ; Forrest, J. D. ; and Sullivan, E. "Abortion
    Services in the United States, 1979 and 1980. " Family
    Planning Perspectives, 1982, 14: 5-15.

Matejcek, Z. ; Dytrych, Z. ; and Schuller, V. "Children

from Unwanted Pregnancies." Acta Psychiatrica Scandi-
navia, 1978, 57: 67-90.

_____. "Follow-up Study of Children Born from Unwanted
Pregnancies." International Journal of Behavioral Development, 1980, 3: 243-251.

_____. "The Prague Study of Children Born from Unwanted
Pregnancies." International Journal of Mental Health, 1979,
7: 63-77.

Simon, Nathan M. "Women Who Are Refused and Who Refuse Abortion." In Abortion: Readings & Research, Paul
Sachdev, ed. Toronto: Butterworths, 1981.

Tietze, C. Induced Abortion: A World Review, 1983. New
York: The Population Council, 1983.

Verny, Thomas, and Kelly, John. The Secret Life of the
Unborn Child. New York: Summit Books, 1981. Also
see "Looking at Life Before Birth," The Evening Tele-
gram, September 28, 1974; "Fetus Deserved Shield of the
Law," Globe & Mail, January 20, 1981; "The Care Before
Birth," Globe & Mail, January 22, 1982; "Is the Fetus a
Patient?," Globe & Mail, February 4, 1983; "Fetus Con-
sidered Separate Being ...," Globe & Mail, May 6, 1983.

Westoff, C. F.; DeJung, J. S.; Goldman, N.; and Forrest,
J. D. "Abortion Preventable by Contraceptive Practice."
Family Planning Perspectives, 1981, 13: 218-223.

Zelnik, M., and Kantner, J. F. "Sexual Activity, Contraceptive Use and Pregnancy Among Metropolitan-Area Teenagers: 1971-1979." Family Planning Perspectives, 1980,
12: 230-237.

PART I:

THEORETICAL ISSUES IN ABORTION

THE HISTORICAL CHARACTER OF ABORTION IN THE UNITED STATES THROUGH WORLD WAR II

By James C. Mohr

Abortion has been practiced in the United States since the founding of the Republic, though both its social character and its demographic impact have varied considerably. In the late eighteenth century, Americans viewed abortion primarily as the recourse of women who wanted to rid themselves of pregnancies that resulted from illicit relationships. Medical guides contained abortion-related information and abortifacient recipes, and physicians could and did terminate pregnancies when confronted with various sorts of medical situations or with requests from their patients. But it is unlikely that abortion played a significant role in regulating the fertility of American women prior to 1800 (Mohr, 1978). Indeed, it is unlikely that anything played a significant role in regulating the fertility of American women prior to 1800, for birthrates in the United States at the end of the eighteenth century exceeded any ever recorded in Europe. As Americans began to reduce those record-high rates, however, the place of abortion in American life changed dramatically.

The most striking change was a sharp rise in the incidence of abortion in the United States after 1830, as the nation underwent a demographic transition to lower birthrates, since recognized as quite typical of modernizing societies. Demographers point out that during the twentieth century abortion has often played a key role in these transitions. Abdel Omran, for example, basing his opinion on the experiences of Japan and Chile, has observed "that when developing societies are highly motivated to accelerate their transition from high to low fertility, induced abortion becomes such a popular method of fertility control that it becomes a kind of epidemic" (Omran, 1971). Students of the modernization of Europe have alluded to similar trends there as well (Glass,

1940; Shorter, 1973). The testimony of scores of nineteenth-century observers now indicates conclusively that the United States was no exception to this common pattern. Contemporaries repeatedly asserted that abortion was a quantitatively significant factor in the reduction of American birthrates during the middle decades of the nineteenth century, and they would almost certainly have agreed with Omran's use of the word "epidemic."

The exact dimensions of that "epidemic" cannot be calculated with precision. Historians must rely upon indirect evidence and contemporary estimates. But the best informed and most systematic observers at the time were convinced that American women were aborting at least one of every five pregnancies by midcentury (Hale, 1866; Storer & Heard, 1968). Many analysts considered that ratio too conservative and placed the incidence of abortion much higher. Contemporaries also agreed that most of the women who were practicing abortion by the middle decades of the nineteenth century were married, white, and native-born. Prominent among them were young wives who wished to delay childbearing and middle-aged women who already had as many children as they wanted. In short, abortion had shifted from being a marginal practice of the desperate few to being a quantitatively significant factor in the effort of American women to regulate their own fertility (Mohr, 1978).

Abortion was certainly not the only, or even the primary, factor in America's demographic transition. Recent research confirms that contraceptive information was also being widely disseminated throughout the United States after 1830 and that some of the techniques advocated were at least partially effective even by modern standards (Reed, 1978). Yet modern demographers have noticed the paradox that an increased use of contraceptive techniques has frequently led to an increase rather than a decrease in abortion rates, at least in the short run. This is explained by the theory that people beginning to use contraceptive techniques have made a commitment to limit the size of their families, but they lack experience with the methods of contraception they have decided to try. The result is a high rate of "mistakes," or unwanted conceptions, and a consequent turning to abortion to erase them. This has occurred in twentieth-century societies, even when the contraceptive techniques themselves were extremely effective, once mastered (Omran, 1971).

In the United States during the nineteenth century several

successive generations of Americans were introduced to new
contraceptive techniques over a period of several decades and
were making mistakes with them.   They were also burdened
with the additional handicap that the techniques themselves
were frequently unreliable even when mastered.   This must
have greatly extended the period of reliance on abortion as
a quantitatively significant backstop for women who sought to
limit the number or to determine the spacing of their children
in nineteenth-century America.   Consequently, the gradual
commitment of Americans to contraceptive practices after the
1830s paradoxically increases, rather than decreases, the
likelihood that contemporary observers who testified to the
existence of a great upsurge of abortion in the United States
during the middle decades of the nineteenth century were
right.

Further evidence of the widespread practice of abortion in the United States during the nineteenth century can be
found in the fact that it became commercialized as early as
the 1840s.   Specialists advertised in the daily press their
willingness to provide abortion services.   Pharmaceutical
firms competed with one another in the lucrative marketplace
of purported abortifacients.   Local apothecaries did a brisk
business in such substances as cottonroot, which was never
prescribed in regular medical practice but had a popular rep-
utation as a mild and effective emmenagogue (Mohr, 1978).

Underlying the increased practice of abortion in nineteenth-century America lay two important factors.   The first
was the nearly universal adherence among Americans to the
old common-law notion of quickening.   The vast majority of
American women did not consider a pre-quickened fetus a
distinct human being with a separate existence of its own.
The historical evidence in support of this point is overwhelming.   Both those who accepted the new role of abortion in
American life and those who abhorred it concurred in this
judgment.   The great dividing line in the minds of most
Americans was set at quickening, the perception of fetal
movement near the midpoint of gestation, not at conception.
Abortions accomplished before quickening were on a continuum
extending back through the various forms of contraception, not
on a continuum reaching forward toward the various degrees
of murder.   Legislators often reflected this popular attitude
by linking abortion and contraception together in the regulatory
statutes they began to pass near midcentury (Mohr, 1978).

The second factor, closely related to the first, was

the legal status of abortion in the United States prior to the Civil War. A few states, frightened by the nation's declining birthrates, had moved to discourage the practice, but not to outlaw it. A few others, offended by the commercialization of abortion services, had enacted anti-advertising laws, but they were pitifully weak. And several states had put forward criminal statutes designed to punish abortionists who harmed their patients. But the quickening doctrine remained in effect in every jurisdiction in the United States as late as 1860, essentially unchanged from the days of British and colonial common law. Under this doctrine, the performance of an abortion, provided it took place prior to quickening and provided the woman was not injured, was not an indictable action (Mohr, 1978).

The second factor was the first to change. The nation's regular physicians, those who favored formal education and scientific research, mounted a major campaign to stamp out the epidemic of abortion in America. They undertook their crusade for a number of complex, interrelated, and overlapping reasons. First, they knew that gestation was a continuous process and that quickening was a relatively unimportant event in the development of a fetus. In the absence of any other dramatic event, they decided that the interruption of gestation at any given point after conception, even early in a pregnancy, was just as logically unjustifiable, and hence immoral, as interruption at any other given point, including late in pregnancy. Second, they considered themselves the supreme champions of life as an absolute value, including fetal life. This was an important part of their ideology and it was embodied in the Hippocratic Oath to which they were pledged. In this context, they were bitterly disappointed that the nation's main-line Protestant denominations quietly but consistently rebuffed their pleas to join the anti-abortion crusade of the post-Civil War era; right through the early decades of the twentieth century medical journals would remain full of grumbling about the reluctance of Protestant clergymen to denounce abortions as sinful under any circumstances. Third, many regular physicians tended to be both nativistic and anti-feminist; they attacked abortion with "race suicide" arguments and "women's place" arguments. Finally, regular physicians recognized in anti-abortion statutes a way to deploy the powers of the state against their irregular rivals in the medical field, especially midwives, botanics, and folk healers. In short, for many nineteenth-century physicians the abortion issue combined both their ideological worldview and their professional self-interest (Dorsett, 1908; Mohr, 1978; Wathan & Stucky, 1904).

Organized under the auspices of the American Medical Association and its affiliates at the state and local level and coordinated by Harvard-trained obstetrician Horatio Robinson Storer, this campaign peaked in the late 1860s and early 1870s. Using their organizational skills, their political influence, and their social standing, the physicians persuaded many state legislators to drop traditional quickening rules from their criminal codes, to revoke common-law immunities for women undergoing abortions, and to enlist the peripheral powers of the state (such as defining what was obscene) in support of the physicians' great crusade to reverse the surging incidence of abortion in the United States. The effect was to proscribe most, but not all, types of abortions as illegal actions carrying criminal penalties. Many of the statutes passed by the separate states during the post-Civil-War period remained literally unchanged through the 1960s; others were altered only in legal phraseology, not in basic philosophy. Taken as a whole, those laws established the official policies toward the practice of abortion that most Americans would live with through the first two thirds of the twentieth century (Mohr, 1978).

Official policy, however, does not always reflect public practice. This, to put it mildly, seems to have been the case with abortion in the United States. A series of events in Chicago neatly illustrate the situation during the first decade of the twentieth century. There, fired by the embarrassing and disturbing anomaly that their city was both the recognized abortion center of the Midwest and headquarters to the American Medical Association, which had spearheaded the drive to outlaw abortion in the United States, members of the Chicago Medical Society voted in January 1904 to explore what might be done to eliminate the practice in their area. Their president-elect believed that some 10,000 abortions were being performed annually in the city, despite prohibitive legislation that dated from 1867 and 1872.

As its first major step, the Medical Society staged a symposium on the problem of abortion in Chicago. It was held November 23, 1904, at the Public Library and proved highly successful. Leading legal scholars, the coroner of Cook County, and a spokesman for the city's Catholic hierarchy joined the physicians in offering papers; the assistant state's attorney, the registrar of vital statistics, the superintendent of the Chicago Home and Aid Society, and chief counsel for the Woman's Protective Association were among the participating discussants. All agreed that abortion was every bit as prevalent as the physicians feared, all agreed that something should be done about it, and all agreed to cooperate with the physicians in their efforts to enforce the state's anti-abortion laws.

During the early months of 1905, members of the Chicago Medical Society, working with the Women's Protective Association, persuaded some of the city's newspapers to drop the thinly disguised abortion-related advertisements they had been carrying. With the help of the state's attorney, the Medical Society also initiated prosecutions of two suspected abortionists in test cases. On the strength of these early successes the physicians decided to make their campaign an ongoing project, and they formally amended the constitution of the Chicago Medical Society in February 1906 to establish the Committee on Criminal Abortion as a permanent standing committee with "the right to co-operate with the proper legal authorities and with similar committees from other organizations whose purpose is the betterment of social conditions." Dr. Rudolph Weiser Holmes, a thirty-five year old obstetrician and gynecologist, became the committee's first permanent chairman. In May, the doctors agreed to back Holmes' efforts financially, should private contributions fail to cover his committee's expenses.

Holmes increased the pressure on Chicago's newspapers by visiting the editorial offices of each one accompanied by an attorney from the Legal Aid Society, a Paulist father, and the Medical Society's own special counsel, Joseph I. Kelly. Their moral suasion induced a few more dailies to suspend abortifacient advertisements and a postal "stop order" that Kelly obtained April 21, 1907, coerced the rest. In May of that year the Holmes committee triumphantly reported to the Medical Society that "the lay press had eliminated from their columns all advertisements pertaining to criminal abortion." Working with the coroner, the Cook County grand jury, and their own special counsel, the Holmes committee had also helped indict six more of the city's most notorious abortionists. Actions were pending against others. At the June meeting of the Medical Society, there was talk of persuading the governor to appoint a special assistant state's attorney, whose sole function would be to carry on the physicians' campaign against abortion in Chicago (Chicago Medical Society, 1907).

But no special assistant state's attorney was ever appointed. Instead, abortion-related advertisements began to reappear in the daily press, and one paper claimed those advertisements were worth some $50,000 per paper per year in revenue. Indictments were dropped for lack of evidence; juries usually refused to convict in the few cases that were carried forward. The press alleged that city officials had begun again to accept payoffs from abortionists in exchange for protection and immunity. A state legislator was said to be financially involved in one of Chicago's largest abortion hospitals. When it became clear that many of Chicago's abortions were being performed by Medical Society members, for whatever reasons, most physicians began to close ranks and to testify to one another's good standing and sound medical judgment. The permanent Committee on Criminal Abortion stopped reporting regularly to the Medical Society. In short, the crusade that seemed so successful in June 1907 was nearly defunct by 1908, four years after it began.

Holmes himself explained what had happened. Responding to a paper on criminal abortion that was read to the American Medical Association convention in 1908, Holmes minced no words:

> I have had the misfortune for three years to be a sort of mentor on criminal abortion work in Chicago. During this period I have presided over a committee of the Chicago Medical Society to investigate, and to attempt to eradicate the evil; I have come to the conclusion that the public does not want, the profession does not want, the women in particular do not want, any aggressive campaign against the crime of abortion.

Holmes' fellow Chicagoan Dr. R. S. Yarros supported the same contention. "To formulate laws and have them enacted is comparatively easy," observed Yarros. "To enforce a law is an entirely different thing. You can not enforce laws, as some of the speakers have already said, with which the public has little sympathy" (Yarros, 1908).

A prominent attorney told the Chicago Gynecological Society in 1910 that the nation's anti-abortion laws were almost invariably enforced for murder, rather than for abortion per se; "the authorities ordinarily do not wake up unless the victim dies." The United States, he concluded, was simply "hypocritical" on the subject of abortion (Zeisler, 1910). Perhaps H. N. Hawkins, a Denver lawyer, put it best. Addressing a symposium on criminal abortion called by the medical society of his city in 1903, he agreed with the physicians that abortion was rampant in Colorado despite adequate legislation designed to prohibit it. Yet only a few people had ever been convicted of performing abortions, and they were incompetents. His explanation for this state of affairs was right on the mark. "The people do not really feel very harshly toward the abortionist. It is only when a bungling job is done, where a woman is killed, that public outcry is heard" (Hawkins, 1903).

Hawkins' assessment of American attitudes at the beginning of the twentieth century was confirmed by what the physicians of Chicago had learned from their crusade, and it remained a reasonably accurate assessment of American attitudes for the next half century. In actual practice, the nation's criminal statutes on the subject of abortion were invoked during the first half of the twentieth century almost exclusively against those who harmed women; invoked, in other words, to regulate the practice of abortion, not to eliminate it. Cynics might even see such highly selective enforcement as a form of quality control, consciously or unconsciously condoned by the physicians, the public authorities, and the people. In any event, beneath the veil of illegality and prohibition, Americans continued to seek and receive abortion services. And most of those services were provided by physicians, notwithstanding the position of the American Medical Association (Taussig, 1936). This is not to say that the social character of abortion did not change in the twentieth century as the result of late nineteenth-century legislation. The practice was no longer commercially visible in the American press, for example, and few voices defended the practice publicly as some of the nation's irregular medical practitioners had done in the nineteenth century. But abortion certainly did not disappear in the United States.

The most significant social shifts in the historical role of abortion in the early twentieth century probably had less to do with official proscription than with two related demographic factors. The first was the spread of contraceptive sophistication among those groups that had accounted for the increased incidence of abortion since the middle decades of the nineteenth century: married, white, native-born women. The economic demographers Paul David and Warren Sanderson, for example, discovered that "native born white women of native parentage living in Rhode Island, Cleveland and Minneapolis had lower cumulative fertility in 1900 than did similar women in the United States in 1970" (David & Sanderson, 1976). Contemporaries and historians agreed that those low rates were attributable primarily to the increased use and effectiveness of contraception. To put it differently, as contraceptive techniques improved, abortion declined as a primary method of family limitation among native-born American women. For most of those people, abortion once again took on the character it had at the outset of the nineteenth century; it was a discreet way to terminate an indiscreet pregnancy. The net result, based upon contemporary observations and impressions, appears to have been a leveling off, and perhaps a modest decrease, in the rate of abortion in the country as a whole during the first three decades of the twentieth century. The most thorough analyst of abortion patterns in the United States between 1900 and 1936, Dr. Frederick Taussig of Washington University, believed that the ratio of abortions in the United States had fallen to fewer than one for every seven confinements by the turn of the twentieth century, and, significantly, that illegitimacy was "the dominant factor" among those who continued to have abortions (Taussig, 1936).

The second factor involves the somewhat contradictory observation that even while leveling off in the nation as a whole, abortion rates probably increased among lower-class, especially immigrant, women in the United States during the first third of the twentieth century. Again, contemporary observers certainly believed that this was the case, as anyone familiar with the career of Margaret Sanger will remember (Kennedy, 1970; Mohr, 1978). Moreover, demographers have witnessed similar patterns in other societies. To quote Omran once again (Omran, 1971):

> In the early stage of transition [to low birthrates], the socially mobile, upper stratum of society adopts small family-size norms more readily and frequently resorts to induced abortion to limit births. With a rise in educational levels and a stabilization of family-size norms, this group turns increasingly to contraception. Yet while the need to resort to abortion decreases for the upper stratum, the abortion wave is maintained, often at epidemic level, because each of the lower strata cohorts also pass [sic] through a state of abortion proneness.

The final significant shift in the historical character of abortion in the United States prior to World War II took place at the onset of the Great Depression. Taussig amassed data that indicate a gradual increase in abortion rates from

1900 through 1928, with a temporary peak during the hard years right after World War I, followed by a sharp and dramatic upsurge as soon as the depression struck. By the mid-1930s Taussig calculated that there was one abortion for every four pregnancies in the United States, and he pointed out that 90 percent of those abortions were being performed upon married women. Abortion had once again become a significant factor in regulating fertility in the United States (Taussig, 1936).

Among the explanations offered for the resurgence of abortion in America during the 1930s, two stand out. One was the obvious fact that far more women found themselves in the plight faced by immigrants two decades before. It was as if Omran's "wave" hit bottom and began to well back up through the social structure. It is unlikely, however, that the increase in abortion during the 1930s represents a conscious choice to abandon contraception as a prime means of fertility control and return instead to abortion. It is more reasonable to assume that the difference between abortion rates in the 1920s and those in the 1930s approximates the national "mistake rate" in the use of contraception. During the 1920s, many women may have been willing, however reluctantly, to accept many of those "mistakes," so abortion rates remained low. In the 1930s, however, too desperate to continue to be willing to do so, they took action to erase the mistakes, thus raising the national abortion rates.

The second factor was the shifting role of women in American society. Both recent research and modern experience confirm Taussig's insightful suggestion that the changing place of abortion in the United States, as early as the 1930s, was also related to what he called "the revolt of womankind against the age-long domination of man" and "to the right of women to control their own bodies" (Taussig, 1936). In short, two of the underlying historical patterns that would help produce a shift in official policy during the 1960s and 1970s-- the renewed importance of abortion as a method of fertility control and the desire of women to determine for themselves without state interference when they wished to carry a pregnancy to term--had already been established by World War II.

References
_____

Chicago Medical Society. Minutes, 1904-1907. Chicago:

Manuscript Division of the Chicago Historical Society. Unpublished manuscript, 1907.

David, Paul A. , and Sanderson, Warren C. "Contraceptive Technology and Fertility Control in Victorian America: From Facts to Theories." Memorandum No. 202. Stanford University: Center for Research on Economic Growth, June 1976.

Dorsett, Walter B. "Criminal Abortion in Its Broadest Sense." Journal of the American Medical Association, 1908, 51 (12): 957.

Glass, David V. Population Policies and Movements in Europe. New York: n. p. , [1940] 1967, pp. 278-82.

Hale, Edwin M. A Systemic Treatise on Abortion. Chicago: n. p. , 1866.

Hawkins, H. N. "The Practiced Working of the Law Against Criminal Abortion." Colorado Medical Journal, 1903, 9 (4): 153-56.

Kennedy, David M. Birth Control in America: The Career of Margaret Sanger. New Haven, Conn. : Yale University Press, 1970.

Mohr, James C. Abortion in America: The Original and Evolution of National Policy, 1800-1900. New York: Oxford University Press, 1978.

Omran, Abdel R. "Abortion in the Demographic Transition". In Rapid Population Growth: Consequences and Policy Implications, edited by the National Academy of Sciences. Baltimore: Johns Hopkins University Press, 1971.

Reed, James W. From Private Vice to Public Virtue: The Birth Control Movement in American Society Since 1830. New York: n. p. , 1978.

Shorter, Edward. "Female Emancipation, Birth Control, and Fertility in European History." American Historical Review, 1973, 78 (3): 605-40.

Storer, Horatio R. , and Heard, Franklin F. Criminal Abortion: Its Nature, Its Evidence, and Its Law. Cambridge, Mass. : n. p. , 1868.

Taussig, Frederick J. Abortion, Spontaneous and Induced: Medical and Social Aspects. London: Kimpton, 1936.

Wathan, W. H. , and Stucky, J. A. In C. J. Aud, "In What Per Cent is the Regular Profession Responsible for Criminal Abortion, and What is the Remedy?" Kentucky Medical Journal, 1904, 2 (4): 95-101.

Yarros, R. S. "Discussion." Journal of the American Medical Association, 1908, 51 (2): 960-61.

Zeisler, Sigmond. "The Legal and Moral Aspects of Abortion," Surgery, Gynecology, and Obstetrics, 1910, 10: 539.

INTELLECTUAL HISTORY OF ABORTION

By Malcolm Potts

In contemporary western democracies, abortion legislation has become a most divisive topic. It is the prototype of single-issue policies in the United States. In several countries it has led to outcomes that run counter to most people's intuition: in Italy a referendum rejected the Pope's plea to outlaw abortion and in Austria, one of the most homogenously Catholic countries in Europe, abortion is permitted on request of the woman during the first trimester of pregnancy. A Life poll taken in the United States (1981) found that only 56 percent of individuals asked felt abortion was morally and licitly acceptable, but 67 percent agreed that women should have access to safe abortion facilities, if needed.

Why has this situation arisen? This chapter explores historical attitudes toward abortion within Western Christendom. A brief review will raise as many questions as it answers, but it is hoped that it will add some depth to current discussions and help those who adopt opposing positions to establish a debate rather than create battle lines.

Any discussion of the rights and wrongs of abortion, in the past or today, has to attempt to build a bridge between whatever knowledge of human embryology exists and current religious beliefs and ethical judgments. While such debates can be traced forward from the classical world, through the Early Fathers of the Church, the Middle Ages, and past the watershed of the Reformation, abortion became a general and insistent theme only as the incidence rose with the urbanization and industrialization of the Western world.

Abortion Techniques

Nearly all societies have some knowledge of abortion tech-

niques (Deveraux, 1960). Herbal remedies for abortion are
virtually universal, although some rely more on the probability of spontaneous abortion occurring and being interpreted
as the result of the medication than on genuine pharmacologic
effects on the uterus or embryo. Trauma to the abdomen is
frequently recognized as a possible precursor of abortion,
and massage abortion is common in the Orient (Narkavonnakit,
1979). In the West, mechanical manipulation of the cervix
followed by deliberate rupture of the fetal membranes has
been the most used method (International Fertility Research
Program [IFRP], 1981). Archaeologic excavation of Roman
sites has uncovered both vaginal speculae and uterine sounds.
The modern technique of cervical dilatation and uterine curettage began to develop in France in the eighteenth century and
was fully evolved by the end of the nineteenth century (Nelson, 1945). Vacuum-aspiration abortion was first described
in 1863 by James Young Simpson, the Edinburgh gynecologist
who helped popularize obstetric anesthesia by giving Queen
Victoria chloroform in 1863. In 1863, in a series called,
Clinical Lectures on Diseases of Women, he described a number of "techniques for the restoration of catamenial [menstrual]
function." Later he wrote:

> I have made frequent use of a tube resembling in
> length and size a male catheter, with a large num-
> ber of thickly set small orifices stretching about
> two inches from its extremity, and have an exhaust-
> ing syringe adapted to its outer lower extremity....
> The use of this instrument is in some cases attended
> with striking results.

Simpson's technique was rediscovered by the Russian
Bykov in 1927, but subsequently it seems to have been lost,
only to be rediscovered by Wu and Wu in China in 1958. Many
Japanese doctors who worked in China during World War II
seem to have known the method (Potts, et al., 1977). By the
late 1950s and early 1960s, it had spread to Japan, Russia,
and eastern Europe. In 1967 Kerslake (Kerslake & Casey,
1967) began to use suction termination in Britain, introducing
the method to much of the English-speaking world. By 1969,
one third of all terminations in England and Wales were performed by vacuum aspiration. In 1937, M. B. Beric had
pioneered outpatient abortion under local anesthesia, using
dilatation and curettage, and in 1966 his son, B. M. Beric,
combined paracervical block with vacuum aspiration, a technique Branch brought to the United States a few years later.
Harvey Karman, a California lay psychiatrist, developed an

outpatient procedure using vacuum aspiration and soft plastic instruments in the early 1960s (Potts, et al. , 1977).

The Ancient World to the Seventeenth Century

Until the seventeenth century, the few people who had the privilege of education shared a common body of knowledge, in which scientific understanding and religious belief were woven together--the biologists looked for the hand of God in the works of nature, and the theologians read Aristotle as well as Aquinas. However, even within this framework, two interpretations of abortion existed. One adopted a gradualist interpretation of development and did not condemn abortion in extraordinary terms; the other emphasized an absolutist view, condemning abortion as equivalent to murder.

Biology, from the time of Aristotle (384-322 B. C.), has supported a gradualist viewpoint. Embryologic knowledge, in large part, was limited to naked-eye observation of an incubated hen's egg broken upon on various days of development. When Aristotle attempted to explain embryology, he was thinking of the chick model. He was to influence the Early Fathers of the Christian Church, and his writings remained important for the next 2,000 years. In On the Generation of Animals (Peck, 1953), Aristotle used the idea of the soul as a causal explanation for embryologic development:

> The problem before us is not Out of What, but, By What, are [embryos] formed? Either something external fashions them, or else something present in the semen or seminal fluid; that is either some part of the Soul, or something which possesses the Soul.

The soul in this context is not too far removed from the modern Aristotelian embryologists' use of the term inducer, or the biochemists' enzyme. Indeed, the action of the soul in embryology was sometimes compared to that of rennet on milk (Needham, 1959), and this concept was passed on later to Jewish thinkers (Job 10:10-12) and into Christian thought (Feldman, 1974).

The Romans, like the Greeks, considered abortion a crime against the husband rather than homicide. The poet Ovid (43 B. C. -A. D. 18) wrote:

> Now she that wishes to seem beautiful harms her womb.

> And rare in these days is the one who would be a
> parent.

There is a disapproving tone, but no suggestion that abortion should be equated with murder.

In the Bible there is only one verse that refers to abortion in any legal or moral sense (Exodus 21: 22-23):

> If men strive, and hurt a woman with child, so that
> her fruit depart from her, and yet no mischief fol-
> low: he shall be surely punished, according as the
> woman's husband will lay upon him; and he shall
> pay as the judges determine.
>
> And if any mischief follow, then thus shalt give
> life for life.

The injunction seems to refer to a wide range of pregnancy stages and might even be interpreted as meaning premature labor. Such an interpretation would fit with the Old Testament theme of God breathing life in man's nostrils at birth and would leave the whole interval prior to childbirth in a separate, less than fully human, category. Augustine (A. D. 354-430), Jerome, Tertullian, and others were to comment on this verse. Augustine states, "the law does not provide that the act pertains to homicide, because still there cannot be said to be a live soul in a body that lacks servation" (Noonan 1965).

The absolutist interpretation of nature that condemns abortion also has a long history. The Hippocratic oath includes a rejection of abortion, although historically it appears to be a less fulsome rejection of the operation than a modern reading might suggest. It is uncertain how much, if any, of the oath associated with the name of Hippocrates (c460-370 B. C.) can be ascribed to the Greek physician and how much is subsequent embroidery on the mantle of his fame. Edelstein (1942) sees the oath as an expression of conflict between the absolutes of the Pythagorean school of philosophers and the general liberality of the rest of the Greek world. Elsewhere, in a work ascribed to Hippocrates, there is a description of a graduated set of dilators similar in shape to those devised by Hegar in Germany only a hundred years ago and still widely used.

Of course, Judeo-Christian doctrine did come to condemn infanticide and child abandonment, ranging against those practices in Roman times (Callahan, 1970; Noonan, 1967). In A. D. 374, more than fifty years after Constantine recognized Christianity, killing an infant was declared homicide. It seems plausible to assume that at this time the treatment of a delayed menstrual period (which no doubt was a hoped for possibility in ancient times, as in nearly all contemporary societies) was still perceived as far removed from the concept of taking a life. In a second-century letter Barnabas writes, "Thou shalt not kill the fetus by an abortion or commit infanticide." The rejection, getting stronger but perhaps still not complete, should be read in the light of the exceptionally limited knowledge of human development available at the time, when absolutist and gradualist interpretations ran side by side. In A. D. 240 Tertullian wrote, "It is not lawful to destroy what is conceived in the womb while the blood is still being formed into a man" [emphasis added]. The Eastern Church was stricter than the Latin tradition. St. Basil the Great wrote in A. D. 376-375, "A woman who deliberately destroys a fetus is answerable for murder. And any fine distinction as to its being completely formed or unformed is not admissible to us." Yet Augustine allowed the distinction between the "unformed" and "formed" fetus. The first systematic attempt to gather ecclesiastical legislation (Gratian's Decretum, A. D. 1140) states, "He is not a murderer who brings about abortion before the soul is in the body." Overall, in the words of Noonan, Catholic theology, "treated the embryo's life as less than absolute, but only the value of the mother's life was given greater weight."

Until the nineteenth century and beyond, the soul was regarded as having a physical location in both the embryo and the adult. The soul was seen as the manufacturing process that created the solid embryo from the liquid semen and also as the force that made the nervous system work. Just as medieval painters saw the soul as an entity flying from Heaven to the womb, so the early anatomists saw the soul as residing in a specific place. (When we say "Bless you!" after a sneeze, we document the once-held idea that the human soul resides in the pituitary gland at the base of the brain. It was thought that the mucus from the nose, which anatomists observed extends to within a fraction of an inch away from the pituitary, contained an essence that it endangered the soul to lose.) Even Leonardo da Vinci could draw a cross-section of a human skull with meridians showing where to find the soul (Brazier, 1979).

The problem of how and when the human soul entered the embryo was also a real and significant one for the classical and medieval thinker. It was again a subject that divided into two themes: was it an instant effect like "Nescafé" or a slow maturity like good wine? The problem was that even the chick embryo manifestly grew and became more complicated, while the soul was absolute, discrete, and immutable. Hence, the tradition grew of a <u>vegetable</u> and a <u>rational</u> soul. Already by the time of Aquinas, there was a need to divide the idea of the soul into parts, which in turn influenced judgments about abortion. The soul was subject to the doctrine of original sin, which can only be washed away by baptism. To quote Augustine:

> Hold fast to this truth, that not only men of rational age, but even babies who, having begun to live in the mother's womb, either die there or, already born, die without the sacrament of baptism in the name of the Father, Son and Holy Ghost, pass from this world to be punished in eternal fire.

Of course, the phrase "begun to live" must be read in the light of what was contemporary embryology. Fertilization was not understood and nothing was known about the first month of development. The doctrine that the unbaptized child went to hell held consistent for over 1,000 years of Western history (Coulton, 1922). In the sixth century St. Fulgentius wrote:

> It is believed beyond doubt that not only men who come to the use of reason, but infants, whether they die in their mother's womb, or after they are born, without baptism ... are punished with everlasting punishment in eternal fire, because though they have no actual sin of their own, yet they carry along with them the condemnation of original sin from their first conception and birth.

Before the Church was split by the Reformation, the Council of Florence (1439) decreed:

> The souls of those dying in actual mortal sin, or in original sin alone, go down at once into hell, to be punished, however, with different punishments.

Seventeenth to Nineteenth Century

The explosion of modern scientific knowledge, the maturing

of the Counter-Reformation and the rise of the modern state
with its emphasis on individual liberties, all had an impact
on the way in which society viewed abortion. The divorce
between the absolutists' and the gradualists' interpretations
of embryology and theology became greater and, in turn, the
disciplines themselves underwent a great separation.

On the whole, embryology lagged behind other aspects
of biology. It required the invention of the microscope, the
unifying idea of the cell theory, and insights into genetics for
embryology to move forward. Sperm were first seen by the
Dutchman van Leeuwenhoek in 1677 (Needham, 1959). In
keeping with the theory that the woman was the field in which
the man sowed his seed, many early microscopists claimed
to see exceedingly minute forms of men with arms, heads,
and legs in each sperm. Such a preformist theory that development was merely concerned with the enlargement of a
perfectly formed miniature human being, had it been confirmed, would have been supported as an absolutist interpretation of abortion.

The understanding of the early stages of mammalian
development was especially slow to develop. Although, William Harvey deduced the nature of the circulatory system,
he failed to understand basic steps in mammalian reproduction. King Charles provided Harvey with deer as experimental animals, unwittingly giving him a species in which egg
implantation is delayed, so there was no visible link between
coital behavior in the autumn and the development of the fawn
after the winter season. Mammalian eggs were only recovered
from the fallopian tubes by Cruickshank in 1797.

The seventeenth-century divorce of science and theology, symbolized by the trial of Galileo, began to move especially far apart in the case of embryology, although the
impact of this division was only to become clear in the nineteenth century and have its maximum impact in the twentieth
century. While the early embryologists were escaping from
the preformist theories of development and recognizing the
processes of epigenesis, or gradual development, that char-
acterize vertebrate development, theologians sought increasingly mechanical and absolutist explanations of the status of
the early embryo. The doctrine of Limbo, as an element
set beside Heaven and Hell, was devised to accommodate the
Fathers of the Old Testament who lived before Christ, vir-
tuous pagans, and Christians who died unbaptized, especially
embryos. Cardinal Roberto Bellarmine (1542-1621), the
Counter-Reformation theologian who moved the trial of Galileo,

wrote at length on the topic (Coulton, 1922). He dismissed, as a Protestant error, the idea that an unbaptized child might merely enter the Kingdom of Heaven, and he refuted the possibility that the fetus might enter a place outside heaven: "Let no man promise unto unbaptized infants any sort of intermediate place of any rest or happiness whatsoever between damnation and the Kingdom of Heaven." At the same time, it seemed intuitively unjust to condemn an unborn child to eternal punishment and doubly contrary to natural justice if the embryo died in utero, making baptism mechanically impossible. Bellarmine and many other theologians softened as much as possible the implications of the argument that unborn children must go to hell:

> I say, therefore, that unbaptized children will feel mental pain, since they will understand themselves to be deprived of bliss, severed from the company of pious brethren and parents, thrust into the dungeon of hell, and destined to spend their lives in eternal darkness.

Intuitively, he wanted to escape the box his absolutes had built, so he went on: "But I hold, for many reasons, that this pain of theirs will be very slight and mild; partly because they had only the remotest disposition toward bliss."

Biologists were also slow to cast off the influence of prior centuries. Descartes held that the soul resided in the pineal gland, Willis, in the white matter of the brain, and, as late as the nineteenth century, the German Pfluger located the soul in the spinal cord. Today, no scientist or theologian would turn to the index of Gray's Anatomy and expect to find a reference to the human soul.

Yet even at its most extreme, the absolutist interpretation did not completely triumph. Both Canon and secular law were forced to make some accommodations and although certain medieval states had imposed the death penalty for inducing abortion (in Germany the man was put to death by the sword and the woman drowned), with the rise of the modern state in the sixteenth century onward, a pragmatic and tolerant legal tradition arose, largely uninfluenced by the speculations of biologists or the assertions of theologians.

English Common Law made a distinction between early and late abortion, drawing the dividing line at quickening. Bracton, in the thirteenth century, only considered abortion to be homicide after animation, or entry of the soul. This distinction also applied in the North American colonies. Prior to 1803 in Britain, abortion before quickening was not regarded as a crime and even abortion later in pregnancy was not severely punished, but in North America a midwife could be dismissed for performing an abortion before or after quickening. The great Elizabethan lawyer Edward Coke believed abortion after quickening was a "great misprison" or misdemeanor, not a murder (Williams, 1958).

At times, some theologians found abortion more easily justified than contraception--for example, Sanchez (1550-1610) and Callahan (1970). The moral philosopher Saint Alphonsus Liguori (1696-1787) also allowed some latitude to the performance of abortion. However, the divorce of natural science and theological science had gone too deep to allow this line of thinking to develop fully.

The polarization of views on abortion was a microcosm of the wider religious issues that led to the Counter-Reformation, yet it was from the scorched earth of the Wars of Religion that the need for religious toleration eventually grew. When Thomas Paine (1737-1809) wrote in the Rights of Man, "Tolerance is not the opposite of intolerance, but is the counterfeit of it. Both are despotisms," the suffering caused by religious conflicts was more visible and his vision correspondingly wider than we sometimes enjoy.

Nineteenth Century to Today

The mammalian egg was first seen in 1827, although a living human egg was not recovered until 1930. Barry described some of the stages in the development of the rabbit blastocyst in 1838. The processes of cellular division were unravelled with the help of Hofmister's work on plants in the 1840s. In 1852, Newport described fertilization in the frog and in the last quarter of the nineteenth century reproductive science began to move forward, although extrapolation from animal observations to the human situation continued to be accompanied by mistakes. (Nearly all nineteenth-century writers assumed that menstruation in women and vaginal bleeding in bitches had a similar relationship to ovulation.) Experimental embryology began in the early twentieth century with work on amphibians, and systematic experiments on mammalian development have really taken off only in the mid-twentieth century and after (Potts, 1982).

The nineteenth century saw the first great upsurge in the number of induced abortions being performed, as Mohr has also noted in tracing the pattern of abortion in the United States in Chapter 1. By 1889 in Britain, Rentoul wrote, "Everyone must notice that, although the number of marriages is on the increase." In 1896 the Chrimes brothers set up a mail-order business in London for the sale of a simple blood tonic that their advertisements implied was an abortifacient. The brothers attempted to blackmail the women who wrote in to purchase the remedy, but their plan was exposed and they were arrested and jailed. In the course of two years, they had collected a file of over 10,000 names. In France, in 1868, one commentator wrote that abortion had grown "into a veritable industry."

Against a background of slow-but-sure expansion of biological knowledge and growing evidence of an epidemic of abortions, the Church, especially the Catholic Church, became increasingly conservative. Tragically, scientists and theologians stopped speaking a mutually understandable language and, at the parish level, the Counter-Reformation doctrines of Bellarmine reached their crudest forms (Coulten, 1922). As late as 1850 a Dublin priest, in a tract with the simple title Books for Children (Furniss, 1850), wrote in short, clear sentences:

> See! It is a pitiful sight. The little child is in this red hot oven. Hear how it screams to come out. See how it turns and twists itself about in the fire. It beats its head against the roof of the oven. It stamps its little feet on the floor of the oven.

One part of the contemporary Western debate on abortion would seem to represent a return to this absolutist tradition in Western thought. When contemporary United States Congressmen set up committees to ask, "When does human life begin?" they are not asking a scientific question but seeking support for a religious belief. They are no more likely to find an embryologist who is able to answer the question than an astronomer who might train his telescope on a specified constellation and locate a physical counterpart of heaven.

At a more sophisticated level, the Catholic Church in the nineteenth century continued to harmonize the reality of abortion with moral absolutes well into the nineteenth century. The distinction between the "formed" and the "unformed" fetus

was not eliminated until 1869, when Pope Pius IX wrote Apos-
tolicae Sedis. The possibility of abortion was written out of
Canon Law in 1917 (Callahan, 1970) at about the very time
that late nineteenth-century developments in medical technology
allowed surgeons to operate for ectopic pregnancy, creating
a new theological challenge. With some logic, the operation
was condemned along the same lines as other abortions, and
in 1902 the Holy Office rejected arguments justifying operations for ectopic pregnancy, even though the woman was virtually certain to die if not operated upon. Subsequently, however, operations to abort an ectopic pregnancy were judged
licit, by involving the principle of double effect (Vermeersch,
quoted by Bouscaren, 1943).

The second half of the nineteenth century saw some
changes in the law as well. Britain passed a restrictive
abortion law in 1861, although there was no discussion of
the Bill on the floor of the House of Commons, or in the
country as a whole, and it may have been a shortcut in draft-
ing, as much as a deliberate legislative action, that removed
the preexisting freedom to perform abortion prior to quickening (Potts, et al. , 1977). Whatever the origin of the law,
it was rapidly disseminated through the British Empire. Restrictive laws, derived from the Code Napoleon, likewise spread
through French colonies, while the emerging nations of Latin
America and even Thailand, Japan, and Iran, which had never
become European colonies, all adopted "Western" restrictive
abortion legislation. Lenin passed the first liberal abortion
law in Europe on November 18, 1920. The philosophy behind
it overlapped with some of the arguments that were to be
made to the United States Supreme Court half a century later:

> During the past decades the number of women re-
> sorting to artificial discontinuation of pregnancy has
> grown both in the West and this country. The leg-
> islation of all countries combats this evil by punish-
> ing the woman who chooses to have an abortion and
> the doctor who performs it. Without leading to
> favorable results, this method of combating abor-
> tions has driven the operation underground ... as
> a result, up to 50% of such women are infected in
> the course of the operation, and up to 4% of them
> die.

It is important to note that the Russian law was changed on
the basis of female equality and in recognition of a woman's
right to control her own fertility and was without demographic

considerations. Lenin believed women should have the right "of deciding for themselves a fundamental issue of their lives" (David, 1970, p. 206).

By contrast, the totalitarian regimes of the 1920s and 1930s condemned abortion. In a change that may yet adumbrate contemporary attitudes in North America, the Russian law was reversed in 1935, and on June 27, 1936, the Council of the People's Commissars decided, with a few defined exceptions for health and inherited disease, "to forbid the performance of abortion whether in hospitals, special institutions, or in the homes of doctors and the private homes of pregnant women." Violations of the law were to be punished by two or three years' imprisonment. Maternity homes and kindergartens were made more numerous and alimony regulations stricter.

Elsewhere in Europe abortion remained illegal, except in Iceland, where a reform law was passed in 1935. However, abortion became especially common during the Depression. In Hamburg, for example, in 1930 it was estimated that there was one abortion for every birth (Taussig, 1936). In Germany as a whole it was thought between 600,000 and 800,000 illegal operations took place annually, or twice the rate of legal abortions in the contemporary United States. The National Socialist party attempted to stem this tide:

> Women inflamed by Marxist propaganda claim the right to bear children only when they desire, first furs, radio, new furniture, then perhaps a child. The use of contraceptives means a violation of nature, a degradation of womanhood, motherhood and love. Nazi ideals demand that the practice of abortion shall be exterminated with a strong hand.
> Adolf Hitler (quoted by Davis, 1938).

Five years before Hitler invaded Sudetenland in 1938, he had invaded the bedroom of every citizen of the Third Reich. In a series of moves designed to "protect" the family, the equality of women was curbed, religious education in schools made compulsory, homosexuality punished, and marriage loans and child allowances initiated. A woman with eight or more children was given a gold Honour Cross of the German Mother "since the risks to health and life she incurs for Volk and Fatherland are the same as those equal of the soldier in the thunder of battle." Above all, the Fascists tightened up anti-contraception and anti-abortion legislation, beginning in Italy in 1927. In Germany, immediately after the Nazis came to power in 1933, every family planning clinic was closed, jail sentences of six to fifteen years were imposed on doctors convicted of performing abortions, and a unique effort was made to register all pregnancies. Even the nonpregnant women who attempted an abortion could be prosecuted. Penalties of solitary confinement and hard labor for life were imposed (Greenberger, 1971). Ernst Grafenberg, one of the pioneers of intrauterine devices (IUDs), had to flee the country (Lehfeldt, 1975).

During World War II and within a few months of signing the Armistice with Hitler, Marshal Pétain of the Vichy Government of France found time to pass a law making abortion a capital offense, and Madame Giraud, a laundress who had performed twenty-six abortions, went to the guillotine in February 1942 for her crime. With Teutonic logic, a similar law was passed in Germany in 1943. (Fedou, 1946; Watson, 1952). For a few years and under extreme circumstances, the absolutist interpretation of abortion had found its logical expression.

Conclusions

The two sides in contemporary abortion debate have roots that can be traced far back in the history of Western thought. It will be difficult but may not be impossible to bring them into harmony. It is notable that, from biblical times through the early Fathers of the Church and the Counter-Reformation, an absolutist interpretation--outlawing all abortions under all circumstances--has never held sway for long without being challenged by a more gradualist theme. Conversely, although the philosophy that abortion is a woman's right is more recent, it must also come to be blunted by the facts of biology and the realities of social life, just as the United States Supreme Court ruling of 1973 recognized that after "some point in time another interest, that of the health of the mother or her potential human life, becomes significantly involved."

Few people who support liberal abortion legislation actually believe a woman has a absolute right over the embryo at all stages of pregnancy and conversely pro-life supporters back away from the suggestion that abortion legalization should outlaw IUDs and oral contraceptives, which in some cases act after fertilization.

Despite the bleak outlook, it still may be possible to

reconcile apparently irreconcilable divisions. The Abortion
Parley organized by the University of Notre Dame in 1979
recognized that current divisions cause anguish on both sides.
Father Hesburgh, in attempting to "elevate the present state
of affairs from a strident shouting match to serious discussion of fact and principle," commented:

> We have witnessed the fact that political candidates
> who agree 95 percent with Catholic principles of
> social justice in most issues of public policy have
> been defeated by their opposition on this one issue
> and have been replaced by candidates who, agreeing
> superficially on this issue of abortion, disagree with
> us on about every other issue bearing on justice and
> equality. Even worse, many candidates who agree
> with our position on abortion in this country advocate
> foreign policy positions that increase the likelihood
> that women in the Third World will seek abortion.
> A life is a life--whether it be in the United States,
> Colombia, or Sri Lanka.

Neither pro-choice nor pro-life attitudes are monolithic, and
history shows that in the past absolutist beliefs on abortion
have always eventually yielded to gradualist interpretation.

One of the triumphs of intellectual and human history
in the past two centuries has been the spread of religious
tolerance. The Catholic Church, in the statement that grew
out of Pope John's great Second Vatican Council (1962-1963),
stated:

> The Synod further declares that the right to religious
> freedom has its foundation in the very dignity of the
> human person, as this dignity is known through the
> revealed Word of God and by reason itself.
> (quoted by Abbott, 1965)

In January 1973, the United States Supreme Court
struck down all restrictive state laws on grounds of religious
toleration; Britain (1967) and Canada (1968/69) liberalized
laws to deal with hard cases. The Supreme Court's philosophy
was different and the judgment of the Supreme Court of the
United States, Roe vs. Wade, 22 January 1973, states:

> We need not resolve the difficult question of when
> life begins. When those trained in the respective
> disciplines of medicine, philosophy and theology are

unable to arrive at any consensus, the judiciary, at this point in the development of man's knowledge, is not in a position to speculate as to the answer.

The Supreme Court did not casually toss aside the rights of the embryo and fetus but recognized that, within a country that values freedom of religious belief but where there are sincere disagreements about the status to be conferred on the human conceptus, then freedom of choice must obtain. The Court stated, "we do not agree that, by adopting one theory of life, Texas [the case under appeal involved a woman from Dallas, Texas] may override the rights of the pregnant woman that are at stake."

The solution to the abortion debate lies in the accommodation society must make when people of different religious persuasions live together and practice their own life-styles. Some religious groups oppose abortion and others regard it as licit. The Canadian Churchman wrote in 1968 (de Valk, 1981):

> In the area of abortion, contraception and homosexuality, the choice is governed by individual conscience. If his church is opposed then he has a moral obligation to obey his church's rules, but he has no right to impose those rules on people of other faiths or no faith at all.

In many ways the debate is similar to other differences over religious beliefs that so convulsed Europe in the sixteenth and seventeenth centuries. The First Amendment to the United States Constitution was passed when memories of religious wars were foremost in the minds of statesmen. Unfortunately, political familiarity can breed philosophic contempt, and today we forget too easily what a noble testimony to human enlightenment it is to find a synagogue, a mosque, and a church side by side in the same city. It should be no more remarkable, and in many ways an equal measure of religious toleration, to find an abortion clinic in a community where a significant number of people are sincerely and totally opposed to abortion. The pragmatism that appears to accompany abortion does not grow from any looseness in moral philosophy but is the outcome of the community in the aggregate, creating the optimum environment in which individuals can arrive at difficult decisions about abortion: it recognizes the individual's need to follow his or her own conscience in a complex, solemn, and important area.

References

Abbott, W. M. , ed. The Documents of Vatican II, n. p. , 1965.

Bouscaren, A. Ethics of Ectopic Operations. Milwaukee: Bruce, 1943.

Brazier, M. A. B. "Challenges from the Philosophers to the Neuroscientists." In Brain and Mind. Cuba Foundation Symposium 69. Amsterdam: Excerpta Medica, 1979.

Burtchaell, J. T. , ed. Abortion Parley. Kansas City: Andrews and McNell, 1981.

Callahan, D. 1970. Abortion: Law, Choice and Morality. New York: Macmillan, 1970.

Coulton, G. C. "Infant Perdition in the Middle Ages." Medieval Studies, 1922, n. p. : 61-32.

David, H. Family Planning and Abortion in the Socialist Countries of Central and Eastern Europe. New York, Population Council, 1970.

Davis, D. "The Law of Abortion and Necessity." Modern Law Review, 1938, 2: 126.

de Valk, A. In "Abortion Politics: Canadian Style." Paul Sachdev, ed. Toronto: Butterworths, 1981.

Deveraux, G. A Study of Abortion in Primitive Societies. London: Yoseloff, 1960.

Edelstein, L. The Hippocratic Oath. New York: Columbia University Press, 1962.

Fedou, G. L'avortement: de sa répression et de sa prévention dans le Code de la Famille et les lois posterieures. Villeurbanne, France: Impremeries Marques, 1946.

Feldman, D. M. Marital Relations, Birth Control and Abortion in Jewish Law. New York: Schocken Books, 1974.

Furness, J. Books for Children Book X, The Sight of Hell. Dublin: Duffy, 1850.

Greenberger, R. The 12-Year Reich. A Social History of Nazi Germany: New York: Holt, Rinehart & Winston, 1971.

International Fertility Research Program. Traditional Abortion Practices. North Carolina: IFRP., 1981.

Kerslake, D. and Casey, D., "Abortion Induced by Means of the Uterine Aspirator." Obstetrics & Gynecology, 1967, 30: 35-45.

Lehfeldt, H. "Ernst Grafenberg and His Ring." Mount Sinai Journal of Medicine, 1975, 42 (4): 345-352.

Life (November 1981), 45-59.

Needham, J. A History of Embryology. New York: Abelard-Schuman, 1959.

Nelson, M. R. "History of the Uterine Curette." Contributions from the Department of Gynecology of the City of New York, 1945, 8: 72.

Noonan, J. T. "Abortion and the Catholic Church: A Summary History." Natural Law Forum, 1967, 12: 85-131.

_____. "An Almost Absolute Value in History." In Morality of Abortion: Legal and Historical Perspectives, John T. Noonan, ed. Cambridge: Harvard University Press, 1970.

_____. Contraception. Cambridge: Harvard University Press, 1965.

Ovid. Nux Elegia, lines 23-24.

Paine, T. Rights of Man, Henry Collins, ed. Harmondsworth: Penguin Books, 1969.

Peck, A. L. Aristotle: Generation of Animals. In Greek and English translation. Cambridge: Harvard University Press, 1953.

Potts, M. "History of Contraception." In Fertility Regulation, J. J. Sciarra; M. J. Daly; and G. I. Zatuchni, eds. Philadelphia: Lippincott, 1982.

_____; Diggory, P.; and Peel, J. Abortion. Cambridge, England: Cambridge University Press, 1977.

Rentoul, R. R. Causes and Treatment of Abortion. Edinburgh: Pentland, 1889.

Simpson, J. Y. Clinical Lectures on Diseases of Women. Philadelphia: Blanchard & Len, 1863.

Taussig, F. J. Abortion, Spontaneous and Induced: Medical and Social Aspects. London: Kimpton, 1936.

Narkavonnakit, Tongplaew. "Abortion in Rural Thailand." Studies in Family Planning, 1979, 10: 223-229.

Vermeersch, A. Theologiae Moralis (4th Edition). Rome: Gregorian University Press, 1947 [quoted by John T. Noonan, ed. in Morality of Abortion: Legal and Historical Perspective, 1970], p. 112.

Watson, C. "Birth Control and Abortion in France Since 1937." Population Studies, 1952, 5: 261-270.

Williams, G. The Sanctity of Life and the Criminal Law. London: Faber and Faber, 1958.

THE ROOTS OF CONTEMPORARY ANTI-ABORTION ACTIVISM

By Stephen L. Markson

Hundreds of people are jammed into Gardner Auditorium at the State House in Boston, Massachusetts, for a public hearing on a proposed anti-abortion bill. The sentiments expressed on the many placards, banners, and buttons displayed throughout the hall are vivid testimony to the divergence, depth, and intransigence of the beliefs of the opposing camps. A tottering decorum gives way to a series of unbridled outbursts as the speaker at the podium boldly compares pro-choice supporters to Adolf Hitler:

> We have the gall to criticize Hitler for slaughtering 6 million Jews, at least he let them die with dignity--he let them walk into the ovens.

Her analogy is met with shouts of outrage from many in a shocked audience. Yet the speaker refuses to budge at all in retreat from her position, adding:

> I think we have more than a few Hitlers in the room here today ... if you kill this bill this is what you'll be doing....

She suddenly thrusts a paper bag above the podium and emphatically proceeds to empty onto the stage the disembodied pieces of a rubber doll!

This incident indeed may have been the most melodramatic of the morning session. Yet the extreme sensitivity and emotionality apparent on both sides of the abortion issue permeate the more calmly delivered opinions as well:

> One must question the social utility of neglected children, unabating poverty and the return of "back-alley" abortions performed by filthy butchers....

> A society that blandly accepts the killing of the un-
> born without a moral qualm is certain to become
> less reluctant to accept cruelties committed against
> children, the infirm, disabled, defective and eld-
> erly....

On January 22, 1973, the United States Supreme Court, by a vote of 7 to 2, ruled that the restrictive state abortion laws under challenge in Texas and Georgia were unconstitutional. The judgment was grounded in the rights to personal privacy guaranteed by the 9th and 14th amendments. The momentous Roe vs. Wade decision has been summarized as follows:

> (1) For the stage prior to approximately the
> end of the first trimester, the abortion decision
> and its effectuation must be left to the medical judge-
> ment of the pregnant woman's attending physician.
> (2) For the stage subsequent to approximately
> the end of the first trimester, the State, in pro-
> moting its interest in the health of the mother, may,
> if it chooses, regulate the abortion procedure in
> ways that are reasonably related to maternal health.
> (3) For the stage subsequent to viability, the
> State, in promoting its interests in the potentiality
> of human life, may, if it chooses, regulate, and
> even proscribe abortion except where it is neces-
> sary, in appropriate medical judgment, for the pre-
> servation of the life or health of the mother.
> (Babcock, et al. , 1975:958).

The right to abortion granted by this decision was not unqualified; clinics and hospitals could still refuse to abort unless no other facilities were within a "reasonable" distance, and private doctors still retained the right to refuse to abort private patients without referral. Although the ruling clearly did not legalize abortion "on demand," it did, however, represent a stunning judicial victory for pro-choice forces. Organizations such as the Association for the Study of Abortion (ASA), the National Association for Repeal of Abortion Laws (NARAL), the Women's National Abortion Action Coalition, and Planned Parenthood have spearheaded a two-decade campaign for the availability of safe, legal abortions. [1] Mounting public pressure to repeal restrictive abortion statutes demanded and ultimately received legitimation from the summit of our judicial system. Yet, as is so often the case, given the dialectical nature of moral controversies, the apparent

triumph served only to energize a determined counterattack
from anti-abortion forces--an offensive which has continued
to gather momentum with each passing year. A nascent anti-
abortion movement predated the 1973 court decision. Both
the National Right-to-Life Committee (NRLC) and Birthright
had been formally organized and chartered in 1968. Additionally, various state and local groups had rallied for public
support in their fight against abortion prior to the nationally
based and coordinated organizational efforts.[2] However, it
was the Supreme Court decision of January 22, 1973, cursed
as cataclysmic by anti-abortionists, which generated in the
movement a sense of urgency and militancy characteristic of
a crusade. Orrin Klapp captures such zeal in arguing that
"the goal of a crusade is to defeat an evil, not merely to
solve a social problem" (Klapp, 1969:274). That goal is perhaps better seen as a "calling"--a goal not merely good, but
ennobling in purpose.

The reaction to the judgment was swift and uncompro-
mising: New York's Cardinal Terence Cooke decreed it to be
"a tragic utilitarian decision" adding that "judicial decisions
are not necessarily sound moral decisions." James Lenehan,
chairman of the newly formed Connecticut Right-to-Life Committee feared "the wholesale slaughter of unborn children,"
comparing the ruling to the 1857 Dred Scott decision in its
willingness to "compromise humanity." Boston Bishop Hum-
berto Madeiros referred to abortion as "the new barbarism,"
while threatening excommunication for Catholics in the medical profession who participated in the procedure.

The call to action most assuredly did not go unheeded.
The National Right-to-Life Committee boasted a membership
by 1980 of 11 million with affiliate organizations in all 50
states. Minnesota alone has some 200 community chapters
of "Citizens Concerned for Life." Furthermore, the burgeoning anti-abortion movement clearly had a powerful impact upon
the sweeping redefinitions of public policy on abortion which
occurred in June 1977.

In a triad of abortion decisions, the Supreme Court
ruled initially that Title XIX of the Social Security Act did
not require states to fund the cost of all abortions permitted
under state law and could limit reimbursement to "necessary"
and "therapeutic" abortions. Secondly, the court held that
states participating in the medicaid program were not con-
stitutionally required to pay for "nontherapeutic" abortions
because they subsidized the cost of childbirth, thus upholding

the states' "strong and legitimate interest in encouraging normal childbirth." Finally, the court decided that the constitution did not require that public hospitals perform elective abortions even though they provide care for childbirth.

Congress quickly followed suit with legislation banning the use of federal funds for abortions, with three exceptions: (1) when a woman's life is endangered, (2) when, in the opinion of two physicians, pregnancy would cause "severe and long-lasting physical health damage," and (3) when the pregnancy resulted from rape or incest reported within 60 days. The growing influence of the anti-abortion movement and such ideological allies as the self-proclaimed "moral majority" were perhaps evidenced even more persuasively when several senators whom they had targeted as "pro abortion" were defeated in their bids for reelection in 1980. Despite such clear indicators of the powerful presence of anti-abortion forces, simple journalistic accounts of the movement's growth are virtually all that exist to explain this phenomenon of such impressive magnitude. Moreover, I suspect that these limited narrative accounts have consistently failed to capture effectively the essence of anti-abortion activism due to their lack of historical perspective. As C. Wright Mills insisted in The Sociological Imagination, "any social study that does not come back to the problems of biography, of history, and of their intersections within a society has not completed its intellectual journey" (Mills, 1959:15). The social activism and pronounced cultural turbulence of the late 1960s and early 1970s in the United States supply, I believe, the necessary historical context and analytical base to enable one to construct an explanation for the reemergence of abortion as a prominent moral and political controversy in the mid-1970s. The cultural aftershocks of that tumultuous period in United States history continue to shape and influence the contours of contemporary events. Placing current anti-abortion activism in such a context does much to clarify an issue rooted in cultural clashes generated years before abortion was transformed into a normative battle zone of competing moralities.

In the late 1960s and early 1970s, political activism, strident demands for sweeping change, and calls for a more equitable distribution of privilege and opportunity swept through the United States in great waves of protest. The protests were voiced virtually in unison by such diverse constituencies as racial minorities, women, students, homosexuals, and the disabled. However, despite the intensity and scope of the dissidence, it could be argued persuasively that the challenges

failed to instigate the fundamental reforms which were sought
in the primary political and economic institutions of the social
structure. But at the cultural level the status quo was far
less resistant to radical intrusion. The decade of protest had
a profound attitudinal impact upon this society and dramatically
altered the normative contours of the cultural system. Traditional values and long-accepted definitions of morality were
repeatedly assailed on several fronts as being hopelessly out-
dated and out of touch with contemporary reality. To some
in the society these pervasive challenges to tradition represented a welcome and overdue dissolution of irrational constraints. But to others, as is now apparent, the boundaries
being eroded by change and the barriers being scaled by non-
traditional life-styles represented the very pillars and founda-
tions of social order. The era, as interpreted by the anti-
abortion movement, inaugurated a precipitous decline in the
intensity of our society's traditional commitment to family
ideals. The "progress" hailed by the activists of that era
represent to the contemporary activists on the Right little
more than the exaltation of the individual at the expense of
the communal. When in 1973 the Supreme Court based its
Roe vs. Wade decision upon the rights to personal privacy
guaranteed by the 9th and 14th amendments, a doctrine of individual rights quite apart from familial rights and obligations,
was promoted. Such a doctrine is profoundly threatening to
those of the anti-abortion movement, for it represents the
desanctification of the traditional concept of family they have
so firmly embraced. Unwavering attachment to family had
suddenly been questioned, perhaps devalued, by an emerging
emphasis upon individual autonomy and self-actualization.
The traditional family norms and values to which they had
faithfully adhered no longer seemed to command the universal acceptance and reverence they had once enjoyed.

   The institutions of marriage and the family have indeed
undergone considerable change and revision in the last 15 years
or so. While the fact of change may be virtually indisputable,
the meanings imputed to such change are widely divergent.
Skolnick and Skolnick in Intimacy, Family and Society (1974)
provide some evidence of fluctuations in demographic patterns
which may reflect an alteration of underlying attitudes concerning the family. They initially note a dramatic drop in
the birthrate. The child-centeredness of the 1950s--that ro-
mantic doctrine of togetherness, portrayed so poignantly by
the Father Knows Best, Make Room for Daddy, and Leave It
to Beaver television genre of the day,--seems to have waned
considerably. Subscription to what might be termed the "nu-

clear family ideology" with the traditional configuration of housewife-mother, breadwinner-father, and children-at-home now represents a statistical minority. Both husband and wife are now apt to work outside the home even when young children are present. Furthermore, the increased acceptance without stigma of children born out of wedlock and heightened tolerance of nontraditional forms of family life are recent phenomena as well. The status quo clearly has not been maintained in reference to the contemporary American family, which may be a more diversified entity than ever before in our history.

These variations of family organization, structure, and style have recently prompted a spate of scholarly attention. The mass media have also addressed these issues of late, often under the provocative headline (or some reasonable facsimile): "Is the Family Falling Apart?" However, few scholars of the family, with the notable exception of Christopher Lasch in Haven in a Heartless World: The Family Besieged (1977), have found convincing evidence of the imminent collapse or dissolution of the American family. Kenneth Keniston in All Our Children (1977) and Mary Jo Bane in Here to Stay: American Families in the Twentieth Century (1976) persuasively argue that the changes we have witnessed were the necessary adjustments that had to be made in order to bring the current organization of family life in line with the cultural and economic reality of contemporary American society. Both Keniston and Bane agree that to cling to rigid tradition amidst pervasive and sweeping social change, in order to salvage a romanticized vision of the family in the "good old days," would be akin to nailing down the hands of a clock in order to halt the flow of time. Thus, the conclusions they reach are not at all suggestive of impending doom for the familial institution. Reorganization prompted by a confluence of powerful social forces rather than disorganization prompted by a loss of commitment to family best summarizes their findings. Yet, even if such an assessment, which focuses on the family as successfully adapting to broadbased societal change, can ultimately be sustained as the correct interpretation, its accuracy will not diminish the status threat of the change to those who are firmly committed to the traditional image of the family. Issues relating to sexuality, women's roles, and life-style options in general are also germane to an understanding of the status resentment generated by recent social change.

One can assuredly find, in the era, evidence of a dis-

tinct cultural drift toward a marked expansion of the parameters of legitimacy in respect to life-style choices. Concerning sexuality, the changes were indeed considerable as noted
by the wide availability of contraception, increased acceptance
of cohabitation without marriage, and the proliferation of coed
dormitories at major universities across the nation. Gay-
rights organizations mobilized campaigns for anti-discrimination
legislation in the area of sexual preference. Sex education
became commonplace in public schools, while at the same
time the constitutionality of school prayer was denied and
public funding of parochial education lost whatever legal standing it had previously possessed. However, it was the marked
resurgence of the women's rights movement that may have
raised most significantly the central challenge to traditionally
defined values.

The issues articulated throughout the rebirth of American feminism, such as sexual discrimination in employment,
equality of legal protection, and the debilitating effects of
sexual stereotyping, squarely confronted and contested the
legitimacy of women's second-class citizenship. The feminist critique of male hegemony threatened traditional norms
at their most fundamental level. To insist, as women's rights
activists did, that the roles of the sexes were socially created in order to facilitate and solidify sexual inequality, rather
than being the natural evolution of a divinely inspired blue-
print for life, was to defy the very basis of traditional order.
Consequently, the crux of feminist criticism was the overall
masculinization of American society--that the traditional roles,
values, and ideals at the normative core of mainstream American culture have been masculinely defined, wherein men create the cultural contexts that define women's place. The per-
ceptible erosion of popular support for clearly demarcated
sex roles that the women's movement fostered adds a critical
dimension to this analysis of the impact of the era of the
late 1960s and early 1970s upon anti-abortion activism. The
critical dimension to which I refer is that of social status
and its distribution within a society.

Joseph Gusfield in Symbolic Crusade (University of Illinois, 1963) empirically demonstrated that moral controversies rooted in people's desires to defend deeply held value
commitments can prompt the development of a social movement as energetically as the class and economic issues more
commonly viewed as the major themes of collective action.
The quest for social esteem and status, perhaps independent
of economic standing, can also motivate social-movement mo-

bilization. As Weber (Gerth & Mills, 1946) noted, "status honor" is not inevitably hinged upon nor necessarily linked to formal class position. Those collectively engaged in a moral reform movement may be bound by common value orientations and shared moral commitments which distinctly traverse established social class differentiations. A latent by-product of the normative revisions and cultural changes that I have traced to this 1960s-1970s era has been the pressing challenge presented to those who have maintained allegiance to the precepts of traditionally defined morality. When people begin to perceive their own cherished values as being displaced by alternative moralities, specific issues are likely to be embraced as tests of status, symbolic of the confrontation between competing conceptions of morality. As Gusfield maintained:

> Discontents that arise from the status order are often as sharp and as powerful as those that emerge in the struggles over income and employment. As the cultural fortunes of one group go up and those of another group go down, expectations of prestige are repulsed and the ingredients of social conflict are produced.
>
> (Gusfield, 1963:80)

The legal standing of abortion has been embraced by the contemporary right-to-life movement as a summary symbol of the divisive rift in United States culture generated by the realignment of the structure of normative values that the social activism discussed earlier had presaged. As viewed through the ideology of the anti-abortion movement, the basic theme characteristic of the previous decade's protests represented the hasty dissolution of our cultural commitment to the sanctity of family and community--the affirmation of individual rights at the expense of traditional social responsibilities. To those in United States society who held firmly to traditional normative standards, the "rules of the game" had been suddenly and dramatically changed. The change, it would appear, seemed to accord considerably less prestige to their life-style choices and value commitments than once enjoyed. This idea of status threat is explained by Zurcher and Kirkpatrick:

> Change upsets old hierarchies, develops new collective aspirations and challenges long-established values and norms with potential obsolescence. When the individual is threatened with the impact of social

change upon his self-concept, especially upon the prestige and respect he has enjoyed and come to expect as associated with his espousal of traditional values and norms, he will resist both the change and those he perceived to be the agents of change. (Zurcher and Kirkpatrick, 1976:262)

The legal standing of abortion as a moral and political issue has come to symbolize such a status threat and consequently is imbedded within a far wider constellation of beliefs. The crusade against abortion has come to represent to its participants the defense of traditional conceptions of morality and conventional values against the threat posed not simply by the legality of abortion but also by the normative realignment in American culture that was its forerunner. To those embroiled in the conflict, the issue is virtually the fulcrum upon which the balance of power has come to rest.

When the contemporary debate over abortion is viewed in historical perspective as an extension and outgrowth of normative battles which flared more than a decade ago, considerable insight can be gained. The interpretation that I have proposed stresses that the controversy we are now witnessing is a reflection of cultural clashes and discord running to significantly greater depth than is immediately apparent. While it is likely that the abortion issue will be resolved and will consequently recede from a position of intensive public scrutiny, it is highly unlikely that the status conflicts which it symbolizes will similarly disappear from the scene. The process of social change will continue to unfold and will continue to disturb established value systems and hierarchies, and since the cultural realignments can be expected to generate new status threats, people are certain to launch new campaigns to defend staunchly their status interests. Unhappily, then, I conclude that crusades as bitter, divisive, and vitriolic as that over abortion are yet to be waged.

Notes

1. A concise history of the "pro-choice" abortion reform movement can be found in Armand Mauss, Social Problems as Social Movements (New York: Lippincott, 1975, pp. 465-480).
2. A New York State Right-to-Life Committee entered the arena of political activity in 1965.

References

Babcock, Barbara Allen; Ann E. Freedman; Eleanor Homes Norton; Susan C. Ross. Sex Discrimination and the Law. Boston: Little, Brown and Company, 1975.

Bane, Mary Jo. Here to Stay: American Families in the Twentieth Century. New York: Basic Books, 1976.

Blumer, Herbert. "Collective Behavior." In Principles of Sociology, 2nd edition, Alfred McClung Lee, ed. New York: Barnes and Noble, 1969, 65-121.

_____. Symbolic Interactionism: Perspective and Method. New Jersey: Prentice-Hall, 1969.

Crawford, Alan. Thunder on the Right: The "New Right" and the Politics of Resentment. New York: Pantheon Books, 1980.

Gerth, Hans and C. Wright Mills. From Max Weber: Essays in Sociology. New York: Oxford University Press, 1946.

Gusfield, Joseph R. Protest, Reform and Revolt: A Reader in Social Movements. New York: Wiley, 1970.

_____. Symbolic Crusade. Illinois: University of Illinois Press, 1963.

Keniston, Kenneth. All Our Children: The American Family Under Pressure. New York: Holt, Rinehart and Winston, 1977.

Klapp, Orrin E. Collective Search for Identity. New York: Holt, Rinehart and Winston, 1969.

Lasch, Christopher. Haven in a Heartless World: The Family Besieged. New York: Basic Books, 1977.

Markson, Stephen L. "Normative Boundaries and Abortion Policy: The Politics of Morality." In Research in Social Problems and Public Policy, Vol. 2. Michael Lewis, ed. Connecticut: JAI Press, 1982, 21-33.

Mauss, Armand L. Social Problems as Social Movements. New York: J. B. Lippincott, 1975.

Mills, C. Wright. The Sociological Imagination. New York: Oxford University Press, 1959.

Rubin, Lillian B. Worlds of Pain. New York: Basic Books, 1976.

Skerry, Peter. "The Class Conflict Over Abortion," The Public Interest, 1978, 52:69-84.

Skolnick, Arlene and Jerome H. Skolnick. Intimacy, Family and Society. Boston: Little, Brown and Company, 1974.

Zurcher, Louis A. and R. George Kirkpatrick. Citizens for Decency: Anti-Pornography Crusades as Status Defense. Texas: University of Texas Press, 1976.

ABORTION POLITICS AND PUBLIC POLICY

By Philip R. Lee and Lauren B. LeRoy

The Supreme Court's 1973 ruling in the case of Roe vs. Wade established a woman's constitutional right to have an abortion, but as Dierdre English notes, for supporters of the Court's decision "The victory, it turns out, took place before the battle" (English, 1981, p. 23). Despite the Supreme Court decision, the debate over abortion policy is far from settled. The form a policy takes does not end with its first expression in a formal policy statement (e. g. , a new law, a court decision). Rather, it is shaped by all those involved in its implementation, including those who disagree with the policy and are working simultaneously to change it. Such is the case with abortion policy which presents sharply divergent, indeed irreconcilable, views on the morality of abortion.

Since 1973, the ability of women to exercise their legal right to an abortion has depended on the sum of interactions between women and physicians and a host of agencies and institutions in both the public and private sectors. A central factor in the development of abortion policy in the United States since 1973 is the failure of key actors in both the health care system and government to exercise leadership in the implementation of abortion policy. This is particularly so with the medical profession, the hospital leadership, and the federal government. The inadequate response of these groups to the responsibilities placed on them by the Supreme Court decision created a policy vacuum which the right-to-life movement has sought to fill. The developments following the 1973 decision have been described in considerable detail (Jaffe, et al. , 1981). We will begin with a summary of those developments and then explore more closely, particularly at the federal level, efforts to secure passage of policies to restrict access to legal abortion.

Legal abortion has gradually become available to women

44

in the United States since 1973. In 1972, the Center for Disease Control reported 586,760 legal abortions in 28 states (U. S. Department of Health and Human Services, 1979). Almost half of those abortions were performed in New York and California. In 1980, 1,553,890 legal abortions were performed and only 28 percent were in New York and California (Henshaw, et al., 1982). In 1973, one quarter of all women seeking legal abortions had to travel outside their home state. In 1977, only one woman in eleven had to do this to obtain a legal abortion (Forrest, et al., 1980).

These may seem to be impressive accomplishments, but national statistics mask regional, state, and local differences in the delivery of abortion services. Today, almost ten years after the Supreme Court decision, the majority of abortions are performed by a relatively small number of physicians in a relatively small number of clinics and hospitals, mostly in urban areas. In 1980, nearly 78 percent of the U. S. counties, containing 28 percent of all women of reproductive age, had no identified abortion service provider (Henshaw, et al., 1982).

One of the most crucial aspects of the Roe vs. Wade decision involves the critical role it assigned to the medical profession. The Court said: "The abortion decision in all its aspects is primarily and inherently a medical decision, and basic responsibility for it must rest with the physician" (Roe v. Wade, p. 50). The Court thus created a decision-making process in which women and the medical profession are coparticipants.

The response to this mandate by the two national organizations whose members most directly affect the implementation of abortion policy--the American Hospital Association (AHA) and the American Medical Association (AMA)--might best be described as one of self-protection. Less than three weeks after the Supreme Court ruled, the AHA recommended legislation to give member hospitals and individual physicians a right to refuse to participate in abortions (American Hospital Association, 1973). Neither then nor subsequently has the AHA addressed any other aspect of the subject.

Similarly, official actions by the AMA have been limited primarily to statements like the one in June 1973 urging that abortions be performed only by licensed physicians and that physicians with conscientious objections to abortion be free not to participate in performing them (American Medical

Association, 1973). Since then, the AMA has taken no initiative to assure implementation of the Supreme Court ruling. Only the American College of Obstetricians and Gynecologists (ACOG) has assumed a role that could serve as an example for the rest of the medical profession. Since the 1973 decision, ACOG has consistently taken positions in the abortion debate, issued official statements on government policies, prepared reports and guidelines on the medical dimensions of abortion, and presented educational programs related to abortion at its meetings (American College of Obstetricians and Gynecologists, 1973).

The response of state professional associations mirrored that of their national counterparts. Prior to 1973, 19 state medical societies had voted to recommend liberalization of their states' abortion laws. Following the Court's decision, only 17 state medical societies issued guidelines or statements on the new situation. Sixteen took no action and the remainder generally confined their statements to very narrow issues only (Alan Guttmacher Institute, 1976:a). The reaction of state hospital associations also was limited, with the majority taking no action or adopting recommendations that objecting hospitals and physicians be exempted from providing abortion services (Alan Guttmacher Institute, 1976:b).

The grudging response of the medical profession and hospital leadership to the Supreme Court's 1973 decision is not difficult to explain. Abortion is controversial. Physicians and hospital administrators and trustees--like the leaders of other professional and business establishments--try to avoid controversy whenever possible. Physicians today mostly favor the continued legalization of abortion as defined in the 1973 Supreme Court decision. There are a number of factors, however, that influence whether or not a physician is willing to perform an abortion or to speak out on the subject. Some health professionals, like many Americans, bitterly oppose abortion on religious, moral, or philosophic grounds. Approval of abortion as a means of coping with an unwanted pregnancy coexists with negative attitudes particularly among older professionals who received their training when the procedure was illegal. Local peer pressure or politics in a particular hospital or community may influence physician behavior. Physicians may feel threatened by the degree to which birth control and abortion have contributed to changing roles and opportunities for women. In the words of one physician: "Legal abortion makes the patient truly the physician: She makes the diagnosis and establishes the therapy" (Hospital

Practice, 1970). In these circumstances, it was charged, the physician becomes "merely" the technician, carrying out the patient's wishes.

Abortion raises a number of issues that relate to the consumer's role in health care. It is in fact a precursor to other situations in which the traditional authoritarian relationship between doctor and patient is being challenged. Given these dilemmas, it is not difficult to see that significant underlying moral, religious, and professional attitudes largely explain the health system's failure to respond to a woman's right to abortion and a physician's right to perform abortion legally. To attribute the medical system's failure to moral controversy, however, does not relieve the profession of its responsibility. The fact remains that a significant social change occurred in the 1960s and early 1970s and was reflected in the Supreme Court's 1973 decision on abortion. That change involved the health system, but the system has failed to respond in ways commensurate with its social role and responsibility.

State public health authorities, faced with concrete legal and adminstrative questions after the 1973 decision, tended to react more directly than their private sector counterparts. These state efforts varied widely, however. Some state departments of public health issued guidelines that were long and detailed; others issued brief and general statements. In about half the states, the official health agency still has not issued any guidelines, even for procedures in late pregnancy where the Supreme Court clearly defined a role for government. In some cases, state regulations included provisions designed to circumvent or negate aspects of the 1973 decision, but these have been invalidated by federal courts.

Local government has many areas of responsibility that directly affect, and can be used to limit, community-based abortion services. Some local authorities have enacted or attempted to enact strict regulations governing many facets of abortion clinics' operations. Some provisions, such as the well-publicized restrictive abortion ordinance enacted in Akron, Ohio, have sought to intrude directly into the physician-patient relationship in a manner that is unprecedented for a local government. Although most of these local roadblocks have been thrown out by the courts, they confront potential providers with the prospect of long delays, high legal fees, and community controversy, and they continue to generate publicity for the anti-abortion cause.

The federal government, for its part, has taken a step backward in recent years after initially moving only slowly to establish policies in the programs it runs or funds. The 1973 Supreme Court decision legalizing abortion throughout the United States initially posed a challenge and provided an opportunity to many agencies of the Department of Health, Education, and Welfare (HEW) to articulate through professional example and practice the meaning of the law. For the most part, however, these federal agencies have avoided involvement whenever possible.

HEW failed to set an example in its own medical care programs, such as the Public Health Service hospitals and clinics and the Indian Health Service. Two years after Roe vs. Wade, many of these providers still were not complying with the decision. In the years between 1973 and the enactment of the first ban on federal funds for abortion in 1976, HEW took no steps to clarify abortion's place in the Medicaid program, although large numbers of women receiving welfare, the program's primary adult beneficiaries, could have been expected to seek abortions. HEW permitted considerable uncertainty to develop about how programs receiving federal funds, such as family planning and maternal health programs and community and migrant health centers, were to proceed with regard to abortion services, counseling, and referral.

HEW's actions following the enactment of the Hyde amendment in 1976, which barred federal funding for Medicaid abortions, is illustrative of prevailing federal policy. When implementation of the Hyde amendment was blocked initially by a federal court order, HEW issued no policy statements to its regional offices or grantees for a full week and refused to answer inquiries from frantic state administrators who did not know whether or not to reimburse abortions obtained by Medicaid recipients. The situation was very different, however, one year later when HEW Secretary Joseph Califano made a nationwide announcement of HEW's restrictions within one hour of the removal of the restraining order.

The lack of any vigorous attempt by federal and state governments to implement the 1973 Supreme Court decision, coupled with their rapid response to subsequent efforts to restrict abortions, signaled to abortion opponents that government was reluctant to act on this sensitive issue and was susceptible to their political pressures. Initially, the anti-abortion forces did not go unopposed in their attempts to overturn the Supreme Court ruling. In fact, the abortion rights activists were more experienced politically, although they, like the right-to-life forces, were better organized in the states than nationally. The 1973 decision, however, served to galvanize the opposition, while having the opposite effect on most supporters of legal abortion.

Unlike the right-to-life groups, those supporting abortion rights represented a diverse group of organizations whose primary concerns were broader than the single issue of abortion. With the legalization of abortion, many felt the battle was won and turned their attention to other issues. It was left to a handful of political-action and legal-defense organizations to counter attempts to enact abortion restrictions after 1973. These groups were no match for the right-to-life movement with its financial and organizational support from the Catholic Church. The more broadly based organizations began to speak up again only after abortion rights had begun to be eroded by restrictions on public funding and efforts to block the availability of abortion for all women.

The immediate response of the anti-abortion groups to the 1973 decision was to press for constitutional amendments to invalidate the ruling. By early 1974, 58 amendments were introduced that could be categorized into four types (Donovan, 1981; Paul & Klassel, 1981):

(1) Human Life Amendment--to bar abortions except to save the pregnant woman's life;
(2) "Paramount" Human Life Amendment--to place an absolute ban on abortion;
(3) State's Rights Amendment--to return the power to regulate abortions to the states; and
(4) Human Life Federalism Amendment--to give states and the federal government concurrent power to regulate abortion.

Although unified in their position against abortion, there has been considerable disagreement since 1973 among factions of the anti-abortion movement over which of these approaches to follow.

Beginning in early 1974, hearings on pending proposals for abortion-related constitutional amendments were held before subcommittees in both houses of Congress. These hearings, which lasted more than a year, failed to produce approval for any such proposal. Only once in 1975, through the

maneuvers of Senator Jesse Helms (R-North Carolina), did
a human life amendment reach the floor of the Senate, where
it was tabled (Paul & Klassel, 1981).

Their inability to gain a quick reversal of the 1973
decision was a disappointment to anti-abortion activists. Anti-
abortion leaders recognized the need to redirect efforts toward
interim goals and to create a political base. In 1975, the
National Conference of Catholic Bishops unanimously approved
the Pastoral Plan for Pro-Life Activities calling for all Church-
sponsored and identifiably Catholic organizations to undertake
a comprehensive "pro-life" legislative campaign of political
mobilization at the grass roots level to win passage of state
and federal legislation, and ultimately a constitutional amendment, giving maximum protection to the unborn child.

At the same time, right-to-life leader Randy Engel
called for a new strategy to seek restrictive riders on "any
and all federal legislation related directly or indirectly to
health" in order to keep the abortion issue visible and to build
support. She further argued that such efforts would provide
abortion opponents with political experience, educate the public, force members of Congress to put their positions on record, and force supporters of abortion to expend resources
opposing each rider (Planned Parenthood Washington Memo,
1975).

The 1976 presidential campaign marked an accelerated
involvement by anti-abortion groups in electoral politics. That
effort was facilitated by 1974 election reforms permitting formation of political action committees for funding election campaigns (Oliker, 1981). The National Right-to-Life Committee
has established such a political action arm called the Life
Amendment Political Action Committee (LAPAC). Abortion
emerged as an important issue in the 1976 campaign and received disproportionate attention in the media because of the
entry of Ellen McCormack as an anti-abortion candidate in
the Democratic primary race. Anti-abortion activists remained frustrated in their attempts to convince the Democratic
Platform Committee to support a constitutional amendment;
but they were more successful with the Republican Party.
While President Gerald Ford gave only a half-hearted endorse-
ment--saying he would "support but not seek" a states' rights
amendment--the Republican Party Platform went further in
calling for an amendment "to restore the protection of the
right to life for unborn children" (New York Times, Septem-
ber 29, 1975).

Since that time, the National Right-to-Life Committee has increasingly articulated its goals in political terms. This development has been accompanied by a hardening of positions, leadership changes, and increasingly prominent identification with conservative lobbying and political action groups.

The failure of Congress to adopt a human life amendment probably was the decisive factor in redirecting anti-abortion forces toward interim strategies. At the same time, the right-to-life movement and the church have by no means abandoned their primary goal, which they continue to pursue simultaneously. Finding no satisfaction in Congress, the right-to-life forces focused their effort in the mid-1970s on convincing state legislatures to pass resolutions calling for a constitutional convention to consider a human life amendment. This method of amending the Constitution requires two thirds of the states to call for a convention and three quarters of the states to ratify any amendment proposed by the convention. Such a constitutional convention is unprecedented. Many constitutional experts argue that the lack of rules or guidelines for conducting such a convention make it a dangerous undertaking. Thus far, 19 of the required 34 states have passed resolutions calling for a constitutional convention, but none has done so since May 1980 (Donovan, 1981).

Meanwhile, action in Congress shifted from consideration of constitutional amendments to passage of narrower restrictive legislation. Committed anti-abortion congressmen had been launching attacks on Medicaid funding since the 1973 Supreme Court decision. However, they were unsuccessful until 1976 when, without warning, freshman Representative Henry Hyde (R-Illinois) proposed an amendment to the HEW-Labor appropriations bill banning federal funds "to pay for abortion or to promote or encourage abortion." While supported in the House, the proposal initially was defeated in the Senate. A compromise that allowed an exception to protect the life of the mother was reached and the proposal was adopted.

It is noteworthy that 72 representatives who had voted against a comparable amendment in 1974 now voted for the Hyde amendment in the heat of the election campaign. Observers have suggested that the Senate's similar willingness to support the amendment reflected a well-calculated political gamble that the Supreme Court, in forthcoming decisions on two Medicaid cases, would declare such funding restrictions unconstitutional. Their expectations initially were confirmed when U.S. District Court Judge John F. Dooling issued an injunction against implementation of the 1976 Hyde amendment on the first day of the new fiscal year.

The following year, Representative Hyde introduced a similar amendment to the 1978 HEW-Labor appropriations bill. A week later, the Supreme Court ruled that states could deny Medicaid funding for "nontherapeutic" abortions. Subsequently, Judge Dooling lifted his temporary injunction. While the House again adopted the new Hyde amendment, the Senate held that Medicaid should pay for "medically necessary" abortions, as it pays for other necessary medical services. The phrase "medically necessary" then became the focus of debate for six months, holding up passage of the $60 billion appropriations bill.

Despite the time and effort consumed, this debate was the antithesis of deliberative, legislative decision-making. None of the substantive committees responsible for the basic legislation held even a day of hearings on the ban. Not a single witness was heard. Virtually no factual evidence was presented. The most visible outside participant in the process was Mark Gallagher, lobbyist for the Bishop's National Committee for a Human Life Amendment.

A compromise amendment finally was adopted which banned federal funds for abortion with exceptions to protect the life of the mother, in cases of rape or incest, or to protect the mother from severe or long-lasting physical health damage. This compromise satisfied no one, least of all Representative Hyde, who voted against it because he was "unwilling to trade unborn life for a health condition or for any other circumstance, except to save another human life" (Congressional Record, December 7, 1977).

After enforcement of the Hyde amendment and its state counterparts began in August 1977, a number of cases challenging its legality and constitutionality were filed. Among the most important was McRae vs. Secretary of DHEW, heard by Judge Dooling in 1980, which was the only suit to challenge the legality and constitutionality of the Hyde amendment directly. Judge Dooling ruled that the effect of the Hyde amendment was to violate the First Amendment guarantees of free exercise of religion or conscience and the Fifth Amendment rights of privacy, due process, and equal protection of the laws for poor women eligible under the Medicaid program. The decision was appealed to the Supreme Court which, by a one-vote majority, affirmed the constitutionality of the Hyde amendment.

The 1980 Supreme Court decision gave the anti-abortion forces new hope. It served to legitimize not only the Hyde amendment but various other restrictions Congress subsequently imposed on federal funding for abortion (e. g. , Department of Defense, Peace Corps, and Legal Services). In addition, the political effectiveness of the anti-abortion movement has been enhanced significantly by its growing alliance with the political right. There are strong links between the leaders of the "new right" (e. g. , Paul Weyrich, founder of the Committee for the Survival of a Free Congress; Richard Viguerie, publisher of the "new right" Conservative Digest; Howard Philips, head of the Conservative Caucus) and the leadership of the anti-abortion movement (Oliker, 1981). The conjunction of "new right" and right-to-life interests was evident in the pursuit of key federal legislators targeted for defeat in the 1980 election campaign on the "hit lists" of both right-to-life and "new right" organizations.

The relationship between right-to-life forces and the political right has proven mutually beneficial. It has been suggested that the increased receptivity of Congress to an anti-abortion position is due more to the swing toward conservative candidates than to a singular commitment against abortion (Granberg, 1981). On the other hand, the political right has much to gain from the alliance as well. English argues that "the abortion issue has become the conscience of conservatism. It is the only issue in which the New Right can claim the cloak of altruism" (English, 1981, p. 17). It "sanctifies a movement" that otherwise is willing to ignore basic human rights and social-justice concerns. The anti-abortion movement also offers the political right its extensive organization from the national to grass roots levels, a massive membership, and the support of the Catholic Church in mobilizing and financing the movement (Oliker, 1981).

The conservative sweep in the 1980 elections appeared to improve dramatically the chances for bold anti-abortion initiatives at the federal level. No president has offered stronger support to the anti-abortion forces than President Reagan. The 97th Congress is considerably more conservative than its predecessors with key pro-choice supporters having been replaced by anti-abortion activists. Moreover, the Republican majority in the Senate has placed abortion opponents in crucial committee chairmanships. Senator Orrin

Hatch (R-Utah) replaced the defeated Senator Birch Bayh as Chairman of the Judiciary Subcommittee on the Constitution, and Senator Strom Thurmond (R-South Carolina) replaced Senator Edward Kennedy (D-Massachusetts) as Chairman of the full Senate Judiciary Committee.

Within this new political context, many of the proposals for a constitutional amendment have reappeared. The human life amendment (which provides an exception to save the mother's life) was proposed by Senator Jake Garn (R-Utah) and Representative James Oberstar (D-Minnesota). Senator Helms introduced the "paramount" human life amendment banning all abortions. Senator Hatch has been joined by abortion opponents Senators Jeremiah Denton (R-Alabama), Don Nickles (R-Oklahoma), and Rudy Boschwitz (R-Minnesota) in cosponsoring a human life federalism amendment.

Despite the gains made by anti-abortion forces in the 1980 elections, it soon became evident that they do not have the votes to secure passage of a human life amendment--the ultimate objective of the right-to-life movement. This has led, once again, to a search for an interim strategy and the proposed approaches have divided the anti-abortion movement.

One approach is that proposed by Senator Hatch in the Human Life Federalism Amendment. Hatch contends that this proposal represents a more reasonable approach designed to appeal to moderates in the Congress without whom no amendment can be passed. While he remains committed to the traditional human life amendment, he sees this compromise as a major first step toward achieving the ultimate goal. The strategy underlying the Hatch amendment comes from a "confidential," but widely publicized, memo by David O'Steen, executive director of the Minnesota Citizens Concerned for Life (O'Steen, 1981). In that memo, O'Steen outlines a three-step strategy including two constitutional amendments. First, an amendment would be proposed that simply gave Congress and the states the authority to protect all human life. O'Steen contends that such a seemingly reasonable proposal would be difficult for anyone to oppose. Following ratification of the first amendment, Congress could move forward to enact, by a simple majority vote, legislation for protection of the unborn child "consistent with that desired in the ultimate amendment." It is assumed that this statutory restriction on abortion gradually would create the public consensus needed for the final step: passage and ratification of a human life amendment.

Departing from its long-standing policy of not supporting specific atni-abortion proposals, the National Council of
Catholic Bishops has backed the Hatch amendment as an
"achievable solution" (Roberts, 1981, p. 1). Other support
within the ranks of the anti-abortion movement, however,
has not been forthcoming. Shortly after the Hatch amendment was introduced, the National Right-to-Life Committee
leadership voted unanimously to support a human life amendment (Fisher, 1981). A coalition of over 60 pro-life and
pro-family organizations announced its opposition to the Hatch
amendment and called on President Reagan to press for passage of another interim proposal, the Human Life Statute
(Human Life Statute Coalition).

The Human Life Statute was introduced by Senator
Helms and Representative Hyde as a means to circumvent
the process of amending the Constitution in order to overturn
the 1973 Supreme Court decision. The Helms-Hyde statute
would define the word "person" in the Fourteenth Amendment
to include the unborn from the moment of conception and therefore extend the protection of due process of law to the unborn "person." This statute also would strip the lower federal courts of their jurisdiction over abortion cases.

The appeal of a human life statute is that it requires
only a simple majority vote in each house of Congress and
the President's signature to become law. While it has gained
support from a number of pro-life groups, the Helms-Hyde
statute has been widely criticized (Donovan, 1981; Paul &
Klassel, 1981). Many question its constitutionality and view
such an attempt by Congress to overturn a Supreme Court
ruling by statute as setting a dangerous precedent. Both
pro-choice and anti-abortion groups also have denounced the
proposal, on the grounds that it is inappropriate for Congress
to determine when life begins.

At no time since the 1973 Supreme Court decision
have the prospects for passage of restrictions on abortion
appeared greater. Yet, groups within the anti-abortion movement cannot agree on how best to proceed. Some want to
capture the moment and pursue interim policies that have
greater chance of passing. Others refuse to compromise
when the momentum seems to be in the direction of ultimate
victory. The proposals currently before Congress reflect the
disagreements within the anti-abortion movement and among
its supporters in Congress.

The lack of consensus within the right-to-life movement diminishes the likelihood of any anti-abortion measure being adopted in the near future. It also provides an opportunity for pro-choice groups to strengthen their efforts to protect the rights won by women in the 1973 Supreme Court decision. Those efforts, however, must not be confined only to proposals on abortion. Many believe that the attack on abortion is simply the first step in an assault on reproductive rights and the gains made by women in the past decade. More generally, it is seen as part of a larger attempt to impose a conservative set of morals and values held by a small minority on the rest of the population. The inconsistency between this attempt and conservative claims to be the champions of individual liberty and freedom of choice should not go unnoticed.

References

Alan Guttmacher Institute. A 1976 State Hospital Association Survey. New York: Alan Guttmacher Institute, 1976.

_____. (b) 1976 State Medical Society Survey. New York: Alan Guttmacher Institute, 1976.

American College of Obstetricians and Gynecologists. Policy Statement, February 10, 1973.

American Hospital Association. House of Delegates Resolution, February 7, 1973.

American Medical Association. House of Delegates Resolution, June 1973.

Congressional Record. House of Representatives, December 7, 1977, p. H12773.

Donovan, Patricia. "Half a Loaf: A New Antiabortion Strategy." Family Planning Perspectives, 1981, 13, (6): 262-268.

English, Dierdre. "The War Against Choice: Inside the Antiabortion Movement." Mother Jones, 1981 6 (2): 16-24.

Fisher, P. A. "NRLC Board Unanimously Approves Paramount HLA." The Wanderer, October 15, 1981, pp. 51-60.

Forrest, J. D. , Henshaw, S. ; Sullivan E. ; and Tietze C. "Abortion 1977-1979: Need and Services in the United States. " New York: The Alan Guttmacher Institute, 1980.

Granberg, Donald. "The Abortion Activists. " Family Planning Perspectives, 1981, 13 (4): 157-163.

Henshaw, Stanley K. , Forrest, J. D. ; Sullivan, E. ; and Tietze C. "Abortion Services in the United States, 1979 and 1980. " Family Planning Perspectives, 1982 14 (1): 5-15.

Hospital Practice, 1970, 5 (8): 19. "Abortion Training Policies Hold Spotlight at AMA. "

Human Life Statute Coalition. Press release, Washington, D. C. (no date).

Jaffe, Frederick S. ; Lindheim, Barbara L. ; and Lee, Philip R. Abortion Politics: Private Morality and Public Policy. New York: McGraw-Hill, 1981.

National Conference of Catholic Bishops. Pastoral Plan for Pro-Life Activities. November 20, 1975.

New York Times, excerpt, September 29, 1975, p. 21.

Oliker, Stacey. "Abortion and the Left: The Limits of 'Pro-Family' Politics. " Socialist Review, 1981 56: 71-95.

O'Steen, D. N. "The Case for a New Pro-Life Strategy-- Two Amendments. " Confidential memorandum, 1981.

Paul, Eve W. and Dara Klassel. "Outlawing Abortion: Proposed Constitutional Amendments and 'Human Life' Statutes Analyzed. " New York: The Planned Parenthood Federation of America, Inc. , October 1981.

Planned Parenthood Washington Memo. "Abortion Foes Differ on Strategy in Wake of Defeat of Constitutional Amendment," October 17, 1975.

Roberts, S. V. "Catholic Bishops Support a Move Allowing States to Ban Abortions. " New York Times, November 6, 1981, p. 6.

Roe v. Wade, 410 U. S. 113 (1973), p. 50.

U. S. Department of Health and Human Services, Center for Disease Control. "Abortion Surveillance: Annual Summary, 1977" (Table 1). Atlanta: Center for Disease Control, 1979.

ABORTION POLICIES: THE VIEW FROM THE MIDDLE

By L. W. Sumner

Abortion remains the most perplexing and intractable moral problem of our time. The issues it raises are encountered at two distinct levels. For those actually or potentially involved in the practice of abortion--women faced with unwanted pregnancies, friends or counsellors attempting to give them advice, health professionals debating whether to perform or assist at abortions--the problem is direct and personal. The basic moral question at this personal level is whether undergoing, or performing, an abortion is morally justifiable. Although this question will be confronted by many individuals, and perhaps by most women, over the course of their lives, for others it may never arise at all. The personal question does not generalize to all members of society.

At the second level abortion is a matter of public policy. Every society must decide whether, and how, it will regulate abortions. A society may decide that abortion requires no special regulation--no constraints beyond those applicable to all medical procedures--or it may decide to treat abortion as a special case. The basic moral question at this social level is whether undergoing, or performing, an abortion is to be legally permissible. Whatever the shape of a society's abortion policy, settling on one policy or another is unavoidable and thus at the social level the moral perplexities created by abortion are unavoidable. The choice of an abortion policy is the legitimate concern of all members of society capable of participation in the political process. Unlike the personal problem, the social problem raised by abortion does not confront us only when we are involved as participants. It is addressed to all of us simply as citizens.

The personal problem raised by abortion is commonly felt by those who confront it as a moral problem. That the social problem is also a moral one can be disguised by the

fact that it can seem merely political. Thus in a democracy
it may be said that we discover which policy is to be preferred by determining which will be selected by the appropriate
procedure: the legislature, an authoritative court, a referendum, or whatever. The selection of an abortion policy thus
becomes a question of social choice. Now it is certainly true
that some political procedures confer a greater degree of legitimacy on policies than do others, but no procedure can en-
sure that the policies it selects are morally justifiable. The
most impeccable of political systems (including democracies)
are capable of generating morally abhorrent policies. Thus
beyond the political questions concerning the choice of a policy
there is always a further and independent moral question. It
is this moral question, as it applies to abortion policies,
which this paper will address. The question may be put thus:
Of all the possible abortion policies that a society might select and enforce, which is morally acceptable?

It will help to begin with a short survey of the available alternatives. Broadly speaking, abortion policies divide
into three sorts. A policy is permissive if it treats abortion
at every stage of pregnancy as a form of minor surgery.
Permissive policies will impose on abortions only those constraints applicable to medical procedures in general, concerning for instance the competance of the practitioner, the standards of the facilities, and the informed consent of the patient.
A policy is restrictive if it treats abortion at every stage of
pregnancy as a form of homicide. Restrictive policies will
either prohibit abortions outright or severely limit their justifying gounds, for instance to cases in which continuation of a
pregnancy threatens the woman's life. A policy is moderate if
it falls somewhere between the extremes defined by permissive and restrictive policies. Moderate policies commonly
impose two sorts of special constraint on abortion, concerning the stage of pregnancy at which an abortion is performed
and the reason for performing it. These constraints may take
different forms and may be combined in different ways. The
result is that while permissive and restrictive policies are
much of a piece, moderate policies are a mixed bag. Depending on their ingredients moderate policies may tend toward
either the permissive or the restrictive extreme of the range
of available alternatives.

Although it is analytically useful to distinguish the social problem of abortion from the personal, they are obviously
connected. The morality of abortion policies is partially (not
wholly) determined by the morality of abortion itself. A view

of the morality of abortion will typically address both problems. The public debate over abortion is a conflict among such views. The debate in most countries is dominated by two groups, whom we may for convenience call liberals and conservatives. Each group begins with an assessment of the moral status of the fetus, since it is the fact that abortion results in the death of the fetus that is the source of our moral qualms about it. Liberals believe that human fetuses have no greater intrinsic moral significance than body parts. Abortion is therefore morally on a par with the removal of an appendix or the pulling of a tooth. As a method of population control it is morally no more problematic than contraception. It therefore requires no special regulation, and the only appropriate policy is a permissive one. Conservatives, on the other hand, believe that human fetuses have as much intrinsic moral significance as adult members of the species. Abortion is therefore morally on a par with murder or manslaughter. As a method of population control it is morally no less problematic than infanticide. It therefore requires special regulation, and the only appropriate policy is a restrictive one.

These established views are both simple and internally coherent. Beginning from diametrically opposed valuations of the fetus, they progress inevitably in diametrically opposed abortion policies. The conflict between the established views defines the public abortion debate in most countries. Faced with this polarization, it is easy to conclude that the established views exhaust our available options. Either abortion is the moral equivalent of contraception or it is the moral equivalent of infanticide. Against the simplicity and power of the extreme views, more moderate positions appear muddled and indecisive.

But it is the very simplicity of the established views, apparently their greatest virtue, which is in fact their main defect. The moral problems, personal and social, raised by abortion do not appear to be simple. The established views treat as an illusion the intricacies and convolutions that most of us find so puzzling. We should be wary of those who contend that apparently complicated matters are really quite straightforward. For evidence of the complexities of the moral problems of abortion we need look no further than the flourishing of the established views themselves. If the problems really were as simple as both sides claim, it would be quite inexplicable that two diametrically opposed solutions to them should each attract a substantial and committed following.

For all their obvious differences, the two established views share one important feature. Each defends a uniform abortion policy, on which all abortions are treated alike. Each bases its policy on a uniform view of the morality of abortion, on which all abortions are placed in the same moral category. And each bases its evaluation of abortion in turn on a uniform view of the moral status of the fetus, on which all (human) fetuses are assigned the same moral status. It is this uniformity which makes possible the simplicity of the established views. But it is also this uniformity which is most at odds with common-sense attitudes toward abortion. We should not allow the high public profile of the established views to mislead us into thinking that either commands majority support in most societies, or indeed that they do so jointly. Opinion polls in the Western democracies tend to show that only a small minority of respondents supports either the liberal or the conservative position (Badgley, 1977 and Lane, et al., 1974). Most persons with views on abortion seek out some middle ground which attaches significance to two factors ignored entirely by both of the established views: when an abortion is performed, and why. The common-sense view appears to be that early abortions are morally less objectionable than later ones, and that some grounds for abortion are less objectionable than others. Neither of these ingredients can find a place within a uniform view of abortion. The uniformity--and the resulting simplicity--of the established views renders them repugnant to common sense.

Common-sense attitudes toward abortion can be put into practice only by a moderate abortion policy. But the fact that common sense will not have either of the established views nor either of the extreme policies they promote, does not take us far. Moral problems are not solved by appeals to opinion polls. If the view from the middle is to be given an adequate defense, some considerations in the favor must be found in addition to its congeniality to common sense. And here again moderate policies appear to be at a disadvantage. It is easy to see how to defend a permissive or a restrictive policy: the established views show us how. But it is not easy to see how to defend a moderate policy. If our intuitions favor such a policy, how can we enlist reason as well on our side?

A closer critique of the established views may reveal their deficiencies more clearly so that we may also see more clearly how they are to be avoided. The heart of each view is its assignment of moral status to the fetus. We should remind ourselves that although we conveniently use the label "fetus" to cover all human beings in that period between conception and birth, the label conceals the spectacular changes that a fetus undergoes during gestation and thus conceals the enormous differences between fetuses at different stages of development. A fetus begins its life as a single-celled animal and ends its (fetal) life as a medium-sized and highly complex mammal. Each of us has undergone qualitatively greater changes during the first nine months of our lives then we will experience during our entire remaining duration. A fetus at conception is as different in function and structure from a full-term fetus as an amoeba is from the family dog. Yet both of the established views assign to them the same moral status at all times, regardless of their level of development.

Liberals believe that all fetuses are mere things with no moral standing in their own right. This view is attractive if we attend to the earlier stages of fetal development, since it produces the plausible result that the use of a "morning-after" pill or an intrauterine device (both of which are abortifacients) is as morally innocuous as the use of a contraceptive. But it becomes much less attractive when we move on to the later stages of development, since it produces the implausible result that abortion shortly before birth is morally innocuous while infanticide immediately after birth is not.[1] For the liberal, although conception has little or no moral significance, birth has enormous significance. But it is difficult to see why an event that is basically the severing of the life-support connection between two bodies should be thought to be so important. How can it be that the fetus has no moral significance whatever as long as it is attached to its mother, but it suddenly acquires such significance as soon as this attachment ends? How could anyone think that being attached to another deprives one of moral standing? The liberal view, which works so well for the beginning of gestation, breaks down entirely for its end. Liberals can distinguish late abortion from infanticide only at the cost of investing birth with a moral salience it does not merit.

Conservatives believe that all fetuses have full moral standing--the same status as a normal adult. This view is attractive if we attend to the later stages of fetal development, since it produces the plausible result that the abortion of a full-term fetus is as morally serious as infanticide. But it becomes much less attractive when we move back to the earlier stages of development, since it produces the implausible result that abortion shortly after conception (including the "morning-after" pill and the intrauterine device) is morally serious while the prevention of conception is not.[2] For the conservative, although birth has little or no moral significance, conception has enormous significance. But it is difficult to see why an event that is basically the union of two sex cells (gametes), each with a half complement of chromosomes, should be thought to be so important. How can it be that the gametes have no moral significance whatever as long as they exist separately, but they suddenly acquire such significance as soon as they unite? How could anyone think that having a partial complement of chromosomes deprives one of moral standing? The conservative view, which works so well for the end of gestation, breaks down entirely for its beginning. Conservatives can distinguish early abortion from contraception only at the cost of investing conception with a moral salience it does not merit.

Each of the established views assigns more weight to one of the temporal boundaries of pregnancy than it can reasonably bear. Each is forced to do so by its refusal to assign any weight to fetal development. The common failure of the established views suggests that they must be superseded by a hybrid--liberal for the earlier stages of gestation and conservative for the later. A uniform view of the moral status of the fetus is thus abandoned for a differential one, in which moral status is correlated with level of development. A differential view will locate some threshold during gestation at which the fetus begins to acquire instrinsic moral importance. However, although the failure of the established views provides some motivation for seeking such an alternative, we still lack a positive rationale for it. Where is such a threshold to be located? Why at one stage rather than another? The acquisition of which characteristic during normal prenatal development begins to entitle the fetus to moral standing?

These questions can be answered convincingly only if we look beyond the confines of the abortion issue itself. We need a general criterion of moral standing that will identify the characteristics or capacities whose possession by human beings entitles them to moral consideration. Any number of candidates can be advanced--rationality, the capacity for autonomous choice, moral agency--but the higher the standard is set the larger the class of those who will be excluded by it; the young, the mentally retarded, the mentally ill, the senile, among others. A high standard makes it very diffi-

cult to explain, or support, the common opposition to such
practices as infanticide or the selective "euthanasia" of the
mentally handicapped. If we are to explain and support our
common moral convictions concerning human life then we need
to cast the moral net very widely indeed. We can do this
only if we select as our criterion for inclusion within the
moral realm a characteristic which is widely shared by human beings. One such characteristic is sentience--the capacity for experiencing pleasure and pain, enjoyment and suffering, satisfaction and frustration. If we grant that any creature
that possesses this capacity (or set of capacities) has a claim
upon our moral attention--has moral standing--then we can
easily explain why we distribute such standing so readily across
all of the (postnatal) members of our species. We can also explain why we commonly regard members of higher animal
species, and especially other mammals, as objects of moral
concern who can be wronged by our actions. If we are to
distribute moral standing widely within our own species than
consistency requires that we distribute it as well over other
species.

Selecting sentience as our criterion of moral standing
thus enables us to explain and support many of our common
moral beliefs and practices. It will serve us equally well
for the issue of abortion. An early, undeveloped fetus is
nonsentient; thus it lacks moral standing. For it the liberal
view is applicable. A late, developed fetus is sentient; thus
it possesses moral standing. For it the conservative view
is applicable. Since sentience is acquired at some stage during gestation, its use as a criterion enables us to locate somewhere during prenatal development the threshold at which
moral standing is initially acquired. This criterion therefore
grounds a differential view of the morality of abortion, and
a differential abortion policy. The uniformity that was the
fetal defect of both of the established views is avoidable. We
are able to manage more than simply grafting these views
together into an ungainly hybrid; we can show how a plausible
general criterion of moral standing requires just such a differential approach to abortion. The common-sense intuitive
preference for a middle ground, and for a moderate abortion
policy, has a rational foundation.

It follows that any acceptable abortion policy must sa-
tisfy three conditions.

(1) It must set a time limit that divides early from
late abortions. The threshold of moral standing is the acqui-

sition of sentience. The capacities that constitute sentience-
including the most primitive of them, such as the experience
of pleasure and pain--are not acquired suddenly. The threshold of moral standing is thus a stage, and not a point, in
fetal development. This fact introduces some borderline
vagueness into the morality of abortion, since it will be unclear whether some fetuses are to count as sentient. This
moral vagueness, which is matched by similar gray areas in
other moral issues involving human development, is quite
tolerable. An abortion policy, however, is unworkable if it
is vague. It must therefore establish a reasonably precise
time limit. Any such limit will inevitably be somewhat arbitrary, in the same way that age qualifications for driving
or voting are arbitrary. It is enough that the limit be located within the appropriate threshold stage. We need more
and better information on when a fetus becomes sentient, but
it is reasonably safe to assume that this capacity is normally
acquired sometime during the second trimester of pregnancy.
In that case it will be defensible to locate the time limit at
any point in that trimester--that is, between thirteen and
twenty-six weeks of gestation. A variety of moderate policies
is thus defensible, depending on the location of the time limit.

(2) It must be permissive for early abortions. Before the time limit a fetus is not itself an object of moral
concern. An abortion during this period is thus, as liberals
contend, a private matter--the moral equivalent of contraception or elective minor surgery. [3] For this period no special
abortion policy is necessary, or justifiable. This moral parity between abortion and other comparable medical procedures
must extend to the financing of abortions. If a society possesses a comprehensive health care program it is obliged to
include abortions within its scope. Failure to do so will impose special impediments on those who seek abortions, and
no such discriminatory treatment can be justified.

(3) It must be restrictive for late abortions. Any
time limit set during the second trimester will allow women
sufficient time both to discover their pregnancies and to decide whether they wish to carry them through. (A time limit
later in the second timester obviously allows a longer period
for discovery and decision than an earlier limit and is to be
preferred on this ground.) After the time limit has passed
an abortion will not be available without inquiry into its grounds.
If we are to take seriously protection of fetal life beyond the
time limit, these justifying grounds must be restrictive (though
not as restrictive as conservatives commonly urge). Two

grounds are defensible: (a) where continuation of a pregnancy will pose a serious threat to the life or health of the mother, and (b) where a serious fetal abnormality has been diagnosed. What is to count as serious in both cases is open to interpretation; again a range of policies will be possible. However, each ground must be construed fairly strictly, for neither may serve as a covert device for continuing a permissive policy past the time limit. It would be at least appropriate, and perhaps mandatory, to establish some screening mechanism for abortion requests beyond the time limit--within a hospital, a therapeutic abortion committee to apply general guidelines to particular cases.

These three conditions impose limits on what can count as an acceptable abortion policy. They exclude entirely policies that are uniformly permissive or restrictive. They also exclude moderate policies that require justifying grounds at all stages of pregnancy. In emphasizing the importance of a time limit and of grounds for late abortions they capture the common-sense conviction that it matters both when abortions are done and why they are done.

The central issue of the abortion problem is the moral status of the fetus. No abortion policy is morally justified unless it is grounded on a defensible position on this issue. A moderate policy is the only sort which can be thus grounded. If we look beyond this central issue the merits of a moderate policy become even more conspicuous. Moderate policies protect the freedom of women to control their own reproductive processes and to determine the uses to be made of their bodies. Every woman who becomes pregnant will have the opportunity to decide whether she wishes to continue the pregnancy. Moderate policies also encourage early abortions (before the time limit). Early abortions are demonstrably safer than later ones--and safer also than childbirth (Cates, et al. , 1977). By requiring no screening of abortions before the time limit, moderate policies eliminate delays which result in later and more hazardous abortions. Moderate policies also protect maternal life and health by allowing the termination of hazardous pregnancies even after the time limit. Finally, by permitting the abortion of severely handicapped fetuses, moderate policies reduce the anguish suffered by parents who give birth to such infants.

Moderate abortion policies that meet the conditions of acceptability are not rare, but they are also far from universal. Although they may have been adopted in some countries as matters of principle, in many others they have been the outcomes of political compromise between the opposed demands of liberals and conservatives. Moderate policies have obvious political advantages. What is more important is that they also have a moral justification independent of the political prodecures by means of which they come to be adopted. No conscientious person, no one prepared to take seriously the moral issues raised by abortion, should be prepared to accept a policy that lacks such a justification. In the choice of abortion policies the only moral way is the middle way.

* * *

The contentions of this paper are presented in greater detail in the author's book Abortion and Moral Theory (Princeton, N. J.: Princeton University Press, 1981).

Notes

1. I assume here that a liberal on the abortion question does not wish also to approve infanticide. This pair of views is inconsistent. The liberal can recover consistency by abandoning opposition to infanticide, but this is a high price to pay for maintaining a view of abortion.
2. I assume here that a conservative on the abortion question does not wish also to condemn contraception. This pair of views is inconsistent. The conservative can recover consistency by abandoning approval of contraception, but this is a high price to pay for maintaining a view of abortion.
3. Most contraceptives are cheaper, safer, and less traumatic than most abortifacients. These advantages justify a birth control policy which encourages contraception as the primary line of defense, but they are practical and not moral advantages.

References

Badgley, Robin F. Report of the Committee on the Operation of the Abortion Law. Ottawa: Supply and Services Canada, 1977.

Cates, W., Jr.; Schulz, K. F.; Grimes, D. A.; and Tyler, C. W., Jr. "Legal Abortion Mortality in the United States:

Epidemiologic Surveillance, 1972-1974," Journal of the American Medical Association, 1977, vol. 237 (5): 452-455.

Lane, The Hon. Mrs. Justice, et al. Report of the Committee on the Working of the Abortion Act. London: Her Majesty's Stationery Office, 1974.

PART II:

ABOUT THE ABORTION SEEKERS

THE EPIDEMIOLOGY OF ADOLESCENT ABORTION IN THE UNITED STATES

By Nancy V. Ezzard, Willard Cates, Jr. , and Kenneth F. Schulz

Introduction

During the 1970s, the United States was reported to have one of the highest teenage fertility rates in the world (Alan Gutt-macher Institute [AGI], 1981). In addition, teenagers had accounted for most of the increase in childbearing among un-married women in the United States between 1965 and 1970 (Sklar & Berkov, 1974), and the out-of-wedlock birthrate for teenagers continued to increase throughout the 1970s (Bald-win, 1981). Although fertility rates for teenagers declined during this time (Baldwin, 1981), the reported pregnancy rate increased slowly and the abortion rate doubled from 20 to 44 abortions per 1,000 15- to 19-year-old women (See Figure 1). Thus, legal abortion had played an inportant role in teen-age fertility control.

In 1978, approximately 1.2 million reported pregnan-cies (including 460,000 abortions) (Centers for Disease Con-trol [CDC], unpublished data: a) occurred among women less than age 20 in the United States, of whom 5 million were es-timated to be sexually active (AGI, 1981); approximately 200,000 additional pregnancies ended in spontaneous miscarriages and stillbirths (Tietze, 1978). Most (77%) of the pregnancies were unintended (AGI, 1981) and almost half (44%) of the births were delivered out-of-wedlock (National Center for Health Statistics [NCHS], 1980). At 1976 rates, almost 40 percent of today's 14-year-olds in the United States will experience one pregnancy before they are 20, and 15 percent will have legal abortion (Tietze, 1978).

In this chapter, we will discuss the changing patterns

73

FIGURE 1

Reported Pregnancy Rate and Legal Abortion Rate for Teenagers, by Age at Conception, United States, 1972-1978

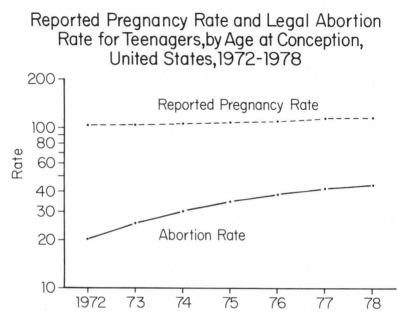

Note: Reported pregnancies (live births plus legal abortions) to women less than 20 years of age per 1,000 15- to 19-year-old women.

Sources: Centers for Disease Control, unpublished data (a); U. S. Bureau of the Census. Current population reports. (Series P-25, 721 & 870). Washington, D. C.: Department of Commerce, 1978 & 1980.

---

of abortion use by teenagers in the United States, the medical risks of abortion for teenagers, and the public health impact in the United States of the increasing availability of legal abortion for teenagers.

Characteristics of Teenage Abortion Use

Although attitude surveys indicate that teenagers are less likely to approve of abortion than are women in their middle reproductive years (Zelnik & Kantner, 1975), a disproportionate number of abortions are obtained by teenagers. Abortion ratios (abortions/ 1,000 live births) are one indicator of the proportion of pregnancies that are unplanned. In this chapter, we present abortion ratios calculated by the mother's age at conception, because artificially high ratios result for teenagers when such ratios are calculated by her age at the time of abortion (Tietze, 1981); age at time of abortion was reduced by 3 months and age at time of birth by 9 months. Even after this age correction, abortion ratios for teenagers in the United States are higher than those for every age range except 35 to 39 and 40 and older (Tietze, 1981).

In 1972, white teenagers less than 15 years of age had the highest legal abortion ratio among teenagers (Ezzard, Cates, Kramer, & Tietze, 1982). The abortion ratio for white teenagers decreased with increasing age. Legal abortion ratios for black and other minority teenagers in each age category were lower than those for white teenagers of corresponding ages. By 1978, all abortion ratios for teenagers had increased, and age- and race-specific differences had narrowed; the range in abortion ratios indicated that 37-40 percent of reported pregnancies were ending in abortion. In 1978, the least race-specific difference in abortion ratios occurred for teenagers less than 15 years of age for whom abortion ratios were essentially equal; the ratios for this age group were also lower than at least one ratio for older teenagers of the same race. Since more of the pregnancies to teenagers less than 15 years of age in 1978 were unplanned and out-of-wedlock (AGI, 1981; NCHS, 1980), factors other than planning status must contribute to their less-than-expected use of abortion. Young teenagers are more negative about abortion than are older teenagers (Zelnik & Kantner, 1975), have a greater tendency to delay abortion (Cates, 1980), and are more dependent on parents for source of payment (Torres, Forrest, & Eisman, 1980).

The higher a teenager's socioeconomic status, the more likely she is to terminate a pregnancy by abortion. In 1978 in Rhode Island, 56 percent of all pregnancies to teenagers living in the highest socioeconomic-status areas were terminated by abortion as compared with 22 percent of those among teenagers living in poverty areas (AGI, 1981).

Medical Risks of Abortion for Teenagers

As with any other surgical procedure, abortion involves some risk. Teenagers are at no greater risk of complications than are older women, and they have a lower risk of death.

SHORT-TERM MORBIDITY

Teenagers have major complication rates similar to those for older women for surgical evacuation methods (suction curettage and dilatation & evacuation) but significantly lower rates for saline instillation (Cates & Schulz, 1980). For suction curettage procedures performed at 12 weeks' gestation or earlier, the total major complication rate varies between 0.3 and 0.4 per 100 procedures regardless of the woman's age. Teenagers have significantly lower rates for uterine perforation, transfusion for hemorrhage, and unintended major surgery, but they have higher rates for cervical injury.

After 12 weeks' gestation, the type of method used affects the rates of short-term major complications for teenagers. Abortions performed by dilatation and evacuation (D & E) have significantly lower short-term major complication rates for teenagers (0.5/100 procedures) than do those performed by either saline instillation (1.2) or prostaglandin instillation (2.0). Although rates for cervical injury are higher following D & E than instillation, routine use of laminaria reduces the rate of cervical injury following D & E (Cates, Schulz, Gold, & Tyler, 1979; Grimes & Cates, 1979).

MORTALITY

Between 1972 and 1978, 29 teenage women died following legally induced abortion and 14 died following illegally (nonphysician) induced abortion. Teenagers of black and other minority races represented a higher proportion of the deaths following illegal abortion (80%) than those following legal abortion (35%); however, 9 of the 11 deaths to minority teenagers following illegal abortion occurred in 1972 and 1973.

a. Illegal Abortion

Because illegal abortion is a clandestine event, no accurate denominators are available to calculate death-to-case rates for teenagers compared to older women. Among black and other minority women, the proportion of teenage deaths after illegally induced abortion (20%) was similar to the proportion after legally induced procedures (14%); among white women the proportion of teenage deaths after illegally induced abortion (12%) was much lower than the proportion after legal procedures (29%) (CDC, unpublished data: b). If these numerators are accurate reflections of the denominators, this indicates that black and other minority teenagers were neither more nor less likely than older women of the same race to be using illegally induced abortion, whereas white teenagers were less likely than older white women to be using illegally induced abortion. In 1972-1978, the major causes of death to teenagers following illegal abortion were the same as those for older women; the majority (64%) died from infection and a smaller proportion (21%) died after an embolus.

b. Legal Abortion

Between 1972 and 1978, the death-to-case rate for legal abortion decreased (CDC, 1980). The crude death-to-case rate for teenagers between 1972 and 1978, 1.3 deaths per 100,000 procedures, was significantly lower than the rates for older women (LeBolt, Grimes, & Cates, 1982). The rate for black and other minority teenagers (1.5) was not significantly different than the rate for white teenagers (1.1). Moreover, standardized death-to-case rates for abortion and childbirth between 1972 and 1978 show that the teenagers' risk of death from pregnancy continuation was nearly 6 times higher than that from pregnancy termination (LeBoldt, Grimes, & Cates, 1982). The relative risk of death from childbirth remains higher than that for legal abortion until gestational ages of 16 weeks or later (Cates & Tietze, 1978).

Gestational age at the time of abortion is the most important determinant of abortion complications (Cates, Schulz, Grimes, & Tyler, 1977); the risk of death increases by 50 percent for each week of delay after 8 weeks of gestation (Cates & Tietze, 1978). In 1978, teenagers were still twice as likely as older women to obtain abortions after 12 weeks' gestation (Table 1). Almost half (44%) of the abortions performed after 12 weeks' gestation in 1978 were to teenagers (CDC, 1980). In addition, younger teenagers were twice as likely as older teenagers to obtain their abortions at 16 weeks of gestation or later, when the risk of complications and death is the greatest (See Table I).

In a study of fatal septic abortion from 1975 to 1977, the risk of death from infection following legal abortion was found to be inversely related to a woman's age and directly related to gestational age of the time of abortion (Grimes, Cates, & Selik, 1981). Teenagers had a death-to-case rate from infection following legal abortion 6 times higher than that for women 25 years of age or more. Accordingly, causes of death following legal abortion from 1972 to 1978 were dif-

TABLE I:

Percent Distribution of Legal Abortions, By Woman's Age and
Weeks of Gestation, United States, 1978

Weeks of Gestation	Years of Age		
	< 14	15-19	> 20
≤8	32. 7%	40. 8%	54. 3%
9-12	44. 3	46. 1	38. 3
13-15	8. 7	6. 1	3. 7
≥16	14. 4	7. 1	3. 7
Total	100. 0%	100. 0%	100. 0%

Source: Centers for Disease Control. Abortion Surveillance,
1978. Atlanta, Ga. : Author, 1980.

___

ferent for teenagers than for older women. Teenagers were
more likely to die from infection but less likely to die from
hemorrhage (See Table II). These trends were greatest for
teenagers of black and other minority races, where 60 percent of the deaths were from infection. Death from infection
in teenage women was usually related to unrecognized retained
products of conception after a uterine evacuation procedure.
Underestimation of gestational age by at least 4 weeks was
a factor in 3 of the 12 teenage deaths due to infection between 1972 and 1978 (Cates & Grimes, manuscript submitted
for publication). Nine of the young women delayed seeking
treatment of postabortion symptoms, possibly because of reluctance to let their parents know that they had had an abortion procedure (Cates, 1980).

Two types of delay, then, are associated with increased medical risk of abortion for teenagers: 1) delay in
seeking the abortion procedure, and 2) delay in seeking treatment for postabortion complications. Distance from the abortion facility and legal requirements for parental notification
or approval are among the factors that contribute to delay in
obtaining abortions (Bracken & Kasl, 1975). Although the
Supreme Court has ruled unconstitutional any law requiring
abortion facilities to ask for parental consent before providing abortion services to minors, almost one third of the facilities in 1980 required parental consent or notification for
women 17 years of age or younger (AGI, 1981). Some of the

TABLE II:

Primary Causes of Death Following Legally Induced Abortion, By Race and Age, United States, 1972-1978

Cause of Death	Teenagers			Older Women		
	White (N=19)	Black & Other (N=10)	Total (N=29)	White (N=46)	Black & Other (N=63)	Total (N-109)
Infection	32%	60%	41%	13%	25%	20%
Embolus	37%	0%	24%	26%	22%	24%
Anesthesia reaction	10%	20%	14%	11%	19%	16%
Hemorrhage	5%	0%	4%	15%	19%	17%
Other	16%	20%	17%	35%	14%	23%
Total	100%	100%	100%	100%	100%	100%

Source: Centers for Disease Control, unpublished mortality data.

factors that contribute to delay can be eliminated through health education programs and increased availability of abortion services. However, an analysis of delayed abortion in an area where abortion was readily available found that much of the delay was related to individual-oriented factors (Burr & Schulz, 1980); a history of irregular periods was the strongest single determinant for seeking a late abortion. Thus, continued efforts are needed to make late abortion procedures safer, cheaper, and more readily available. Following the abortion procedure, teenagers in particular need to be counseled about the signs and symptoms of infection and urged to obtain treatment promptly; treatment facilities that can respond to complications in a confidential manner, without involving parents, need to be available.

EMOTIONAL COMPLICATIONS

In comparison to older women, some studies have shown that teenagers are at higher risk of short-term psychological sequelae: anxiety, depression, sadness, guilt, and regret (Bracken, Hachamovitch, & Grossman, 1974). However, a study in 1975 based on the entire population of Denmark found that first admission rates to psychiatric hospitals within three months after delivery or abortion were lower for teenagers than for older women (David, Rasmussen, & Holst, 1981). Teenagers had a higher admission rate following abortion (11.4 admissions/10,000 women) than did teenagers following delivery (6.2) or all other teenagers in Denmark (4.9). The importance of a stable partner relationship was stressed in this study. Other factors influencing a teenager's reaction to abortion are the level of parental support, her preabortion psychological state, attitudes and support of the attending medical staff, the degree of her ambivalence about abortion, and the opportunity for her to make her own decision regarding the abortion.

The type of abortion procedure also affects the psychological sequelae; uterine curettage procedures are associated with more favorable postabortion reactions than are labor-like instillation procedures (Kaltreider, Goldsmith, & Margolis, 1979; Rooks & Cates, 1977). Since teenagers are more likely to delay abortion until the later gestational ages, when instillation procedures may be used, clinicians should be aware of the emotional impact of the particular method used.

LONG-TERM EFFECTS

Studies of adverse outcomes (low birth weight, short gestation, and spontaneous abortion) of pregnancies after induced abortions have had conflicting conclusions. A recent review of the available studies found significantly increased risks of adverse outcomes after a single abortion in only 2 of 29 study groups; both of these groups used surgical (sharp) curettage as the method of abortion (Tietze, 1981). A review of 10 studies could demonstrate no consistency about whether repeated abortions produce increased risks of adverse reproductive outcomes in subsequent desired pregnancies. Again, those studies that demonstrate higher risks have primarily implicated the type of abortion procedure--especially sharp curettage (Cates, Hogue, & Tietze, 1981).

Although both issues are unresolved, several clinical recommendations can be made (Cates, 1979). First, teenagers considering pregnancy termination should be encouraged to make their decision as early as possible; this will reduce both the short- and possible long-term risks of the abortion or will allow proper prenatal care early in pregnancy. Secondly, if a nulliparous teenager with a small cervix requests an abortion that would require dilatation of 11mm or more, serious consideration should be given to the use of laminaria tents. Thirdly, teenagers who have had one induced abortion should be counseled regarding the safety and effectiveness of the various medical birth control methods and urged not to rely on abortion as their primary method of birth control.

Public Health Impact of Legal Abortion on Teenagers

The availability of legal abortion for teenagers has had a positive impact on three public health parameters: deaths, births, and patterns of teenage marriage.

DEATHS

After 1973, the reported number of teenage deaths following illegal abortion declined sharply. This probably means that most teenagers are now choosing to terminate unplanned pregnancies through safer, legal channels rather than resorting to the less safe self-induced or nonphysician-induced procedures. In addition, the risk of death following legal abortion has also declined as physicians become more experienced with abortion procedures and management of complications.

BIRTHS

Use of abortion has been associated with the level of a state's teenage fertility rate. In 1974, state-to-state variation in fertility rates for 15- to 19-year-olds was significantly associated with the ratios for abortions-to-live-births for the same age group; states with the highest abortion ratios had the lowest teenage fertility rates (Brann, 1979). Although out-of-wedlock birthrates for teenagers have increased, the proportion of intended births among teenage out-of-wedlock first births has also increased, from one in five in 1971 to one in three in 1976 (Zelnik & Kantner, 1978:b). The most likely explanation is the increase in the proportion of unintended pregnancies that are terminated by abortion.

Teenagers apparently have not substituted use of abortion for medical methods of contraception but have used a combination of both to lower their birthrates. A study of the interstate variation in fertility of teenage girls showed that use of both family planning programs and abortion played roles in reducing levels of teenage fertility rates between 1970 and 1974 (Brann, 1979). In 1976, young unmarried women who became pregnant and had an abortion were no less likely to be using contraception at the time of conception than young women who became unintentionally pregnant and did not have an abortion (Zelnik & Kantner, 1978:a). Contraceptive use following abortion apparently increased during the 1970s; young unmarried women whose first pregnancy ended in abortion in 1976 showed a substantial reduction in the risk of repeat pregnancy over the 24-month period following the abortion in comparison with this risk in 1971 (Zelnik, 1980).

Although use of medical methods of contraception has increased among teenagers, the average delay between a teenager's initiation of sexual activity and her first visit to a family planning clinic in 1980 was 16 months (Zabin & Clark, 1981). More than one third of the teenagers suspected pregnancy on their initial visit. The two major reasons teenagers gave for delaying were procrastination and fear that their parents would find out. Since half of all initial premarital pregnancies occur in the first 6 months of sexual activity, and more than one fifth in the first month (Zabin, Kantner, & Zelnik, 1979), current programs providing contraceptive services for teenagers will not eliminate the need for abortion.

In addition, the risk of a premarital first pregnancy

for teenage users of contraception increased between 1976 and 1979 (Zelnik & Kantner, 1980). Part of the increase was caused by a decline in use of oral contraception and a corresponding increase in use of the less effective nonprescription methods (Aved, 1981; Zelnik & Kantner, 1980). Without the option of legal abortion, these women would have to choose between illegal abortion or an unplanned birth.

MARRIAGE TRENDS

The availability of legal abortion has also affected teenage marriage rates. In the United States, before 1969, trends in crude marriage rates among states with different levels of legal abortion services were similar (Bauman, Koch, Udry, & Freeman, 1975). Beginning in 1970, states with high abortion ratios had significantly greater declines in teenage marriage rates than did states with low ratios (Bauman, Anderson, Freeman, & Koch, 1977). In 1979, the proportion of premaritally pregnant teenagers who married during the course of their first pregnancy was half the proportion who married in 1971 (Zelnik & Kantner, 1980). This suggests that liberalized abortion policies might be providing teenagers with an alternative to marriage forced by premarital pregnancy.

Because marriage and childbearing during the teenage years have greater negative repercussions than later marriage and childbearing, these lower marriage rates may have a positive public-health impact. Teenage parents acquire less education than their contemporaries, their marriages are less stable, and they eventually have more children than they consider ideal (Card & Wise, 1978; Menken, 1972; Trussell & Menken, 1978). The effect of truncated education on later job satisfaction and income is more serious for the adolescent mother than father (Card & Wise, 1978). As long as education and childbearing continue to be mutually exclusive activities, it will be difficult for these young women to catch up with their peers.

Conclusions

Use of legal abortion by teenagers in the United States doubled between 1972 and 1978. In 1972, the year before legal abortion became nationally available, white teenagers had higher legal abortion ratios than did black and other minority teenagers; in addition, white teenagers made relatively less use of illegal abortion in comparison with older white women, whereas no age differential for use of illegal abortion occurred among black and other minority women. By 1978, age- and race-specific differences in abortion ratios for teenagers had narrowed. The annual number of illegal abortion-related deaths among teenagers declined considerably after 1973. The risk of death for teenagers following legal abortion also decreased during this time and became at least one-sixth lower than the risk of death following a term birth. Infection continued to be the primary cause of abortion-related death for teenagers. Many of these deaths could have been prevented if teenagers had obtained abortions at earlier gestational ages and if they had promptly reported symptoms of postabortion complications. A single abortion using suction curettage is apparently not associated with harmful effects on later desired pregnancies; the scientific literature is inconclusive about later effects of repeat abortions. Although current programs providing contraceptive services for teenagers have made an impact on teenage fertility rates, they will not eliminate the need for abortion. Since 1970, legal abortion has allowed teenage women in the United States to control their reproductive outcomes more effectively. Without it, the alternatives of either illegal abortion or an unplanned birth place teenagers at higher risk of morbidity.

*   *   *

The authors would like to thank Elaine Rodenhiser and Joyce Maze for their help in assembling the data.

References

The Alan Guttmacher Institute. Teenage Pregnancy: The Problem That Hasn't Gone Away. New York: Alan Guttmacher Institute, 1981.

Aved, B. M. "Trends in Contraceptive Method of Use by California Family Planning Clinic Clients Aged 10-55, 1976-1979." American Journal of Public Health, 1981, 71: 1162-1164.

Baldwin, W. "Adolescent Pregnancy and Childbearing--An Overview." Seminars in Perinatology, 1981, 5: 1-8.

Bauman, K. E.; Anderson, A. E.; Freeman, J. L.; and Koch, G. G. "Legal Abortions and Trends in Age-Specific Marriage Rates." American Journal of Public Health, 1977, 67: 52-53.

Bauman, K. E.; Koch, G. G.; Udry, J. R.; and Freeman, J. L. "The Relationship Between Legal Abortion and Marriage." Social Biology, 1975, 22: 117-124.

Bracken, M. B.; Hachamovitch, M.; and Grossman, G. "The Decision to Abort and Psychological Sequelae." Journal of Nervous and Mental Disease, 1974, 158: 154-162.

Bracken, M. B., and Kasl, S. V. "Delay in Seeking Induced Abortion: A Review and Theoretical Analysis." American Journal of Obstetrics and Gynecology, 1975, 121: 1008-1019.

Brann, E. A. "A Multivariate Analysis of Interstate Variation in Fertility of Teenage Girls." American Journal of Public Health, 1979, 69: 661-666.

Burr, W. A., and Schulz, K. F. "Delayed Abortion in an Area of Easy Accessibility." Journal of the American Medical Association, 1980, 244: 44-48.

Card, J. J., and Wise L. L. "Teenage Mothers and Teenage Fathers: The Impact of Early Childbearing on the Parents' Personal and Professional Lives." Family Planning Perspectives, 1978, 10: 199-205.

Cates, W., Jr. "Adolescent Abortions in the United States. Journal of Adolescent Health Care, 1980, 1: 18-25.

_____. "Late Effects of Induced Abortion--Hypothesis or Knowledge?" The Journal of Reproductive Medicine, 1979, 22: 207-212.

_____, and Grimes, D. A. "Deaths from Second-Trimester Abortion by Dilatation and Evacuation, United States, 1972-1978." Manuscript submitted for publication.

_____; Hogue, C. R.; and Tietze, C. "Repeat Induced Abortions: Do They Affect Future Childbearing?" Paper presented at the meeting of the American Fertility Society, Atlanta, Georgia, March 1981.

_____, and Schulz, K. F. "The Risks of Teenage Abortion." Presented at the Thirteenth Annual Meeting of the Society for Epidemiologic Research, Minneapolis, Minnesota, June 19, 1980.

_____; Gold J.; and Tyler, C. W., Jr. Complications of Surgical Evacuation Procedures for Abortions After 12 Weeks' Gestation." In Pregnancy Termination: Procedures, Safety and New Developments, Zatuchni, G. I.; Sciarra, J. J.; and Speidel, J. J., eds. Hagerstown, Md.: Harper and Row, 1979.

_____; Schulz, K. F.; Grimes, D. A.; and Tyler, C. W., Jr. "The Effect of Delay and Method Choice on the Risk of Abortion Morbidity." Family Planning Perspectives, 1977, 9: 266-273.

_____, and Tietze, C. "Standardized Mortality Rates Associated with Legal Abortion: United States, 1972-1975." Family Planning Perspectives, 1978, 10: 109-112.

Centers for Disease Control. "Abortion Surveillance, 1978." Atlanta, Ga.: Centers for Disease Control, 1980.

_____. (a) (Unpublished) "Births and Abortions to Teenagers Calculated by Age at Conception." Atlanta, Ga.: CDC

_____. (b) (Unpublished) "Mortality Data." Atlanta, Ga.: CDC David, H. P.; Rasmussen, N. K.; and Holst, E. "Postpartum and Postabortion Psychotic Reactions." Family Planning Perspectives, 1981, 13: 88-92.

Ezzard, N. V.; Cates, W., Jr.; Kramer, D. G.; and Tietze, C. "Race-Specific Patterns of Abortion Use by American Teenagers." American Journal of Public Health, 1982, 72: 809-814.

Grimes, D. A., and Cates, W., Jr. "Complications from Legally-Induced Abortion: A Review." Obstetrical and Gynecological Survey, 1979, 34: 177-191.

_____; and Selik, R. M. "Fatal Septic Abortion in the United States, 1975-1977." Obstetrics and Gynecology, 1981, 57: 739-744.

Kaltreider, N. B.; Goldsmith, S.; and Margolis, A. J. "The Impact of Midtrimester Abortion Techniques on Patients and Staff." American Journal of Obstetrics and Gynecology 1979, 135; 235-238.

LeBolt, S. A.; Grimes, D. A.; and Cates, W., Jr. "Mortality from Abortion and Childbirth: Are the Populations Comparable?" Journal of the American Medical Association, 1982, 248: 188-191.

Menken, J. "The Health and Social Consequences of Teenage Childbearing." Family Planning Perspectives, 1972, 4: 45-53.

National Center for Health Statistics, Advance Report, Final Natality Statistics, 1978. Monthly Vital Statistics Report, Vol. 29, no. 1. (DHHS publication no. (PHS) 80-1120). Hyattsville, Md.: National Center for Health Statistics, April 28, 1980.

Rooks, J. B., and Cates, W., Jr. "Emotional Impact of D & E Versus Instillation." Family Planning Perspectives, 1977, 9: 276-278.

Sklar, J., and Berkov, B. "Abortion, Illegitimacy and the American Birth Rate." Science, 1974, 185: 909-915.

Tietze, C. Induced Abortion: A World Review, 1981. New York: The Population Council, 1981.

_____. "Teenage Pregnancies: Looking Ahead to 1984." Family Planning Perspectives, 1978, 10: 205-207.

Torres, A.; Forrest, J. D.; and Eisman, S. "Telling Parents: Clinic Policies and Adolescents' Use of Family Planning and Abortion Services." Family Planning Perspectives, 1980, 12: 284-292.

Trussell, J., and Menken J. "Early Childbearing and Subsequent Fertility." Family Planning Perspectives, 1978, 10: 209-218.

Zabin, L. S., and Clark, S. D., Jr. "Why They Delay--A Study of Teenage Family Planning Clinic Patients." Family Planning Perspectives, 1981, 13: 205-215.

Zabin, L. S.; Kantner, J. F.; and Zelnik, M. "The Risk of Adolescent Pregnancy in the First Months of Intercourse." Family Planning Perspectives, 1979, 11: 215-222.

Zelnik, M. "Second Pregnancies to Premaritally Pregnant Teenagers, 1976 and 1971." Family Planning Perspectives, 1980, 12: 69-76.

_____, and Kantner, J. F. "Attitudes of American Teen-agers Toward Abortion." Family Planning Perspectives, 1975, 7: 89-91.

_____. (a) "Contraceptive Patterns and Premarital Preg-nancy Among Women Aged 15-19 in 1976." Family Plan-ning Perspectives, 1978, 10: 135-142.

_____. (b) "First Pregnancies to Women Aged 15-19: 1976 and 1971." Family Planning Perspectives, 1978, 10: 11-20.

_____. "Sexual Activity, Contraceptive Use and Pregnancy Among Metropolitan-Area Teenagers: 1971-1979." Family Planning Perspectives, 1980, 12: 230-237.

TRENDS IN LEGAL ABORTIONS AND ABORTION RATES IN CANADA, 1970-1980

By S. N. Wadhera and C. R. Nair

Introduction

The practice of induced abortion is an area of human concern. As a profound social, moral, and legal issue it involves a great risk of personal and collective bias influencing approach, the interpretation, and the use of "facts." Although induced abortion is an indisputable fact of life, the way this issue is seen by a people is reflected in the nature of a nation's laws, the type of information routinely collected, analyzed, and published, and the use to which this information is put (Badgely, 1977).

Changes in Abortion Laws

Over the past fifteen years, a number of countries liberalized their abortion laws to various degrees. At present nearly two thirds of the world's population reside in countries allowing abortion at the request of the pregnant woman, without specifying reasons, or authorizing it on broadly interpreted social, economic, and personal grounds (Tietze, 1979). Over the past two decades about 37 countries changed their abortion laws--about 33 extended grounds for abortion and 4 in East Europe narrowed them. Some countries now allow abortion on request in the first three months of pregnancy. Table I shows the changing pattern of abortion laws in selected countries. As reflected in this table, abortion laws are most liberal in Denmark, Sweden, and the United States. However, countries like France and West Germany made significant changes in their abortion laws after 1967.

In Canada, prior to August 26, 1969, the mother's life was the only ground for obtaining a legal abortion, but

TABLE I:

Ten Years of Abortion Law Reform, Selected Countries, 1967-1977

Ground for Granting Abortion	Canada	Britain	United States	Denmark	France	Sweden	West Germany
Mother's life	1	1	1	1	1	1	1
Mother's physical health	X	1	X	1	X	1	1
Mother's mental health	X	1	X	1	X	1	X
Health of fetus		X	X	1	X	1	X
Rape or incest			X	1		1	X
Social or Socio Medical				1		1	
Other requests (usually first trimester)			X	X		X	

Legend: 1 = Ground included in laws in force before 1967.
       X = Ground added since 1967.

Source: The Economist, January 29, 1977, pp. 42-43.

on that date the Parliament liberalized the existing abortion law. The new law permits termination of pregnancy in hospital(s) if a committee of not fewer than three physicians, appointed by the hospital board(s), certifies by a majority of its members that the continuation of the pregnancy would or would be likely to endanger the life or health of the pregnant woman. However, by 1980 slightly over one fourth of the 862 public general hispitals had established such committees.

Sources of Information

Various reports issued by Statistics Canada on the subject of therapeutic (legal) abortions for 1970 to 1980 [1-12] are the main source of information. Since the implementation of lib eralized abortion law in Canada on August 26, 1969, Statistics Canada with the cooperation of the provinces and the participating hospitals has coordinated the work relating to therapeutic abortion statistics at the national level. For the period 1970 to 1973 the available information relates to the counts and rates of therapeutic abortions. For 1974 to 1980, information about the selected demographic and medical characteristics of the legally aborted women is also available. International abortion data are based on Dr. Christopher Tietze's Fact Book on Induced Abortions: 1981 (New York: Population Council, 1981).

For Canada the information on induced abortions relates to therapeutic abortions authorized under the amended abortion law. Unless specified otherwise, the term "abortion" refers to a therapeutic abortion in Canada and to a legal abortion as defined by the laws of each country for which induced-abortion data are included in this paper.

Population Characteristics, Canada

The total population of Canada increased from 21.3 million in 1970 to 23.9 million in 1980--an increase of 12.2 percent over the ten-year period of 1970 to 1980. Percent of females to total population increased from 49.9 percent in 1970 to 50.6 percent in 1980 and the percent of females aged 15 to 44 years to total population increased from 21.4 percent in 1970 to 23.8 percent in 1980. The crude birthrate, general fertility rate, and rate of natural increase in population declined from 1970 to 1978 and increased slightly in 1979. The abortion rate progressively increased each year since the amendment in the abortion law. For additional details see Table II.

TABLE II:

Selected Demographic Characteristics of Canadians, 1970-1980

Characteristic	1970	1971	1972	1973	1974	1975	1976	1977	1978	1979	1980
Total Population (million)	21.3	21.6	21.8	22.1	22.4	22.8	23.0	23.2	23.5	23.7	23.9
Female Population (million)											
(a) Total	10.6	10.8	10.9	11.0	11.2	11.4	11.5	11.7	11.8	11.9	12.1
(b) 15-44 years	4.6	4.7	4.8	4.9	5.0	5.2	5.3	5.4	5.5	5.6	5.7
Crude Birth Rate (Per 1000 Population)	17.5	16.8	15.9	15.5	15.6	15.8	15.7	15.5	15.3	15.5	15.5
Rate of Natural increase (Per 1000 Population)	10.1	9.5	8.5	8.1	8.2	8.4	8.4	8.3	8.1	8.4	8.3
General Fertility Rate (Births per 1000 women age 15-49 years)	71.2	67.7	63.4	61.5	60.6	61.2	60.3	59.4	58.0	58.2	57.9
Crude Marriage Rate (Per 1000 Population)	8.8	8.9	9.2	9.0	8.9	8.7	8.4	8.0	7.9	7.9	8.0
Legal Abortion Rate (Per 1000 Population)	0.5	1.4	1.8	2.0	2.1	2.2	2.4	2.5	2.7	2.7	2.7
Legal Abortion Rate (Per 1000 females aged 15-44 years)	2.4	6.6	8.2	8.8	9.5	9.5	10.3	10.6	11.3	11.6	11.5

TABLE III:

Total Abortions and Canadian Residents Obtaining Abortions in Canada, 1970-1980

Year	Total Abortions	Abortions for Canadian Residents	
		Numbers	Percent increase over last year
1970	11,200	11,152	–
1971	30,949	30,923	177.3
1972	38,905	38,853	25.6
1973	43,245	43,201	11.2
1974	48,198	48,136	11.4
1975	49,390	49,311	2.4
1976	54,536	54,478	10.5
1977	57,620	57,564	5.7
1978	62,351	62,290	8.2
1979	65,135	65,043	4.4
1980	65,855	65,751	1.1

Abortions Performed in Canada

In 1970, the first complete calendar year immediately following abortion liberalization, the participating hospitals in Canada performed 11,200 legal abortions. This increased to
30,949 legal abortions in 1971--an increase of 177.3 percent
in one year, the largest annual jump from 1970 to 1980. By
December 1980, about 528,000 legal abortions were reported
to have been performed under the 1969 amended abortion law
in Canada. Of these 99.8 percent were in respect of Canadian residents. See Table III for the annual numbers of total
abortions and abortions to Canadian residents from 1970 to
1980.

Canadians Obtaining Abortions in the United States

The liberalization of legal abortions in several status of the
United States, especially New York State in 1970, and the
United States Supreme Court decision in early 1973 facilitated
the obtaining of legal abortions in that country. Based on
incomplete reports from some of the states in the United
States, the numbers of Canadian women who went to and obtained legal abortions in these states were highest (6,573 abortions) in 1972. It decreased in the succeeding years to 5,501
abortions in 1973; 4,299 in 1974; 4,234 in 1976; 2,300 in
1977; 1,802 in 1978; to only 1,073 abortions in 1979. In
1980 it increased again, to 1,644 abortions.

According to the report of the Badgely Committee on
the operation of abortion law in Canada, in 1974 an estimate
of 20 percent of total abortions in Canada is taken as the
basis of the number of Canadian women who obtained legal
abortions in the United States (Badgely, 1977). For 1974,
this works out to 9,627 legal abortions against 4,214 legal
abortions reported by Statistics Canada. However, in view
of the substantial increases in the annual numbers of legal
abortions in Canada from 48,198 legal abortions in 1974 to
65,855 legal abortions in 1980, it is quite possible that the
number of legal abortions obtained by Canadian women in the
United States had dropped considerably during the years 1974
to 1980.

Abortion Rates, Canada

It is customary to relate abortions to (a) the total population
or preferably the female population of reproductive ages 15
to 44 years and (b) the total number of live births, live births

plus abortions, deliveries, or pregnancies. Measures relating abortions to women (or to the total population) are referred to as rates; whereas measures relating abortions to births plus abortions are called ratios. In this article the abortion rates are per 1,000 women age 15 to 44 years and the abortion ratios are per 100 live births.

Both the abortion rates and the abortion ratios (See Table IV) posted substantial gains during the initial three- to four-year period (1970-1974) immediately following the date of implementation of the amended abortion legislation, and the increases were moderate in the following years. England and Wales and the United States experienced similar patterns immediately following the liberalization of abortion laws in those countries, [13, 14] as shown below.

Item	Canada	England & Wales	United States
1. Year abortion law changed	1969	1967	1970, 1973
2. Percent increase in abortions from 1st to 2nd full calendar year.	177.3% (1970-71)	123.3% (1968-69)	151.1% (1970-71)
3. Percent increase over the first five-year period in terms of			
(a) abortion rate	295.8%	228.6%	266.7%
(b) abortion ratio	363.3% (1970-74)	295.0% (1968-72)	361.5% (1970-74)

Note: 1. Figures in parentheses indicate the time period to which the figures relate.
2. Figures for England & Wales and Canada relate to resident women.

The rise in the numbers and rates of legal abortions in these countries immediately following the liberalization of abortion laws may reflect in part a replacement of illegal abortions by legal abortions. Once the numbers of illegal abortions minimize, the numbers and rates of legal abortions reflect small increases in the subsequent years.

Abortions and Abortion Rates by Provinces

The number of abortions and the abortion rates by province for 1970-1980 are shown in Tables V and VI. Of every 100

TABLE IV:

Abortion Rates per 1,000 Females Aged 15-44 and Abortion Ratios per 100 Live Births, Canada, 1970-1980

Year	Abortion Rate per 1,000 Females 15-44 years		Abortion Ratio per 100 Live Births	
	Alternative I	Alternative II	Alternative I	Alternative II
1970	2.4	2.4	3.0	3.0
1971	6.6	7.8	8.5	10.3
1972	8.2	9.4	11.2	13.1
1973	8.8	10.0	12.6	14.2
1974	9.5	10.5	13.7	15.0
1975	9.5	10.5	13.7	14.9
1976	10.3	11.1	15.1	16.3
1977	10.6	11.1	15.9	16.6
1978	11.3	11.6	17.4	17.9
1979	11.6	11.7	17.8	18.1
1980	11.5	11.8	17.7	18.2

Notes: Alternative I: Rate based on abortions to Canadian residents within Canada.
Alternative II: Rate based on abortions to Canadian residents in Canada and in United States.

TABLE V:

Total Therapeutic Abortion to Canadian Residents, by Province, 1970-1980

Total Therapeutic Abortions

	1970	1971	1972	1973	1974	1975	1976	1977	1978	1979	1980
Newfoundland	25	78	133	193	184	176	418	493	537	645	539
Prince Edward Island	17	39	45	41	50	77	57	43	60	46	23
Nova Scotia	261	643	837	932	1,062	1,017	1,247	1,304	1,454	1,511	1,662
New Brunswick	72	146	183	341	440	379	400	426	454	447	467
Quebec	534	1,881	2,847	3,141	4,453	5,579	7,249	7,583	7,881	8,609	8,940
Ontario	5,568	16,173	20,272	22,603	24,795	24,921	26,768	27,782	29,270	30,671	30,900
Manitoba	238	827	1,178	1,259	1,411	1,298	1,393	1,573	1,869	1,624	1,587
Saskatchewan	215	756	1,043	1,219	1,176	1,282	1,128	1,235	1,490	1,645	1,572
Alberta	1,154	3,116	3,887	4,047	4,391	4,333	4,943	5,642	6,562	6,872	7,131
British Columbia	2,901	7,045	8,179	9,176	10,024	10,076	10,704	11,271	12,483	12,716	12,763
Yukon	6	8	48	76	63	77	79	106	94	113	125
Northwest Territories	-	-	44	51	75	95	90	102	134	141	126
TOTAL CANADA	11,152	20,923	38,853	43,201	48,136	49,311	54,478	57,564	62,290	65,043	65,751
Residence not reported	161	211	157	122	12	1	2	4	2	3	6

TABLE VI:

Legal Abortion Rates in Canada by Provinces, 1970 to 1980 (Therapeutic Abortions for Canadian Residents Performed in Canada Only)

	Legal Abortion Rates (Per 1,000 Females Aged 15-44 Years)											Abortion Ratios (Per 100 Live Births)										
	1970	1971	1972	1973	1974	1975	1976	1977	1978	1979	1980	1970	1971	1972	1973	1974	1975	1976	1977	1978	1979	1980
Nfld.	0.2	0.7	1.2	1.7	1.6	1.5	3.5	3.9	4.2	4.9	4.0	0.2	0.6	1.0	1.6	1.6	1.6	3.8	4.4	5.1	6.3	5.2
P.E.I.	0.8	1.8	2.0	1.8	2.1	3.0	2.2	1.7	2.2	1.7	0.8	0.9	1.9	2.2	2.2	2.6	4.0	2.9	2.2	3.0	2.4	1.2
N.S.	1.7	4.0	5.1	5.5	6.1	5.7	6.9	7.0	7.7	7.8	8.4	1.8	4.5	6.2	7.0	8.2	7.7	9.7	10.5	11.6	12.2	13.4
N.B.	0.6	1.1	1.4	2.5	3.1	2.5	2.6	2.8	2.9	2.8	2.8	0.6	1.2	1.6	3.0	3.8	3.2	3.4	3.7	4.2	4.1	4.4
Quebec	0.4	1.4	2.0	2.2	3.1	3.8	4.8	5.0	5.1	5.6	5.7	0.6	2.1	3.4	3.7	5.0	6.0	7.5	7.9	8.3	8.7	9.2
Ontario	3.4	9.7	11.8	12.9	13.7	13.3	14.2	14.3	14.8	15.2	15.1	4.1	12.4	16.2	18.3	20.0	19.8	21.8	22.6	24.2	25.2	25.1
Manitoba	1.2	4.1	5.8	6.0	6.6	5.9	6.3	6.9	8.1	7.0	6.8	1.3	4.6	6.8	7.4	8.2	7.6	8.3	9.4	11.4	10.0	9.9
Sask.	1.2	4.2	5.9	6.8	6.5	6.8	5.9	6.3	7.4	8.0	7.5	1.3	4.7	6.7	8.2	7.8	8.4	7.1	7.5	9.0	9.7	9.2
Alberta	3.4	8.9	10.8	10.9	11.4	10.8	11.9	12.5	13.9	13.9	13.8	3.6	10.2	13.3	13.8	14.7	13.7	15.0	16.4	18.5	18.6	17.9
B.C.	6.6	15.5	17.2	18.3	19.0	18.4	19.3	19.7	21.3	21.1	20.2	7.9	20.2	23.7	26.7	28.3	27.8	29.9	30.7	33.5	33.1	31.6
Yukon	1.6	2.0	11.2	17.3	14.6	15.7	15.8	19.3	16.8	19.5	21.9	1.3	1.6	10.6	18.1	12.7	18.9	17.6	24.5	21.0	22.6	26.3
N.W.T.	..	..	5.7	6.4	9.4	11.9	11.1	10.2	12.9	13.7	12.2	..	..	3.6	4.2	7.2	8.1	7.6	8.6	11.1	11.0	9.7
CANADA	2.4	6.7	8.2	8.9	9.6	9.6	10.3	10.6	11.3	11.6	11.5	3.0	8.5	11.2	12.6	13.7	13.7	15.1	15.9	17.4	17.8	17.7

TABLE VII:

Total Abortions with Percent Distribution by Selected
Demographic and Medical Characteristics,
Canada, 1974-1980

Characteristics	1974	1975	1976	1977	1978	1979	1980
Total Abortions	41,227	49,033	54,097	57,131	61,806	64,569	65,243
Age							
Under 15 years	1.2	1.2	1.2	1.2	1.0	1.0	0.9
15-19 "	30.3	30.1	29.5	29.6	29.5	29.4	28.8
20-24 "	29.3	29.1	29.6	30.3	30.9	31.5	31.8
25-29 "	18.5	19.4	19.8	19.4	19.3	19.3	19.6
30-34 "	10.7	10.7	10.9	11.2	11.3	11.3	11.6
35-39 "	6.8	6.4	6.1	5.8	5.7	5.4	5.3
39+	3.0	2.8	2.6	2.2	2.1	1.8	1.8
Unknown	0.3	0.2	0.3	0.4	0.3	0.2	0.2
Marital Status							
Single	58.2	58.4	58.4	60.2	61.3	64.0	65.2
Married	31.3	31.5	30.7	29.0	27.3	24.7	23.7
Other & Unknown	10.6	10.2	10.9	10.8	11.4	11.3	11.0
No. of Previous Deliveries							
0	57.2	57.3	57.6	59.0	59.7	61.7	62.4
1	14.3	14.3	15.0	15.6	15.7	15.5	15.7
2	14.2	14.5	14.7	14.0	13.9	13.3	13.1
3	13.0	11.8	10.6	9.3	8.3	7.3	6.9
Unknown	1.4	2.0	2.0	1.9	2.3	2.2	1.9
Gestation Weeks							
Under 9	20.8	22.4	24.1	23.8	24.7	24.5	24.7
9 - 10	32.7	33.7	34.7	36.4	36.2	36.4	36.3
11 - 12	25.3	25.2	24.3	24.0	23.7	24.9	25.1
13 - 15	11.9	11.0	9.5	9.0	9.3	8.6	8.8
16 - 20	8.9	7.5	7.3	6.5	5.9	5.3	5.0
20 +	0.4	0.2	0.2	0.3	0.2	0.2	0.2
Method							
Suction D&C	62.6	70.5	73.5	82.2	84.8	87.7	88.0
Surgical D&C	20.7	13.7	11.0	9.1	7.4	5.9	5.7
Saline	8.6	5.8	5.3	4.0	3.1	2.5	2.7
Hysterectomy/ Hysterotomy	3.4	2.3	1.6	1.1	0.9	0.6	0.4
Prostaglandin	0.2	1.7	2.4	2.8	2.8	2.5	2.0
Urea	0.7	0.8	0.6	0.8	0.9	0.8	0.9
Menstrual Extraction	3.4	5.1	5.7	--	0.1	--	0.3
Other(s)	0.4	0.1	--	--	--	0.1	--

Note: (--) indicates very small figures.

abortions, over the ten-year period, the provincial contributions are: Ontario 50 abortions, British Columbia 21, Quebec and Alberta 10 each, and the rest of the six privinces and the two territories the remaining 9 abortions. For the provinces of British Columbia, Ontario, and Alberta the annual abortion rates and abortion ratios are consistently high, between one-and-one-quarter and two-and-one-half times the national rates ratios respectively. The abortion rates and abortion ratios for the provinces of Nova Scotia, Manitoba, and Saskatchewan range approximately from one third to slightly more than one half the national figures. The abortion rates and ratios for the provinces of Quebec, Newfoundland, and New Brunswick, though still below the national rates, recorded substantial gains from one third of national rates and ratios during 1970-1974 to slightly less than one half of the rates and ratios during 1975-1980.

Characteristics of Women Obtaining Abortions

Canadian women obtaining abortions in Canada, based on the information for 1974 to 1980, were overwhelmingly very young, unmarried, and without previous deliveries. Complete data at national level on the selected demographic and medical characteristics of the aborted women is available starting only in 1974. Table VII shows the number of abortions and the percent distribution of the aborted women by their selected demographic and medical characteristics for 1974 to 1980.

About one third of the total abortions were performed on women under 20 years of age. A slight decrease in the percent of abortions for women under 20 years to total abortions, from 31.5 percent in 1974 to 29.7 percent in 1980, was offset by an increase in the percent for women age 20 to 29 years, from 47.8 percent in 1974 to 51.4 percent in 1980, and an increase in the percent for women age 30-34 years from 10.7 percent in 1974 to 11.6 percent in 1980. The percent of abortions for women age 35 years or over decreased by more than one third over the seven-year period from 1974 to 1980.

The percent of abortions obtained by married women to total abortions declined from 31.3 percent in 1974 to 23.7 percent in 1980. Abortions obtained by women with 3 or more previous deliveries declined from 13 percent of total abortions in 1974 to 6.9 percent in 1980. Gestation period is conventionally defined as the time lapse between the date of last normal menses and the date of pregnancy termination. There is a shift to earlier abortion in Canada. During the seven-year period 1974 to 1980, the percent of abortions with gestation period under 13 weeks to total abortions increased from 78. 8 percent in 1974 to 86. 1 percent in 1980. Along with this trend, use of suction (vacuum aspiration) for abortion increased from 62. 6 percent of total pregnancy terminations in 1974 to 88. 0 percent in 1980.

Facilities for Abortion

The number of hospitals with therapeutic abortion committees performing abortions according to the amended abortion law increased from 143 hospitals in 1970 to 276 hospitals in 1976, roughly one fifth of the total public general hospitals in Canada. There was a slight decrease in the number of hospitals with therapeutic abortion committees in the next two years. The total number of hospitals according to the annual number of abortions performed in these hospitals from 1974 to 1980 are shown in Table VIII. In 1980 about 19 percent of the total hospitals with abortion committees performed no abortions, another 16 percent of the hospitals between 1 to 20 abortions each. About 17 percent of the hospitals, performing more than 400 abortions each, contributed about 76 percent of the total abortions.

Discussion

The Canadian abortion law was liberalized in August 1969. The initial four to five years immediately following this liberalization of the law witnessed an enormous increase in the number of therapeutic abortions, abortion rates, and abortion ratios, and the pace of the increase moderated from 1975 to 1980. England and Wales and the United States had similar experiences immediately following the changes in their respective abortion laws. Although the number of hospitals with therapeutic abortion committees providing legal abortion facilities in Canada considerably increased (from 143 hospitals in 1970 to 271 hospitals in 1980), 19 percent of these hospitals did not perform a single abortion, another 16 percent of the hospitals performed from 1 to 20 legal abortions each. A high percentage (76%) of the total legal abortions were performed in only a small percentage (17%) of the total hospitals.

In terms of the geographical distribution of the legal abortions, the two provinces of Ontario and British Columbia contributed 66. 3 percent of the total legal abortions from 1970

TABLE VIII:

Percent Distribution of the Hospitals with Therapeutic Abortion Committees and Abortions Reported for These Hospitals by Number of Abortions, Canada, 1970 and 1974-1980

Percent of Hospitals

Abortion Range	1970*	1974	1975	1976	1977	1978	1979	1980
All Ranges	100.0 N=143	100.0 N=265	100.0 N=265	100.0 N=276	100.0 N=265	100.0 N=271	100.0 N=271	100.0 N=271
Abortions	21.7	17.4	16.6	18.8	13.6	15.5	17.0	18.8
1-20	49.6	26.8	23.4	22.5	24.5	20.3	19.2	16.2
21-50	16.1	14.3	15.8	13.8	15.8	16.6	14.4	16.6
51-100	7.7	14.0	13.2	13.4	11.3	11.4	10.7	10.3
101-400	2.8	15.0	17.7	18.5	20.7	21.0	21.8	20.6
Over 400	2.1	12.4	13.2	13.0	14.0	15.1	17.0	16.6

TABLE VIII (cont.)

Percent of Abortions for the Hospitals

Abortion Range	1970	1974	1975	1976	1977	1978	1979	1980
All Ranges	100.0 N=4,375	100.0 N=48,736	100.0 N=49,390	100.0 N=54,536	100.0 N=57,620	100.0 N=62,351	100.0 N=65,135	100.0 N=65,855
Abortions								
1-20	9.7	1.7	1.2	0.9	1.0	0.7	0.7	0.5
21-50	16.9	3.0	2.8	2.2	2.4	2.4	1.9	2.5
51-100	18.9	6.2	5.0	4.9	4.2	3.7	3.4	3.4
101-400	16.3	19.2	19.0	19.9	20.9	18.7	17.5	17.8
Over 400	38.2	70.0	72.0	72.1	71.6	74.4	76.5	75.9

(*) Relates to the period August 26, 1969, to August 25, 1970.
(†) Excludes 10 hospitals not reported for 1975.

to 1980. For the provinces of British Columbia, Ontario, and Alberta, the abortion rates were consistently higher than the national rates, and for the rest of the provinces these rates were less than one half the national abortion rates. These disparities in the provincial abortion rates may be due in part to the differences in the available facilities for legal abortion and the interpretation of the abortion law by the hospital committees.

It is extremely difficult to predict the numbers of legal abortions for future years. It is dependent on numerous factors: the abortion laws; facilities for legal abortion; attitudes of the participating doctors, nurses, and other categories of workers; attitude and reaction of the society; and knowledge, attitude, and practice of family planning techniques by the people in fertile ages groups. However, if the current conditions prevail, a moderate rate of 12 abortions per 1,000 females age 15 to 44 years, in Canada would result in 72,000 legal abortions in 1982 and 76,000 legal abortions in 1986. An unknown fraction of these abortions may be performed outside Canada and may not be reported through the current data-collection system.

* * *

The views and interpretations presented are those of the authors and do not necessarily reflect policies of Statistics Canada.

Notes

1. Therapeutic Abortion, Canada, August 26, 1969, to August 25, 1970.
2. Annual reports, Therapeutic Abortions, Canada, Cat. 82-211, 1970-1980.
3. Abortion Statistics, England and Wales, 1977. Office of Population Censuses and Surveys, 1977.
4. Abortion Surveillance, Annual Summary 1976. Issued August 1978. Center for Disease Control, U. S. Department of Health and Human Services.

References

Badgely, Robin F. Report of the Committee on the Operation of Abortion Law, Canada. Ottawa, Minister of Supply and Services Canada, 1977.

Tietze, Christopher. Induced Abortion: 1979, 3rd ed. New York: The Population Council, 1979.

POSTPARTUM AND POSTABORTION PSYCHIATRIC REACTIONS: DANISH NATIONAL REGISTERS AND THE LITERATURE REVIEW

By Henry P. David, Niels Kr. Rasmussen, and Erik Holst

Introduction

Although questions about psychological and psychiatric sequelae of abortion have subsided in recent years, ambivalence and confusion persist regarding relative psychological risks associated with term deliveries and induced abortions (Herzog & Detre, 1976; Lamanna, 1980). One reason for the continuing confusion is the scarcity of epidemiological data on postpartum and postabortion admissions to psychiatric hospitals. Such admissions are not separately tracked in U. S. public health records. They are not cited in the periodic surveys conducted by the National Center for Health Statistics (NCHS); they are not separately recorded by the Biometrics Branch of the National Institute of Mental Health; and they do not appear in the 1979 Diagnostic and Statistical Manual of Mental Disorders (DSM) published by the American Psychiatric Association. Although psychoses associated with childbirth are listed in the International Classification of Diseases and are separately recorded in several European countries, the NCHS surveys combine this category with psychoses associated with other physical disorders. It is the purpose of this chapter to review briefly what is known about postpartum and postabortion admissions to psychiatric hospitals and then to discuss comparative findings from a study of Danish population registers.

Postpartum Psychosis

Postpartum psychosis is generally defined as any mental disorder occurring within three months after childbirth and serious enough to require admission to a psychiatric facility. One likely reason for the resistance to recording postpartum psychosis as a separate statistical entity is that many clinicians do not consider psychotic reactions associated with childbirth to be a distinct clinical condition, with a symptomatology, psychopathology, and prognosis different from other psychoses. That may explain why readers searching for postpartum psychosis in the index of the American Psychiatric Association's Diagnostic Reference Guide are referred to schizophreniform disorders, brief reaction psychosis, atypical psychosis, major affective disorders, and organic brain syndrome (American Psychiatric Association, 1979).

Over 2,400 years ago, Hippocrates observed in the Third Book of the Epidemics that "the bleeding of a nipple of a woman recently delivered of a baby is an ominous sign pointing to a possible onset of mania; the milk of the mother being suppressed, a mental disorder is in the offing" (Jones, 1923; Zilboorg, 1929). Although there is general agreement that postpartum psychotic reactions can be recognized by their acute onset shortly after childbirth, often featuring disordered thought processes focused on the baby (Protheroe, 1969), a review of twentieth-century literature suggests that the syndrome "remains both controversial in definition and elusive in etiology" (Herzog & Detre, 1976; Friederich, 1977; Frate, et al. , 1979).

One of the few epidemiological studies reported from the United States is based on a review of the 1950 case records of public and private mental hospitals in Massachusetts for first admissions of ever-married women 15 to 44 years old who, as of a specific census date, had or had not borne any children (Pugh, Jerath, Schmidt, & Reed, 1963). Compared with non-pregnant controls, the women who had ever delivered were found to have an annual added risk, associated with the first three-month postpartum, of 18 to 25 first admissions to psychiatric hospital per 10,000. While other studies of the incidence of postpartum psychosis have appeared in the U. S. reasearch literature, none has approached the size and scope of the Massachusetts study.

A British study linking the cumulative psychiatric register in the former London borough of Camberwell with the birth registers in the borough catchment area showed a "prominent peak" in new episodes of functional psychoses in the three-month period after childbirth with an annualized rate of 10 psychiatric admissions per 10,000 deliverers (Kendall, Wainwright, Hailey, & Shannon, 1976). Grundy and Roberts (1975) monitored 35,846 consecutive confinements recorded in the Cardiff Birth Survey over a period of eight years from

1965 to 1972. They noted 67 cases of postpartum psychosis, defined as any case of mental disorder referred to a psychiatrist within 28 days of childbirth, an incidence of 19 per 10,000 deliverers. In a 1975-1976 study in the Midlands, Brewer (1977) found an incidence of psychiatric admissions of 17 per 10,000. Differential rates were not provided in any of these studies for separated, divorced, or widowed women.

Postabortion Psychosis

Although more information has become available on the epidemiology of legally induced abortion than on any other surgical procedure in the United States, confusion about psychiatric and psychological sequelae persists (e. g. , Cates, 1982; Potts, Diggory, & Peel, 1977). Inconsistencies of interpretation stem from lack of consensus and misperceptions regarding symptoms, severity, and duration of mental disorder; from single case histories and impressionistic studies disregarding the vast number of women who do not come to psychotherapeutic attention after abortion; and from the lack of a national reporting system, inadequate follow-up monitoring; and attrition of samples (e. g. , Baluk & O'Neill, 1980; David, 1973, 1978, 1981).

One of the few epidemiological studies which produced some data on psychiatric complications in elective abortion was the Joint Program for the Study of Abortion (JPSA), reported by Tietze and Lewit (1977). From July 1, 1970, to June 30, 1971, the 66 participating institutions reported a total of 16 major psychiatric complications from a pool of 72,988 legal abortions. The psychiatric-complications rate recorded in the JPSA data was 2 per 10,000 abortions (without other concurrent surgeries), and 4 per 10,000 abortions for women seen in follow-up evaluations (Institute of Medicine, 1975). In a prospective study conducted during 1975-1976 in the Midlands region of the United Kingdom, Brewer found an incidence of 3 postabortion psychoses per 10,000 legal abortions (Brewer, 1977).

Review of the literature suggests that legal abortions performed in the first trimester of pregnancy do not carry a significant risk of major psychiatric reactions (e. g. , Blumberg & Golbus, 1975; Osofsky, et al. , 1973, 1975; Lamanna, 1980; Figa-Talamanca, 1981). Mild depression, guilt, and regret can occur immediately after termination, especially in situations where considerable ambivalence surrounded the pregnancy, but tend to be of short duration. In the rare instances of psychotic reactions, the degree of emotional adjustment before pregnancy appears to be a major determining mechanism (e. g. , Belsey, et al. , 1977; Zimmerman, 1977). Women having a high degree of social and partner support for their decisions seem to experience much less abortion distress or regret (e. g. , Adler, 1975; Shusterman, 1979). In sum, while abortion can induce a negative emotional aura, for the vast majority of women termination of an unwanted pregnancy in the first trimester engenders a sense of relief and often represents a maturing experience of successful coping with a personal crisis situation.

The Denmark Study

The research literature yields few studies comparing psychological reactions following elective first trimester abortion to other pregnancy-related events. Unique circumstances combined to make possible an assessment of the comparative risks for admission to a psychiatric hospital within three months after either delivery or abortion for all women under age 50 residing in Denmark in 1975 and a comparison of the results with the three-month admission rate to psychiatric hospitals for all Danish women of similar age. Admission to a psychiatric hospital was deemed a measurable event, reflective of severe stress associated in time with delivery and abortion, and less subject to diverse interpretations than individual consultations with clinical practitioners.

Reliable pregnancy testing is readily available and accessible throughout Denmark. A pregnant woman is encouraged to consult with a general practitioner who is empowered to make all necessary arrangements for prenatal care and delivery or early termination of an unwanted pregnancy. Costs are paid by Sundhedsstyrelsen, the Danish National Board of Health. Free follow-up care is provided after delivery or abortion.

Through computer linkages of Danish national registers, data were obtained on admission to psychiatric hospital for 71,378 women carrying their pregnancies to term; 27,234 women terminating unwanted pregnancies; and 1,169,819 women representing the entire female population aged 15 to 44 (David, Rasmussen, & Holst, 1981).

The study was greatly facilitated by the Danish registration system (Lunde, 1980). Either at birth or on moving to Denmark, every individual is given a "person number," which includes the birth date and code for sex. This number is permanently recorded in the Population Register together with additional sociodemographic data including occupation, marital status, number of children, and address. The person number is used for all contacts the individual has with social and medical agencies or service providers. Whenever a person moves, he or she must, by law, report the new address to the Population Register of the new municipality within five days. The Population Register is continually updated. Although an individual's person number and present and past addresses can be obtained by the general public, all other data are usually available only in the form of general statistical reports carefully designed to protect individual confidentiality.

Following an earlier pilot study (Somers, 1979), computerized psychiatric admission records were examined for a period of 15 months before delivery or abortion and for the 3 months immediately after the pregnancy-related event. If was not possible to track psychiatric admission records for earlier periods (that is, before the installation of computers). Data were obtained for five-year age groups (except for those under age 20), marital status, and previous parity. Only first admissions recorded within 3 months after delivery or abortion are reported in this chapter. Women with an admission during the 15 months before delivery or abortion were excluded from the sample. None of the 71,378 women who delivered gave birth twice during the year. Of the 27,234 women who obtained abortions, 26,088 (96%) had one abortion; 561 (2%) had two; and 8 had three (0.02%). The records of the 577 remaining women who had abortions were incomplete. It was decided to link only the first abortion reported to the register for admissions to psychiatric hospitals. Information on marital status and parity was available for all women who delivered, but for only 25,634 (marital status) and 26,057 (parity) women who had abortions.

Data on admissions to psychiatric hospitals for the entire Danish female population aged 15 to 49, representing 1,169,819 women, were obtained from the Sundhedsstyrelsen (1978) for the fiscal year 1974-1975 (April 1, 1974, to March 30, 1975). Only those women were counted who were admitted that year for the first time in their lives. The number of admissions for 12 months was then adjusted to yield a three-month rate, comparable to the rates for women who delivered and who obtained abortions.

The overall findings indicate a postabortion rate of 18.4 admissions per 10,000 women obtaining abortions and a postdelivery rate of 12.0 per 10,000 women carrying to term, compared with a rate of 7.5 admissions per 10,000 for all Danish women aged 15 to 49. For never-married and currently married women, the postpregnancy-related risk of admission is about the same--around 12 per 10,000 abortions or deliveries. The postabortion rate of admission to psychiatric hospitals apparently adds only slightly to the risk of major medical abortion complications (estimated in the United States at 50 per 10,000 abortions), when the procedure is performed by skilled operators using modern methods during the first trimester (Tietze, 1981).

The much higher psychiatric admission rates noted for separated, divorced, and widowed women having abortions (63.8 per 10,000) or carrying to term (16.9 per 10,000), as compared with the rates among currently married and never-married women, may reflect three interacting components: stress, social support, and original intention. Within the present social-cultural context prevailing in Denmark, procedure-related stress is similar among married and never-married women, many of whom may live in stable nonmarital relationships. However, when such stress occurs in a setting of a disturbed or absent-partner relationship, it is greatly magnified by the lack of a social network support. For women deciding to have an abortion, stress can be very intense when an originally intended conception becomes unwanted following the ending of a relationship. Such terminations may well induce more stress than deliveries. The combined effect of marital status and parity remains to be explored.

While specific data on pregnancy intention are not available for the women in this study, such information was obtained in related individual interviews with representative Copenhagen samples of 431 women deciding to carry to term, 441 women terminating unwanted pregnancy, and 485 controls of similar age (Rasmussen, et al., 1981). Of the 431 women who delivered, 74 percent had intended to conceive and had wanted their pregnancies; 93 percent were married or living in stable nonmarital relationships; 91 percent were giving birth to their first or second child; and 89 percent were 20 to 34 years old. Very few experienced ambivalence in their decision to carry to term. Of the 441 women who had abortions, more than 90 percent had not intended to conceive or had not wanted their pregnancies; more than 75 percent decided to terminate within one week of discovering their condition. The difference between the two groups is apparent from the observation that only 18 percent of the women who terminated their pregnancies had the same partner relationship, parity status, and age characteristics shared by 78 percent of the women carrying to term. The Copenhagen observations are similar to those noted in longitudinal studies on intendedness and wantedness of conceptions and induced abortions among women residing in the San Francisco Bay area (Miller, 1981).

In sum, carrying an intended conception to term may represent a dynamic continuation of an original intention and thus be perceived as less psychologically stressful than having an abortion. This finding suggests that special provision should be made to counsel women recently separated from their partners and seeking termination of a pregnancy that was originally intended and conceived in the context of an intact relationship.

*   *   *

Based, in part, on a study conducted with support (Grant HD-09739) from the Center for Population Research, National Institute of Child Health and Human Development, and the Danish Health Insurance Fund. We are pleased to acknowledge the technical assistance of Mogens Trab Damsgaard and the Statistical Research Unit of the Danish Social Research Council and the Danish Medical Research Council; the cooperation of colleagues associated with Sundhedsstyrelsen and the Institute for Psychiatric Demography; and the constructive suggestions of Warren B. Miller, Patricia Steinhoff, and Christopher Tietze. Portions of this essay were adapted, with permission of the Alan Guttmacher Institute, from an earlier paper published in Family Planning Perspectives, 1981, 13: 88-92.

References

Adler, N. E. "Emotional Responses of Women Following Therapeutic Abortion." American Journal of Orthopsychiatry, 1975, 43: 446-454.

_____. "Sample Attrition in Studies of Psychosocial Sequelae of Abortion: How Great a Problem?" Journal of Applied Social Psychology, 1976, 6: 240-259.

American Psychiatric Association. Quick Reference to Diagnostic Criteria from DSM-III. Washington: American Psychiatric Association, 1979.

Baluk, U. , and O'Neill, P. "Health Professional's Perceptions of the Psychological Consequences of Abortion." American Journal of Community Psychology, 1980, 8: 67-75.

Belsey, E. M.; Greer, H. S.; Lal, S.; Lewis, S. C.; and Beard, R. W. "Predictive Factors in Emotional Responses to Abortion: King's Termination Study." Social Science and Medicine, 1977, 11: 71-82.

Blumberg, B. D. , and Golbus, M. S. "Psychological Sequelae of Elective Abortion." Western Journal of Medicine, 1975, 123: 188-193.

Brewer, C. "Incidence of Post-Abortion Psychosis: A Prospective Study." British Medical Journal, 1977, 1 (No. 6059): 476-477.

Cates, W. , Jr. "Legal Abortion in the Public Health Record." Science, 1982, 215: 1586-1590.

David, H. P. "Psychological Studies in Abortion." In Psychological Perspectives on Population, J. T. Fawcett, ed. New York: Basic Books, 1973, pp. 241-273.

_____. "Psychosocial Studies of Abortion in the United States." In Abortion in Psychosocial Perspective: Trends in Transnational Research, H. P. David; H. L. Friedman; J. vd Tak; and M. Sevilla, eds. New York: Springer, 1978, pp. 77-115.

_____. "Worldwide Abortion Trends." In Abortion: Readings and Research, P. Sachdev, ed. Toronto: Butterworths, 1981, pp. 175-192.

_____; Rasmussen, N. Kr.; and Holst, E. "Postpartum and Postabortion Psychotic Reactions." Family Planning Perspectives, 1981, 13: 88-92.

Figa-Talamanca, I. "Abortion and Mental Health." In Abortion and Sterilization: Medical and Social Aspects, J. E. Hodgson, ed. London: Academic Press, 1981, pp. 181-208.

Frate, D. A.; Cowen, J. B.; Rutledge, A. H.; and Glasser, M. "Behavioral Reactions During the Postpartum Period: Experience of 108 Women." Women and Health, 1979, 4: 355-373.

Friederich, M. A. "Psychological Changes During Pregnancy." Contemporary Ob/Gyn, 1977, 9: 27-34.

Grundy, P. F., and Roberts, C. J. "Observations of the Epidemiology of Postpartum Mental Illness." Psychological Medicine, 1975, 5: 286-290.

Herzog, A., and Detre, T. "Psychotic Reactions Associated with Childbirth." Diseases of the Nervous System, 1976, 37: 229-235.

Institute of Medicine. Legalized Abortion and the Public Health. Washington: National Academy of Sciences, 1975.

Jones, W. H. S. Hippocrates--With an English Translation, Vol. 1. London: Heinemann, 1923.

Kendall, R. E.; Wainwright, S.; Hailey, A.; and Shannon, B. "The Influence of Childbirth on Psychiatric Morbidity." Psychological Medicine, 1976, 6: 297-302.

Lamanna, M. A. "Science and Its Uses: The Abortion Debate and Social Science Research." In Abortion Parley, J. T. Burtchaell, ed. Kansas City: Andrews & McMeel, 1980, pp. 101-158.

Lunde, A. S. "The Person Number System of Sweden, Norway, Denmark, and Israel." Vital and Health Statistics, 1980, Series 2, No. 84.

Miller, W. B. The Psychology of Reproduction. Springfield, Va.: National Technical Information Service, 1981.

Osofsky, J. D.; Osofsky, H. J.; and Rajan, R. "Psychological Effects of Abortion: With Emphasis upon Immediate Reactions and Follow-up." In The Abortion Experience, H. J. Osofsky & J. D. Osofsky, eds. Hagerstown, Md.: Harper & Row Medical Department, 1973, pp. 108-205.

_____; and Spitz, D. "Psychosocial Aspects of Abortion in the United States." The Mount Sinai Journal of Medicine, 1975, 42: 456-468.

Potts, M.; Diggory, P.; and Peel, J. Abortion. Cambridge: Cambridge University Press, 1977.

Pugh, T. G.; Jerath, B. K.; Schmidt, W. M.; and Reed, R. B. "Rates of Mental Illness Related to Childbearing." New England Journal of Medicine, 1963, 268: 1224-1228.

Rasmussen, N. Kr.; David, H. P.; Boesen, E. M.; Sidenius, K.; Holst, E.; Falk Larsen, J.; Pedersen, H.; and Wagner, M. Danish Experience with Liberalized Abortion. Copenhagen: Institute of Social Medicine, 1981.

Shusterman, L. R. "Predicting the Psychological Consequences of Abortion." Social Science and Medicine, 1979, 13: 683-689.

Somers, R. L. "Risk of Admission to Psychiatric Institutions Among Danish Women Who Experience Induced Abortion: An Analysis Based on National Record Linkage." Unpublished doctoral disseration. University of California at Los Angeles, 1979.

Sundhedsstyrelsen. Medical report II. Fiscal year 1974/75 Report on Hospitals and Other Institutions for the Treatment of the Sick in Denmark. Copenhagen: Sundhedsstyrelsen, 1978.

Tietze, C. Induced Abortion: A world review, 1981, 4th ed. New York: The Population Council, 1981.

_____ and Lewit, S. "Joint Program for the Study of Abortion. Early Medical Complication of Legal Abortion." Studies in Family Planning, 1972, 3: 97-122.

Zilboorg, G. "Dynamics of Schizophrenic Reactions Related to Pregnancy and Childbirth." American Journal of Psychiatry, 1929, 8: 733-767.

Zimmerman, M. Passage Through Abortion. The Personal and Social Reality of Women's Experiences. New York: Praeger, 1977.

THE EFFECTS OF INDUCED ABORTION ON FUTURE FAMILY GOALS OF YOUNG WOMEN

By Patricia G. Steinhoff

Numerous studies have shown that American women use induced abortion in an attempt to protect the economic, social, and emotional well-being of their families. Women who are already mothers accomplish this directly, by limiting family size or extending the spacing between children. For the majority of American abortion patients, young and childless, the effect on family is indirect. Their reported motives for utilizing abortion reveal both a firm commitment to future childbearing and a strong sense of the obligations of parenthood (Lind, 1974; Steinhoff, 1977). They undergo abortion in order to postpone childbirth to some future time when they are older, better educated, economically better off, and have developed a more stable emotional relationship with a partner. They clearly expect that at some unspecified time in the future they will become more "ready" to be parents as a result of these changes in their lives.

This paper represents a preliminary attempt to assess whether or not women actually carry out their scenarios of a future family and if induced abortion supports their efforts. Women who experienced abortion were compared with women who had a baby or spontaneous abortion at approximately the same time. Two areas of experience were compared. First, subsequent pregnancy exposure and actual pregnancy experienced were examined to determine whether the abortion sample succeeded both in delaying another pregnancy and in achieving one when it was desired. Second, emotions and attitudes associated with the initial and subsequent pregnancy, and some demographic characteristics, were used to evaluate the respondents' sense of "readiness" for parenthood at the time of subsequent pregnancy.

Method

The data used for this analysis were collected as part of a large, multi-disciplinary study of the effects of induced abortion on subsequent reproductive function.[1] Stratified random samples were drawn from the population of women who legally obtained induced abortions in Hawaii from 1970 to 1974 and from the control population of women who experienced live births or spontaneous abortions during the same years. From 1978 to 1980, efforts were made to locate the sampled women, and those located were each asked to participate in an interview. The interview samples used for this analysis include 313 abortion cases and 393 control cases. They are used with weights that adjust the samples to match the age and ethnic composition of the original samples drawn, to correct some biases due to loss to follow-up and interview refusal. Earlier analyses demonstrated that women who were lost to the sample were not significantly different from those who remained in the sample on various behavioral measures, if age and ethnic distortions were accounted for (Chung, et al., 1981).

The primary data for this investigation were collected by means of a timeline technique adapted from a method devised by Miller (1976). Respondents were asked about their contraceptive, menstrual, sexual, and pregnancy history from 1969 up to the date of the interview. Data were recorded in monthly intervals on a timeline that also included educational and employment history, marital history, and other major life and health events. Interviewers were trained to encourage respondents to use recollections from one area of experience to help place other events on the timeline accurately. Interviewers reported high levels of respondent participation, openness, and satisfaction with the technique. A small sample of re-interviews confirmed both respondent satisfaction and general reliability of the technique.

Due to the long timespan covered (11 years) and the retrospective nature of the data collection, the monthly measures cannot be taken as accurate accounts of the exact experiences of the women in a particular month. Yet because women were able to report changes in their behavior and to relate those changes to life events which occurred at specific times, they provide a closer approximation of actual behavior than if consistency during the entire pregnancy interval were assumed.

All interviews were conducted double-blind. The main study, however, employed record-linkage of vital statistics as its major method of data collection. Thus vital statistics could be used to supplement women's reports of reproductive events. The supplemented timeline data were used for a survival analysis of the next pregnancy interval and for a preliminary Box-Jenkins time-series analysis of exposure to pregnancy during the next pregnancy interval.

For the survival analysis, the dependent variable of next pregnancy was derived from the combined vital statistics and the women's reports of next-pregnancy outcome, because there was some underreporting of known induced abortions. Earlier analyses showed the women reported birth dates very accurately but sometimes misdated incomplete pregnancies. Overall, however, there was negligible directional bias due to data errors (Chung, et al. , 1981). Women's dates were used wherever possible, to preserve other relationships in the interview data. The time period used for the survival analysis was the interval between the month of outcome of the induced abortion, birth, or spontaneous abortion for which the woman was included in the study, and the month of conception of her next pregnancy. If she did not conceive subsequently, the interval ended in December 1979, the end of the timeline on which relevant data were collected. The length of possible follow-up for each woman varies from 5 to 10 years. After exclusion of cases with missing data, there were 307 abortion cases and 389 control cases available for the survival analysis.

The Box-Jenkins analysis used the variable "exposure to pregnancy risk," an interval level scale which approximated the percent of time during a month that a woman was exposed to pregnancy risk by a combination of her sexual behavior and contraceptive use. The sexual-behavior component of the scale was the woman's reported frequency of intercourse with all partners. The contraceptive-use component was a combination of the specific methods the woman reported using and her reported consistency of use. The two components were translated from the original verbal-response ranges into decimal scales. When multiplied together, these produce an interval-scaled approximation of exposure to pregnancy risk for the month. The variable was calculated for each woman for each month, and then the scores for all women remaining in the pool for a particular month were aggregated. The mean exposure level for the sample each month comprises the time series. The series was terminated on month 102, at which time there were 30 abortion cases and 31 control cases remaining in the two pools.

The data-collection instruments also included detailed questions concerning each pregnancy during the 11 years under consideration. Women were asked to what extent they had experienced a specified range of emotions in connection with each pregnancy. On the basis of the entire semi-structured interview, the interviewer was asked to assess the wantedness and intendedness of each pregnancy, and the respondent's current satisfaction with the pregnancy's outcome. The latter technique was developed by Miller (1977) to circumvent the social-acceptability bias in women's responses to such questions.

Comparisons were based on all cases available for the initial pregnancy and all cases available for the next birth or spontaneous abortion following the initial pregnancy (ignoring intervening induced abortions). These data were based on a slightly different abortion sample than the previous analyses. Because the attitude and emotion data were based on pregnancies reported by the respondent, they necessarily excluded induced abortions which women did not report to the interviewer. This reduced the size of the abortion sample by 29 percent for the initial pregnancy. To compensate for this loss and also to maximize the number of subsequent pregnancies available for analysis, cases were also included from a special supplemental sample of women who had had abortions and had been record-linked to a subsequent birth or spontaneous abortion. This supplemental sample was drawn at the same time as the original samples, and all subsequent procedures for these cases were identical, but they were not used for analyses in which the extent of subsequent pregnancy in the two samples was relevant, as in the survival and time-series analyses. Sample sizes for the attitudinal and emotional data were 269 abortion cases and 387 control cases for the initial pregnancy; 201 abortion cases and 204 control cases for the subsequent pregnancy.

Results

SURVIVAL ANALYSIS

Survival analysis was performed for 102 months of follow-up calculated in three-month intervals. Survival refers to the length of time a woman remains in the sample because she has not experienced a subsequent pregnancy. Case losses due to other causes (death, interview date, or conclusion of the follow-up period) were adjusted by the procedure. The cumulative proportions of each sample surviving to the end of the interval were nearly identical (.3795 for the abortion sample and .3728 for the control sample), but the median survival times differed considerably: 62.99 months in the abortion sample and 45.21 months in the control sample. The Lee-Desu statistic showed the difference between the two samples as barely significant (P = .0576).

Survival comparisons by age and pregnancy order reveal considerable delay in subsequent pregnancy among young, nulliparous women in the abortion sample. Women under 20 at the initial pregnancy outcome showed the most marked difference in survival rates by sample. Median survival time was 57.0 months in the abortion sample and only 24.9 months in the control sample. The difference between the two groups was significant beyond the .01 level. No other age groups showed significantly different survival patterns by sample, although each age group as a whole had a different level and pattern of survival. The findings quite obviously reflect the social behavior and childbearing intentions of women rather than their physiological ability to conceive.

This interpretation is supported by the findings by pregnancy order. Women who were sampled on their first pregnancy showed significantly different subsequent survival rates by sample, while women with previous pregnancies did not. The survival patterns also differed for women at each pregnancy order, regardless of sample.

The basic limitation of the survival technique is that it can only reflect the experience of fixed subgroups defined at the outset of the time period. While one may infer from the pattern of survival that the behavior or condition of a subsample changed during the interval, these changes cannot be incorporated directly into the analysis so that they can be controlled. The time-series analysis of exposure to pregnancy risk was devised to overcome this limitation in part. In contrast to the life-table or survival method of measuring the length of time specific subsamples remain in the data pool, the time-series method examines the changing composition of the remaining pool. It thus can handle both attribute variables, as the survival method can, and behavioral variables that fluctuate over time for the same individual. In this instance, the survival analysis suggested that exposure to pregnancy risk might be changing over time for specific women during the pregnancy interval. The time-series analysis attempted to capture this fluctuation within the two samples.

TIME-SERIES ANALYSIS

Mean Monthly levels of exposure to pregnancy for the control sample began at about 16.5 percent and sloped steadily down to about 3 percent. The pattern showed a relatively steady removal of women who became pregnant due to exposure, leaving behind a pool of women with very low exposure to pregnancy risk due to the combination of contraceptive practices and frequency of intercourse. The mean level of exposure to pregnancy in the abortion sample began somewhat lower, rose over the first year, and then remained at about the same level, 15 to 16 percent for 3 years, after which it dropped slowly to 7 to 8 percent by the eighth year after the induced abortion.

The generally low-mean exposure levels in both samples reflected substantial use of contraception. Preliminary log linear analyses of the data showed that contraceptive use was substantially independent of intercourse frequency but both were closely related to partner relationship. The patterns of relationship among variables were also significantly different in the two samples. In both samples, some women were highly exposed to pregnancy risk and others reduced their risk substantially by the use of contraception. Only about one quarter of the women who used no contraception, however, were trying to become pregnant.

Behind a mean exposure level of 15 percent, then, lies a complex combination of women trying to prevent or delay pregnancy by contraception, women actively trying to become pregnant, and women who exposed themselves to considerable risk of pregnancy without any clear intention of becoming pregnant. A stable exposure level could be maintained for some period of time by new women shifting from contraception to high exposure, but if the women conceived at normal speed, the pool would eventually become depleted and the mean exposure level would decline.

The data show that the abortion sample remained at a moderate level of exposure for a longer period of time than the control sample. By the end of the time-series, however, the abortion sample had begun to exhibit the same pattern of

declining exposure that was found in the control sample. As
the original pool was depleted of women who became pregnant
upon exposure to risk, the remaining pool consisted increasingly of women with very low levels of exposure, either because of low intercourse frequency or effective contraceptive
practice.

The time-series for both samples showed a significant
degree of auto-correlation, through the 25th lag, which disappeared with one degree of differencing (a moving average
process of one month's lag). While the Box-Jenkins procedure
could be carried through the estimation and forecasting stages
of analysis to predict the point at which the abortion sample
would catch up to the control sample, that refinement is un-
necessary for the present purpose. The patterns of mean
exposure to pregnancy in the two samples indicate quite clearly
that, by reducing their exposure to pregnancy risk, the women
in the abortion sample tended to delay a subsequent pregnancy
longer than the women in the control sample. As their cir-
cumstances--and their exposure level--changed, they became
pregnant and dropped out of the pool.

Time-series analysis of the age and pregnancy order
variables repeated the findings of the survival analysis from
a different perspective. The lower survival rates of younger,
low pregnancy order women were reflected in the time-series
analysis by the changing composition of the remaining samples.
Age patterns in the two samples were nearly identical. The
abortion sample began with a mean age of 24.6. The mean
for the time-series was 30.0. The control sample began with
a mean age of 25.1 and had a time-series mean of 31.3.
Both samples experienced a twelve-year increase in mean
age during the $8\frac{1}{2}$ years of follow-up, which supports the interpretation that younger women were becoming pregnant again,
leaving behind a pool more heavily weighted with older women.
It should be noted, however, that the similar mean ages in
the two samples mask some differences in the actual age dis-
tributions.

The patterns of change in mean pregnancy order in
the two samples mirrored the time-series patterns of mean
exposure to pregnancy. In the control sample, mean pregnancy order rose gradually from 2.2 to 3.3, as lower parity
women dropped out of the sample due to subsequent pregnancy.
In the abortion sample, mean pregnancy order remained very
stable at 2.5 to 2.6 for the first 7 years of follow-up, and
then rose very rapidly to 3.3.

SUBJECTIVE READINESS FOR PARENTHOOD

Interviewers' assessments of the status of the initial and subsequent pregnancies are shown in Table I. The initial pregnancies in the abortion sample were clearly unintended, although both samples showed a substantial amount of accidental but not actively avoided conception. The subsequent pregnancies of the two samples, by contrast, had nearly identical patterns, characterized by a high degree of actively intended pregnancy and a relatively low degree of accidental but not actively avoided conceptions. It is apparent that those women in the abortion sample who had a subsequent pregnancy generally did so deliberately.

Wantedness of pregnancy followed a similar pattern. At the initial pregnancy, many women in the control sample were ambivalent about the birth, while the abortion sample was overwhelmingly negative. At the subsequent pregnancy, the two samples were very similar, though the abortion sample seemed to have slightly more reservations than the controls.

Women were asked whether they had experienced a selected range of emotions during a particular pregnancy. The patterns of comparison follow closely that found for intendedness and wantedness of pregnancy, as shown in Table II. While abortion recipients experienced predominantly negative feelings during the pregnancy that was aborted, their feelings on the subsequent pregnancy were in the same positive range as the controls. In most cases, their responses to the subsequent pregnancy fell between those of the initial and subsequent pregnancies of the control sample. This is probably due to the higher degree of planned pregnancy in the abortion sample's subsequent pregnancies as compared to the control sample's initial pregnancies, plus the fact that the abortion sample was one birth behind, containing predominantly first births in its subsequent-pregnancy category.

At the time of the initial pregnancy, the majority of the abortion patients were unmarried. This makes direct comparison of the economic and social status of the two samples difficult because the family units were different and the abortion sample contained a higher proportion of young women whose position could not readily be inferred from their own social characteristics. Earlier research on samples of women drawn from the same base population demonstrated that, among pregnant single women, those of higher social class families

TABLE I:

Intendedness and Wantedness of Initial and Subsequent Pregnancies, by Sample*

	Initial Pregnancy		Subsequent Pregnancy	
Sample	Abortion	Control	Abortion	Control
Intendedness	%	%	%	%
Intended	2.22	43.78	47.98	50.73
Intended; ambivalent	1.85	6.48	5.05	4.88
Intended; conflict with partner	1.85	1.55	3.03	0.93
Not intended; no contracept.	43.70	32.38	19.70	21.95
Not intended; irreg. contra.	25.56	9.29	11.11	14.63
Not intended; usually contra.	5.19	1.81	3.54	0.98
Not intended; always contra.	19.63	5.70	9.60	5.85
N of cases	270	386	198	205
Wantedness				
Actively wanted; no constraints	2.23	58.29	58.88	67.80
Actively wanted; some constraints	4.83	11.66	16.24	9.76
Passively wanted; no rejection	1.49	26.42	19.29	18.54
Passively wanted; considered rej.	4.09	3.37	3.55	2.44
Unwanted and rejected	87.36	0.26	2.03	1.46
N of Cases	269	386	197	205

*Initial pregnancy is induced abortion for all women in abortion sample. In all other categories, pregnancy outcome is birth or spontaneous abortion.

Source: Hawaii Subsequent Effects of Abortion study, pregnancy modules.

TABLE II:

Emotions Experienced During Initial and Subsequent Pregnancy, By Sample*

Degree of Emotion	Initial Pregnancy					Subsequent Pregnancy				
	Not at All	A Little	Some What	A Lot	N Cases	Not at All	A Little	Some What	A Lot	N Cases
Pride										
Abortion	76.40	11.99	7.12	4.49	267	13.64	13.13	18.69	54.55	198
Control	21.73	16.75	17.54	43.98	382	12.81	10.34	19.70	57.14	203
Anxiety										
Abortion	15.61	14.50	13.75	56.13	269	45.77	30.35	11.44	12.44	201
Control	44.16	26.23	12.21	17.40	385	61.39	22.77	7.92	7.92	202
Happiness										
Abortion	68.28	18.28	7.46	5.97	268	7.00	8.50	16.00	68.50	200
Control	10.08	11.11	16.80	62.02	387	2.96	10.84	15.27	70.94	203
Depression										
Abortion	16.73	21.56	20.07	41.64	269	69.00	20.50	4.50	6.00	200
Control	68.57	16.10	4.94	10.39	385	71.64	17.91	3.98	6.47	201
Acceptance										
Abortion	46.44	15.73	16.10	21.72	267	3.03	5.56	20.71	70.71	198
Control	7.25	7.77	13.73	71.24	386	2.45	6.86	10.78	79.90	204
Anger										
Abortion	48.70	18.96	10.41	21.93	269	89.45	7.04	1.51	2.01	199
Control	86.20	6.51	1.56	5.73	384	88.06	6.97	1.49	3.48	201
Love										
Abortion	51.35	15.83	16.22	16.60	259	7.07	8.59	12.63	71.72	198
Control	8.24	7.45	15.16	69.15	376	5.50	7.00	11.50	76.00	200
Guilt										
Abortion	35.56	20.00	14.07	30.37	270	81.50	13.50	0.50	4.50	200
Control	85.64	7.83	3.39	3.13	383	89.66	5.91	2.46	1.97	203
Relief										
Abortion	85.50	6.11	2.67	5.73	262	46.35	11.98	12.50	29.17	192
Control	48.77	11.99	11.17	28.07	367	41.24	20.10	9.79	28.87	194

*Initial pregnancy is induced abortion for all women in abortion sample. Pregnancy outcomes in all other categories are birth or spontaneous abortion.

Source: Hawaii Subsequent Effects of Abortion study, pregnancy modules.

of origin, with more education and possessing high personal, educational, and economic aspirations, tended to choose abortion (Steinhoff, 1977). The consequences of this initial differential can be seen in the comparison of subsequent pregnancies, at which time the overwhelming majority of women in both samples were married. Over one third of the women in the abortion sample were married to men in professional and managerial occupations, as opposed to one quarter in the control sample. About 90 percent of the husbands in both samples were employed full-time.[2]

All of these various indicators of subjective "readiness" for parenthood suggest that by the time women in the abortion sample had carried to completion their delayed pregnancies, they had achieved a considerably greater degree of "readiness" than they possessed at the time of the abortion. They had developed more stable personal relationships and greater economic security, and then had planned a pregnancy about which they had very positive feelings.

Conclusions

The data provide striking evidence that women who utilized abortion were able to realize their family goals as a result. Young women who delayed the formation of families by utilizing abortion appear to have been quite successful in avoiding subsequent unwanted pregnancy. They have subsequently borne children under more stable economic and social conditions than those prevailing at the time of the abortion. Their subsequent births have been overwhelmingly intended and wanted and have occurred in a positive emotional atmosphere. At the time of their subsequent pregnancies, they are indistinguishable from the control sample in attitudes and emotions, albeit slightly higher in socioeconomic status.

Two other observations may be drawn from the data. The first is that, among very young women, the use of induced abortion leads to a postponement of the first birth well beyond the second birth of women in the control sample. A postponement of this magnitude not only attests to the high use of contraception after induced abortion, it also implies that the long-term demographic effect of induced abortion in slowing generational turnover is probably greater than previously estimated. The assumption that the aborted birth will be followed by another pregnancy at the same interval, as if it had been carried to term, may not be tenable.

The second observation concerns the social-class implications of induced abortion use. It has been apparent for some time that the decision to seek abortion is more often and more easily made by middle-class women. It is now apparent that the use of abortion does indeed serve to preserve or enhance the woman's social status by increasing both her own educational and occupational level and that of her future marriage partner. This effect also carries over to the next generation, by raising the social, educational, and economic level of the household in which the child is brought up. This interpretation may perhaps shed new light on the social sources of opposition to abortion, but pursuit of that question is beyond the scope of the present paper.

Notes

1. This study was supported in part by contract NO1-HD-62801 awarded by the National Institute of Child Health and Human Development, National Institutes of Health, C. S. Chung, principal investigator. The author thanks the sponsor, the principal investigator, the interviewers and respondents, the Department of Sociology, University of Hawaii, and the project staff, especially Alice Beechert and Philip Wehrmann, for research assistance and computer programming well beyond the call of duty.

2. The women's subsequent educational and occupational histories will be considered in a forthcoming paper.

References

Chung, C. S.; Steinhoff, P. G.; Smith, Roy G.; and Mi, M. P. Effects of Induced Abortion on Subsequent Reproductive Function and Pregnancy Outcome. Final Report to Contraceptive Evaluation Branch, Center for Population Research, National Institute of Child Health and Human Development, Contract #NO1-HD-62801. December, 1981.

Lind, Meda. "Motherhood as Option or Destiny." Unpublished Ph. D. dissertation, Department of Sociology, University of Hawaii, 1976.

Miller, Warren B. "The Intendedness and Wantedness of the First Child." In The First Child and Family Formation, W. B. Miller and L. F. Newman, eds. Chapel Hill: Population Center, 1978: 9-24.

_____. "Sexual and Contraceptive Behavior in Young Un-married Women." Primary Care, Vol. 3 No. 3, Septem-ber, 1970: 427-453.

Steinhoff, Patricia G. "Premarital Pregnancy and the First Birth." In The First Child and Family Formation, W. B. Miller and L. F. Newman, eds. Chapel Hill: Carolina Popu-lation Center, 1978: pp. 180-208.

ABORTION: INCIDENCE, MORTALITY, AND MORBIDITY

By Michael E. Kafrissen, Nancy J. Binkin, David A. Grimes, and Willard Cates, Jr.

Introduction

Induced abortion is one of the most commonly performed operations in the world; 30 to 55 million procedures are performed annually (Tietze, 1981). Since the United States Supreme Court decision of 1973 legalizing abortion, over 7 million legal abortions have been performed in the United States (Centers for Disease Control, 1980; 1981). Because of these large numbers and the emotional debate surrounding this operation, abortion is among the most intensively studied of all operative procedures. Today, more is known about the morbidity and mortality associated with legal abortion than with any other operation.

In 1979, the Centers for Disease Control reported 1,238,987 induced abortions in the United States (CDC, 1981). If a total morbidity rate (Tietze, 1981) of 12.3 percent is applied to this figure, over 150,000 women experienced an abortion-related complication in 1979. Thus, although legal abortion is relatively safe, even low morbidity rates deserve public health attention because of the large number of procedures performed.

Morbidity and mortality are the results of complex combinations of interacting variables. These variables include the characteristics of the women obtaining abortions, of procedure, and factors relating to the community and facility. This chapter examines the relationships among these variables and the complications of induced abortion, with special attention to the prevention of complications.

Incidence of Induced Abortion

Before the legalization of abortion, no nationwide data were available on the number of abortions performed in the United States. Gathering information on a clandestine activity is extremely difficult. However, the Arden House Conference participants estimated that the annual number of procedures in the United States ranged from 200,000 to 1,200,000 before the widespread availability of legal abortion (Calderone, 1958).

Since the legalization of abortion, information on the number of abortions has been collected by two organizations --the Centers for Disease Control (CDC) and the Alan Guttmacher Institute (AGI).

The AGI annual estimate of the total number of abortions performed has consistently exceeded CDC's figure by 15 to 20 percent, a difference presumably due to different methods of data collection and to AGI's inclusion of private physician data (CDC, 1981).

In addition to the absolute number of abortions, two other statistical expressions are useful in describing the incidence of abortion in a given population--the abortion rate and the abortion ratio:

> abortion rate = number of abortions per 1,000
> women aged 15 to 44 years;
> abortion ratio = number of abortions per 1,000
> live births.

The reported abortion rate, as tabulated by CDC, has increased from 5 per 1,000 women aged 15 to 44 in 1972 to 23 per 1,000 in 1978. The abortion ratio has increased from 51.9 abortions per 1,000 live births in 1970 to 347.3 per 1,000 in 1978.

Characteristics of Women Obtaining Abortions

AGE

In 1978, approximately one-third of abortions performed were upon women 19 years old and younger, one third upon 20- to 24-year-old women, and one third upon women aged 25 and older (CDC, 1980). While the abortion ratio is high at the age extremes, the abortion rate is relatively low. The under-15 and over-40 groups represent less than 3 percent of all abortions (CDC, 1980).

RACE

Most abortions (67%) were obtained by white women (see Table I). However, among women under 15 years old, 52 percent of abortions were obtained by those of black and other minority races.

Although minority women were more likely than white women to terminate their pregnancies by abortion, the abortion ratio for white women has been increasing more rapidly than that for minority women.

MARITAL STATUS

In 1978, 73.6 percent of women obtaining abortions were unmarried at the time of the procedure (see Table I). This proportion was the same for white women and women of other races.

NUMBER OF PREVIOUS PREGNANCIES

The majority of women obtaining abortions in 1978 had never had a previous live birth (see Table I). The ratio of abortions to live births was highest for women with no previous live births (446 per 1,000 live births), and lowest for those with one previous live birth (201) (CDC, 1980). That is, pregnant women who had no previous live births were the most likely to seek abortion, while pregnant women with one previous live birth were least likely to seek abortion.

Approximately one-fourth of induced abortions are obtained by women who have had one or more previous abortions. From 1974 to 1978, the percentage of repeat induced abortions rose from 13 percent to 29 percent of total abortions (see Table I). In general, women have not relied on abortion in lieu of contraception. This increase in the percentage of repeat induced abortions primarily represents the increasing number of women who have had a first reported abortion and hence are at risk of having another (Tietze, 1978).

GESTATIONAL AGE AT TIME OF INDUCED ABORTION

In 1978, over half of induced abortions were performed at ≤ 8 weeks gestation (see Table I), as determined from the date of the first day of the last menstrual period. Over 90 percent of abortions were performed at ≤ 12 weeks gestation.

TABLE I

Characteristics	Percentage Distribution[1]						
	1972	1973	1974	1975	1976	1977	1978
Residence							
Abortion in-state	56.2	75.8	86.6	89.2	90.0	90.0	89.3
Abortion out-of-state	43.8	25.2	13.4	10.8	10.0	10.0	10.7
Age							
< 19	32.6	32.7	32.7	33.1	32.1	30.8	30.0
20-24	32.5	32.0	31.8	31.9	33.3	34.5	35.0
≥ 25	34.9	35.3	35.6	35.0	34.6	34.7	34.9
Race							
White	77.0	72.5	69.7	67.8	66.6	66.4	67.0
Black and other	23.0	27.5	30.0	32.2	33.4	33.6	33.0
Marital Status							
Married	29.7	27.4	27.4	26.1	24.6	24.3	26.4
Unmarried	70.3	72.6	72.6	73.9	75.4	75.7	73.6
Number of Live Births[2]							
0	49.4	48.6	47.8	47.1	47.7	53.4	56.6
1	18.2	18.8	19.6	20.2	20.7	19.1	19.2
2	13.3	14.2	14.8	15.5	15.4	14.4	14.1
3	8.7	8.7	8.7	8.7	8.3	7.0	5.9
≥ 4	10.4	9.7	9.0	8.6	7.9	6.2	4.2
Type of Procedure							
Curettage	88.6	88.4	89.7	90.9	92.8	93.8	94.6
Intrauterine Instillation	10.4	10.4	7.8	6.2	6.0	5.4	3.9
Hysterotomy/Hysterectomy	0.6	0.7	0.6	0.4	0.2	0.2	0.1
Other	0.5	0.6	1.9	2.4	0.9	0.7	1.4
Weeks of Gestation							
< 8	34.0	36.1	42.6	44.6	47.0	51.2	52.2
9-10	30.7	29.4	28.7	28.4	28.0	27.2	26.9
11-12	17.5	17.9	15.4	14.9	14.4	13.1	12.3
13-15	8.4	6.9	5.5	5.0	4.5	3.4	4.0
16-20	8.2	8.0	6.5	6.1	5.1	4.3	3.7
≥ 21	1.3	1.7	1.2	1.0	0.9	0.9	0.9
Previous Induced Abortions							
0	--	--	86.8	81.9	79.8	76.8	70.7
1	--	--	11.3	14.9	16.6	18.3	22.1
2	--	--	1.5	2.5	2.7	3.4	5.3
≥ 3	--	--	0.4	0.7	0.9	1.5	1.8

---

1. Excludes unknowns.
2. For years 1972-1977 data indicate number of living children.
A dash (--) indicates data not reported.

Source: Centers for Disease Control (1980).

Less than 1 percent of induced abortions were performed after 20 weeks. Younger women tended to obtain abortions later in their pregnancies than older women.

PRE-EXISTING MEDICAL CONDITIONS

When estimating the likelihood of mortality and morbidity from abortion, the physical condition of the woman must be considered. Medical conditions that may predispose a woman to hemorrhage, embolization, or infection can contribute to the likelihood of morbidity. A pregnant woman who has a pre-existing medical condition faces greater risk of mortality and morbidity than a healthy pregnant woman, regardless of the pregnancy outcome (LeBolt, et al. , 1982).

Procedure Variables

Induced abortion includes a wide spectrum of procedures which are associated with differing rates of mortality and morbidity.

Centers for Disease Control defines an abortion-related death as one resulting from problems that become evident within 42 days of the procedure. In the Joint Program for the Study of Abortion, conducted from 1971 to 1975 (JPSA/ CDC), CDC identified a group of 15 complications as major: death; cardiac arrest; convulsions; endotoxic shock; fever for 3 or more days; hemorrhage necessitating blood transfusion; hypernatremia; injury to bladder, ureter, or intestines; pelvic infection with hospitalization for 11 or more days or with 2 or more days of fever and a peak temperature of at least 40° C; pneumonia; psychiatric hospitalization for 22 or more days; pulmonary embolism or infarction; thrombophlebitis; unintended major surgery; wound disruption after hysterotomy or hysterectomy. The term "major complication rate" refers to the percentage of women who sustained one or more of these complications.

The broad categories of induced abortion in current use are instrumental evacuation, labor induction, and major operations. New techniques are being developed in an attempt to minimize the complications, inconvenience, and costs and to enhance the accessibility of legally induced abortion.

Suction curettage is both the safest and the most commonly performed abortion procedure in the United States (CDC, 1980). This procedure results in a major complication rate of 0. 3 percent (Cates and Grimes, 1981).

Instrumental evacuation of the uterus has been extended to progressively later gestational ages. Between 1974 and 1978 the percentage of abortions performed at ≥ 13 weeks' gestation by D & E rose from 32 percent to 51 percent. Most other abortions performed after this gestational age were performed by instillation methods.

Less than 0.1 percent of abortions were performed by hysterotomy or hysterectomy (CDC, 1980). Because the death-to-case rate for hysterectomy and hysterotomy is over 40 deaths per 100,000 abortions, they should be chosen as primary abortion methods only for compelling clinical reasons.

Other factors affect the mortality and morbidity associated with abortion, including the type of anesthesia, method of cervical dilatation, nature of instrumentation, instillation techniques, prophylactic antibiotics, and operator skill.

ANESTHESIA

Anesthesia is an important determinant of abortion morbidity and mortality. For suction curettage, major complication rates associated with the use of local and general anesthesia do not differ significantly (Grimes, et al., 1979). However, the type of major complication associated with each type of anesthesia is different.

The most important distinction between local and general anesthesia is found in the mortality rates (Peterson, et al., 1981). Anesthesia-related complications caused about 15 percent of all abortion-related deaths from 1972 to 1978.

CERVICAL DILATATION

Cervical dilatation may lead to abortion-related morbidity. Too little dilatation may increase the technical difficulty of the procedure as well as the potential for excessive blood loss and retained products of conception. Excessive dilatation may result in cervical laceration and hemorrhage (Peterson, 1979). Rapid dilatation with rigid dilators may damage the integrity of the cervical structure, possibly leading to adverse outcomes in subsequent pregnancies. Laminaria appear to decrease but not eliminate the incidence of cervical laceration, although they also increase the cost and inconvenience.

INSTILLATION TECHNIQUES

The type of agent and method of instillation may affect the mortality and morbidity associated with abortion. The initial JPSA/CDC study comparing saline with prostaglandin amnioinfusion showed a higher rate of major complications associated with prostaglandin as compared with saline (Grimes, et al. , 1977). The infusion of a combination of urea and prostaglandin has been proposed as a safer instillation technique (King, et al. , 1974).

PROPHYLACTIC ANTIBIOTICS

The efficacy of prophylactic antibiotics in preventing morbidity due to infection following abortion is unresolved. A prospective, nonrandomized study found that complications (excluding perforation) were reduced by more than 60 percent (Hodgson, et al. , 1975). No effect was noted except among women with a history of pelvic infection.

OPERATOR SKILL

Operator skill is also a factor that influences mortality and morbidity. Operators may be characterized by their level of training, experience with the procedure being evaluated, and innate ability. Relevant criteria regarding operator skill and complication rates have yet to be defined. The operator's correct estimation of gestational age, careful performance of the appropriate procedure, attention to the quantity and completeness of tissue obtained, and prompt treatment of any complication may reduce mortality and morbidity (Burnhill, 1979).

Community and Other Variables

Community variables affect a woman's ability to obtain a safe and affordable abortion. Many of these community variables result in delayed abortions, which have been shown to be hazardous (Cates, et al. , 1977). Factors that may cause such delay include legal barriers, financial restrictions, geographic barriers, policies of the medical community, and the woman's social and cultural background (Henshaw, et al. , 1981).

EFFECTS OF DELAY IN OBTAINING ABORTION

Because the risk of complications associated with induced abortion increases with each week of gestational age, any delay must be considered potentially threatening to the woman.

After 8 weeks' gestation, the risk of major complications rise 15 to 30 percent each week (Cates, et al., 1977).

The risk of death also increases with advancing gestational age, from a low of 0.4 deaths per 100,000 abortions performed at <8 weeks to 22.1 per 100,000 at ≥ 21 weeks (CDC, 1980).

OTHER BARRIERS

Other important barriers to the reduction of abortion-related mortality and morbidity are failure or absence of contraception, failure of the patient or provider to recognize early pregnancy, and lack of awareness of current options and resources in reproductive health. A study conducted among 1,006 women in an area of easy accessibility to abortion found that the most important determinants of delay were personal factors not readily amenable to public health intervention (Burr & Schulz, 1980).

Facility Variables

The type of facility in which abortions are performed reflects the preferences of the practitioner, the availability of ambulatory surgical centers in the community, and laws operating at federal, state, and local levels.

The type of facility where the abortion is performed does not substantially affect the safety of procedures that can be performed in an outpatient setting (suction curettage and D & E). In fact, hospital and nonhospital procedures have comparable risks of mortality when the rates are adjusted for pre-existing conditions and concurrent sterilization (Grimes, et al., 1981).

Long-term Sequelae

The relation of induced abortion to long-term complications has been frequently studied, with conflicting conclusions (Hogue, et al., in press). Methodologic problems preclude a definitive answer at this time.

Numerous complications noted among women with a history of induced abortion have been attributed to abortion. As technology progresses long-term sequelae that may be associated with one technique, such as rapid dilatation with rigid instruments, may not be associated with another technique, such as the use of laminaria. Hence, conclusions based on studies of older abortion techniques such as dilatation and sharp curettage (D & C) may no longer be relevant.

It has been suggested that induced abortion may be associated with infertility, spontaneous abortion, prematurity, malformations, ectopic pregnancy, placenta previa, and stillbirth. None of these associations has been consistently noted (Hogue, et al., in press).

Conclusions

Although induced abortions occur with or without legal sanction, legal abortions are safer than illegal procedures. Suction curettage and D & E are the safest methods of abortion available at this time. Over 95 percent of legal abortions in the United States are performed at <16 weeks' gestation and are associated with a lower risk of mortality and morbidity than continuing pregnancy to term. Although facilitating access to early and safer procedures will reduce abortion-related mortality and morbidity, further studies are needed to evaluate the evolving technology and long-term sequelae of induced abortion.

References

Burnhill, M. "Reducing Morbidity of Vacuum Aspiration." In Pregnancy Termination: Procedures, Safety and New Developments, Zatuchni, G. I.; Sciarra, J. J.; and Speidel, J. J., eds. Hagerstown, Md.: Harper and Row, 1979, pp. 135-148.

Burr, W. A., and Schulz, K. F. "Delayed Abortion in an Area of Easy Accessibility." Journal of the American Medical Association, 1980, 244 1, 44-48.

Calderone, M. S. Abortion in the United States. New York: P. S. Hoeber, 1958.

Cates, W., Jr., and Grimes, D. A. "Mortality and Morbidity of Abortion in the United States." In Abortion and Sterilization: Medical and Social Aspects, Hodgson, J. E., ed. London: The Academic Press, 1981, pp. 155-180.

Cates, W., Jr.; Schulz, K. F.; Grimes, D. A.; and Tyler C. W., Jr. "The Effect of Delay and Choice of Method on the Risk of Abortion Morbidity." Family Planning Perspectives, 1977, 9: 266-73.

Centers for Disease Control. Abortion Surveillance 1978. November, 1980.

_____. Abortion Surveillance, 1979--, Provisional Statistics. Morbidity Mortality Weekly Report (MMWR) 1981, 31:4, 47-50.

Grimes, D. A.; Cates, W., Jr.; and Selik, R. M. "Abortion Facilities and the Risk of Death. Family Planning Perspectives, 1981, 13: 30-2.

Grimes, D. A.; Schulz, K. F.; Cates, W. Jr.; and Tyler, C. W., Jr. "Local Versus General Anesthesia: Which Is Safer for Performing Suction Curettage Abortions?" American Journal of Obstetrics & Gynecology, 1979, 135: 1030-5.

_____. Midtrimester Abortion by Dilatation and Evacuation." New England Journal & Medicine, 296:1141-45.

Henshaw, S.; Forrest, J.; Sullivan, E.; and Tietze, C. "Abortion 1977-1979: Need and Services in the United States, Each State and Metropolitan Area." New York: Alan Guttmacher Institute, 1981.

Hodgson, J. E.; Major, B.; Portmann, K.; and Quattlebaum, F. W. "Prophylactic Use of Tetracycline for First Trimester Abortions." Obstetrics and Gynecology 1975, 45:5, 574-578.

Hogue, C. J.; Cates, W., Jr.; and Tietze, C. "The Effects of Induced Abortion on Subsequent Reproduction." Epidemiologic Review (in press).

King, T. M.; Atienza, M. F.; Burkman, R. T.; et al. "The Synergistic Activity of Intra-amniotic Prostaglandin F2a and Urea in Midtrimester Elective Abortion." American Journal of Obstetrics and Gynecology 1975, 120-704.

LeBolt, S.; Grimes, D. A.; and Cates, W., Jr. "Mortality from Abortion and Childbirth." Journal of the American Medical Association, 1982, 248:188-91.

Peterson, H. B.; Grimes, D. A.; Cates, W., Jr.; and Rubin, G. L. "Comparative Risk of Death from Induced Abortion at < 12 Weeks' Gestation Performed with Local and General Anesthesia." American Journal of Obstetrics and Gynecology 1981, 141:763-768.

Peterson, W. "Dilatation and Evacuation: Patient Evaluation and Surgical Techniques." In Pregnancy Termination: Procedures, Safety and New Developments, Zatuchni, G. I.; Sciarra, J. J.; and Speidel, J. J., eds. Hagerstown, Md.: Harper and Row, 1979, 184-190.

Sonne-Holm, S.; Heisterberg, L.; Hebjorn, S.; et al. "Prophylactic Antibiotics in First Trimester Abortions: A Clinical, Control Trial." American Journal of Obstetrics and Gynecology 1981, 139:693-6.

Tietze, C. Induced Abortion: A World Review, 1981. New York, The Population Council, 1981.

_____. "Repeat Abortions--Why More?" Family Planning Perspectives 1978, 10(5):286-288.

REPEAT ABORTION

By Christopher Tietze

The issue of repeat abortion is a matter of concern for those who feel that abortion is unacceptable as a primary method of fertility regulation and should be used only as a backup measure when contraception has failed. Others fear that even minor adverse effects on the health of the woman or on the outcome of later pregnancies would be cumulated by multiple abortion experiences. Providers of abortion services, especially health workers involved in counseling, are embarrassed by what they perceive as a failure to educate clients in the successful use of contraceptive methods.

Table I presents the relevant statistics for Canada, England and Wales, and the United States from 1970 to 1980, as available. The data for Canada and England are taken from the reports compiled by the national statistical services [1-3]; those for the United States are estimates by the Alan Guttmacher Institute, [4,5] based on data collected by the Centers for Disease Control, [6] an arm of the United States Department of Health and Human Services, from an increasing number of states (34 in 1980) and the Institute's own nationwide surveys of abortion providers. The series is adjusted for changes in participating states.

Information on prior induced abortions is obtained from women seeking a subsequent termination and are, therefore, subject to response error or even deliberate denial or understatement. In England the recording of prior abortions is limited to those obtained under the Abortion Act of 1967; although Canada and the United States ask for prior induced abortions without qualification, it is believed that few women report abortions obtained in illegal settings. Any inclusion of such abortions would tend to reduce or offset the presumed incomplete reporting of prior legal abortions.

TABLE I:

First and Repeat Abortions: Numbers and Percent

Year	Number		Percent	
	First	Repeat	First	Repeat
CANADA*				
1975	44,945	4,366	91.1	8.9
1976	48,885	5,593	89.7	10.3
1977	50,896	6,668	88.4	11.6
1978	54,037	8,253	86.8	13.2
1979	55,719	9,324	85.7	14.3
1980	55,094	10,149	84.4	15.6
ENGLAND AND WALES				
1970	74,743	1,219	98.4	1.6
1971	92,206	2,364	97.5	2.5
1972	104,530	4,035	96.3	3.7
1973	105,265	5,303	95.2	4.8
1974	103,068	6,377	94.2	5.8
1975	99,287	6,937	93.5	6.5
1976	93,931	7,981	92.2	7.8
1977	94,592	8,085	92.1	7.9
1978	102,105	9,746	91.2	8.8
1979	109,224	11,387	90.6	9.4
1980	115,763	13,164	89.8	10.2
UNITED STATES				
1974	762,060	136,510	84.8	15.2
1975	822,080	212,090	79.5	20.5
1976	911,320	267,980	77.3	22.7
1977	972,530	344,170	73.9	26.1
1978	996,460	413,140	70.7	29.3
1979	1,025,340	472,330	68.5	31.5
1980	1,042,960	510,930	67.1	32.9

*Women with number of prior abortions not reported (2.1 - 2.7%) were distributed pro rata.

TABLE II:

Women at Risk of First and Repeat Abortion:
Numbers and Percent

Year	Est. Number (1,000)		Percent	
	First	Repeat	First	Repeat
CANADA				
1975	5,013	183	96.5	3.5
1976	5,068	229	95.7	4.3
1977	5,149	277	94.9	5.1
1978	5,201	327	94.1	5.9
1979	5,250	379	93.3	6.7
1980	5,289	445	92.2	7.8
ENGLAND AND WALES				
1970	9,210	101	98.9	1.1
1971	9,142	183	98.9	2.0
1972	9,086	278	97.0	3.0
1973	9,052	379	96.0	4.0
1974	8,992	477	95.0	5.0
1975	8,945	570	94.0	6.0
1976	8,941	656	93.2	6.8
1977	8,962	737	92.4	7.6
1978	9,008	816	91.7	8.3
1979	9,060	899	91.0	9.0
1980	9,109	985	90.2	9.8
UNITED STATES				
1974	44,392	2,216	95.2	4.8
1975	44,602	3,004	93.7	6.3
1976	44,864	3,857	92.1	7.9
1977	45,034	4,780	90.4	9.6
1978	45,181	5,740	88.7	11.3
1979	45,082	6,934	86.7	13.1
1980	45,343	7,705	85.5	14.5

TABLE III:

Index Numbers of Repeat Abortions and Women at Risk (1975 = 100) and Abortion Rates per 1,000 Women at Risk

| Year | Index Numbers | | | Abortion Rates | |
	Repeat Abortions	Women at Risk		First	Repeat
CANADA					
1975	100	100		9. 0	23. 9
1976	128	125		9. 6	24. 4
1977	153	151		9. 9	24. 1
1978	189	179		10. 4	25. 2
1979	214	207		10. 6	24. 6
1980	232	243		10. 4	22. 8
ENGLAND AND WALES					
1970	18	18		8. 1	12. 1
1971	34	32		10. 1	12. 9
1972	58	49		11. 5	14. 5
1973	76	66		11. 6	14. 0
1974	92	84		11. 5	13. 4
1975	100	100		11. 1	12. 2
1976	115	115		10. 5	12. 2
1977	117	129		10. 6	11. 0
1978	140	143		11. 3	11. 9
1979	164	158		12. 1	12. 7
1980	190	173		12. 7	13. 4
UNITED STATES					
1974	64	74		17. 2	61. 6
1975	100	100		18. 4	70. 6
1976	126	128		20. 3	69. 5
1977	162	159		21. 6	72. 0
1978	195	191		22. 1	72. 0
1979	223	231		22. 7	68. 1
1980	241	256		23. 0	66. 3

Numbers of repeat abortions increased rapidly in all three countries during the period covered by available statistics, the average annual increment ranging from 18 to 26 percent. The share of repeat abortions among all abortions also grew, but somewhat more slowly because the total numbers of legal abortions were larger in later years.

These rapid increases do not reflect a progressive change from contraception to abortion as the primary method of fertility regulation but rather, to a large degree, the fact that growing numbers of women who have had a first legal abortion are at risk of having a repeat abortion. Table II illustrates this situation. Unfortunately, statistics on repeat abortions were not collected in any of the three countries during the first few years following liberalization of the abortion laws. It was, therefore, necessary to estimate the numbers of first legal abortions by extrapolating the percentage of repeat abortions backwards. After cumulating the numbers of first abortions, appropriate corrections were made to subtract women who had reached the end of the childbearing period or had died during the interval.

The first two columns of Table III show index numbers of repeat abortions and of women at risk using the year 1975 as a baseline of 100. The trends match almost perfectly in each of the three countries.

The last two columns of Table III reveal for Canada and the United States much higher rates of repeat abortions, per 1,000 women at risk, than of first abortions at the same time. This finding should not be interpreted as evidence for a deterioration of contraceptive practice after the first abortion. Rather, the difference reflects the heterogeneity of the female population in regard to the need for and use of abortion as a method of fertility control. With and without contraception, the incidence of unintended pregnancies varies with age, parity, and marital status. For example, the large numbers of women in Table II who had not yet experienced any abortion include many teenagers and some adult women who had not yet become sexually active and were, therefore, not at risk of either pregnancy or abortion. In both countries access to abortion services varies among localities and socioeconomic groups. In addition, attitudes and behavior range as a continuum from complete rejection of abortion under all circumstances, to acceptance of abortion in some situations (e. g. , for termination of out-of-wedlock pregnancy or for family limitation, but not for childspacing within marriage), to the acceptance of abortion of all unintended pregnancies. Other factors being equal, the difference between first-abortion rates and repeat-abortion rates increases with the degree of heterogeneity of the population with regard to abortion practices.[7]

In England and Wales the differences between rates of first abortions and of repeat abortions, per 1,000 women at risk, are in the same direction as in Canada and the United States, but much smaller, especially in recent years. Three possible explanations (or a combination thereof) suggest themselves: (1) The population may be less heterogeneous in regard to abortion; (2) women may find it more difficult to obtain authorization for a second or higher order termination; or (3) under-reporting of repeat abortions may be more severe and in any case is not offset by inclusion of pre-1968 abortions in the statistics. None of these explanations can be established as correct, but the third may be the most important.

Differences in regard to surgical sterilization performed concurrently with the abortion procedure have probably not contributed much, if anything, to the narrow gap between first-abortion rates and repeat-abortion rates in England, as compared with Canada. During the period for which data on concurrent sterilization are available for both countries (1972 to 1980), the combined procedure was more often used in Canada than in England. In addition concurrent sterilization typically involves multiparous older women who would not have contributed much to the aggregate risk of repeat abortion.

Notes

1. Canada: Statistics Canada. Therapeutic Abortions [1975-] 1980. Ottawa, [1977-] 1982.
2. United Kingdom: Office of Population Censuses and Surveys. The Registrar General's Statistical Review of England and Wales. Supplement on Abortion [1970-] 1973. London, [1972-] 1974.
3. United Kingdom: Office of Population Censuses and Surveys, Abortion Statistics. England and Wales [1974-] 1980. London, [1977-] 1982.
4. Henshaw, S. K., et al. Abortion 1977-1979: Need and Services in the United States, Each State and Metropolitan Area. New York: Alan Guttmacher Institute, 1981.

5. Henshaw, S. K. and K. O'Reilly. "Characteristics of abortion patients in the United States, 1979 and 1980." Family Planning Perspectives 1983, 15 (1): 6-16.
6. United States: Centers for Disease Control. Abortion Surveillance [1974-] 1978. Atlanta, [1976-] 1980.
7. Tietze, C. and A. K. Jain. "The Mathematics of Repeat abortion: Explaining the Increase." Studies in Family Planning, 1974, 9 (12): 294-299.

THE HABITUAL THERAPEUTIC ABORTER:
SOCIOPSYCHOLOGICAL CHARACTERISTICS

By Ellen W. Freeman

Although legal first-trimester abortion entails low risk of mortality (0. 6 deaths per 100,000 abortions) and morbidity (U. S. Dept. HHS, 1980), abortion continues to be complicated by conflicting attitudes toward its social and ethical implications. Issues in medical care reflect these conflicts. Abortion services are unevenly distributed in the country; in 1977, there were identified abortion providers in only 23 percent of U. S. counties (Seims, 1980). A survey by Nathanson and Becker (1980) showed that the effect of physicians' attitudes on the number of abortions performed in hospitals is strong and independent of factors such as hospital size and community needs for abortion services. The Hyde amendment made costs for obtaining abortion services greater than costs of delivering a pregnancy for women eligible for Medicaid (Trussell, et al. , 1980). There are widespread concerns about whether women use abortion rather than contraception and whether the numbers of repeat abortions will continue to increase.

Abortion Frequency

About one in seven women of childbearing age in the U. S. has had a legal abortion. In 1979, approximately 30 percent of pregnancies were terminated by induced abortions (Henshaw, et al. , 1981). Twenty-nine percent of abortions obtained in 1978 were repeat abortions (U. S. Dept. HHS, 1980).

Tietze's models estimated the rate of repeat abortions that could be expected from total abortion rates. With assumptions that abortion risk is constant and independent of prior experience, the model showed that the proportion of repeat abortions increases over time as more women have had a first abortion until a steady state is reached (Tietze and Jain, 1978). Another model--predicting repeat abortions based on current contraceptive effectiveness rates--estimated that a majority of women using contraceptives with 90 to 95 percent effectiveness will have a repeated contraceptive failure within five years (Tietze, 1974). Clinical data show some fit with these models but also challenge assumptions of the models: Contraceptive usage is not independent of prior abortion experience; contraceptive failures subsequent to a first abortion are not all aborted (Steinhoff, et al. , 1979).

Risk of Repeat Abortions

Medical concerns now focus on potential effects of abortions on reproductive capacity. Legalized Abortion and the Public Health, a report of the Institute of Medicine (1975), stated that conclusions about long-term complications were unwarranted based on existing data. Since the Institute's report, there have been findings of perinatal complications and fetal loss associated with induced abortions (Richardson & Dixon, 1976; Harlap & Davies, 1975) but other studies failed to confirm such findings (Daling & Emanuel, 1977; Hogue, 1975; Oronsaye, 1979). In a record-linkage analysis, Steinhoff, et al. (1979) showed that women in the low socioeconomic status categories were about $2\frac{1}{2}$ times more likely to experience repeat abortions than women in the high socioeconomic status categories. Many pregnancy-related problems such as low birthweight and perinatal mortality are correlated with these same social-class factors. These studies suggest the importance of controlling for the strong socioeconomic bias of the population of repeat aborters when investigating the effects of induced abortion on subsequent pregnancies.

Recent data collected by the World Health Organization (1979) from eight countries allowing legal abortion showed an increased incidence of miscarriages associated with prior D & C, but not with vacuum aspiration procedures. Other epidemiological data showed that women with two or more induced abortions had 2 to 3 times greater risk of miscarriage, premature deliveries, and low-birthweight infants in subsequent pregnancies than women who had one abortion or one live birth (Maine, 1979). Further analysis of the WHO data also showed that both the type of previous induced abortion and the woman's characteristics were more important factors in subsequent miscarriages than the number of abortions (Cates, et al. , 1981).

Risks from the mental-health perspective appear low.

Studies from a number of theoretical orientations showed that abortion is not a psychologically damaging procedure for most women (Osofsky & Osofsky, 1973; Bracken, et al. , 1974). In U. S. clinical studies, psychiatric conditions were less than 10 percent and associated with pre-existing conditions (Friedman, et al. , 1974). Apart from psychiatric conditions, it is common to experience depression, guilt, anxiety, or anger with an unwanted pregnancy and the processes leading to its termination. These emotional distress symptoms typically diminish shortly after or within several months following abortion procedures (Payne, et al. , 1976; Freeman, 1978).

There are few data on emotional distress factors in repeated abortion. In our clinical studies, self-reported emotional distress levels prior to abortion procedures did not differ significantly between first and repeat aborters (Freeman, et al. , 1980). However, following abortion procedures, emotional distress levels declined less among repeat aborters. The data showed that the experience of unwanted pregnancy and abortion was as stressful for repeaters as for those who experienced it for the first time, although we inferred that postabortion relief of emotional distress was less intense for those who had experienced abortion previously.

Abortion and Contraceptive Use

Abortion is an inefficient method of fertility regulation when contraception is available. Costs, inconvenience, and distress are generally experienced by those involved. Statistically, 9. 6 abortions per female are needed to reduce the natural fertility rate to replacement level (Tietze, 1979).

Repeat induced abortions in the United States appear to result from failures rather than non-acceptance of contraceptives (Tietze, 1978). Clinical reports show high contraceptive acceptance and use of more effective methods following abortions (Miller, et al. , 1977; Fylling and Svendsby, 1979). Repeat aborters reported significantly higher frequency of contraceptive use than first aborters (Bracken, et al. , 1972; Brewer, 1977). Shepard and Bracken (1979) found prior abortion was associated with greater use of all methods of contraception, except among women on welfare. However, Schneider and Thompson (1976) found that the increased contraceptive use following abortions became less persistent over time; women repeating abortions used contraceptives less in the months preceding abortion than sexually active, nonpregnant women. Data from conception cohorts suggested two abortion-use patterns, differentiated by users' long-range planning orientations and highly correlated with socioeconomic status: (1) Women of higher socioeconomic status used abortion to postpone first births and to prevent later births, usually after the second child, and (2) Women of lower socioeconomic status showed a retrospective approach to fertility control and used abortion to delay births after the first child and prevent births after four or more children (Steinhoff, et al. , 1979).

Contraceptive Failure

Reasons for contraceptive failures are complex, as suggested by Rovinsky's estimates that 61 percent were patient failures, 24 percent method failures, and 15 percent institutional failures (Rovinsky, 1972). The interrelationships of these categories and associated predictive factors are poorly understood.

Psychological studies have focused narrowly on individual characteristics and found contraceptive failures associated with unstable personal relationships and social situations (Bracken, et al. , 1972; Jacobsson, et al. , 1976); motivational problems including denial, guilt, game-playing, and fear (Rader, et al. , 1978); and perceived inability to control events, particularly those relating to sexuality and reproduction (Leach, 1977).

In a recent questionnaire study of 1,500 women having abortions (Howe, 1979), the major reasons given by abortion repeaters for not using contraceptives when conception occurred were medical contraindications and lack of supplies. Another study found that 17 percent of abortion repeaters had stopped contraception because of fears resulting from the negative publicity about oral contraceptives (Daily, et al. , 1973).

The role of sex frequency is unclear. Howe, et al. (1979) asserted that abortion repeaters had a greater risk of pregnancy since repeaters reported more frequent sexual activity than women having first abortions. However, this cannot be accepted without calculating the effect of contraceptive use in each group. Statistically, the risk of pregnancy with coitus once per month, at random and with no birth-control usage, is about equal to that of coitus 2 to 3 times a week with 90 percent-effective contraception (Tietze, 1974).

Emotional Distress and Repeated Abortions

Our studies of first and repeat aborters investigated whether emotional distress factors--identified readily with the use of patient self-assessment forms--had predictive usefulness in identifying women at risk of repeat abortions. First-trimester induced-abortion patients were sampled in 1973, 1977, and 1978, with the last sample reassessed at two weeks and one year post-abortion (Jacobs, et al., 1974; Freeman, et al., 1980; Freeman, et al., in press). In the last sample, 35 percent of the women were repeating abortion.

The sample discussed here was young--65 percent were under age 25, a proportion similar to the U.S. abortion profile (U.S. Dept. HHS, 1980), although only 27 percent were teenage patients compared to 33 percent nationally. Thirty-four percent had education beyond high school, 44 percent had completed high school, and 22 percent had not completed high school. The subjects were predominantly unmarried (71% were never married; 16% were separated, divorced, or widowed; 13% were married); of low parity (44% had no living children; 49% had 1 or 2 children; 7% had 3 or more children); and black (78% were black, reflecting the surrounding residential area; 22% were white). Seventy-seven percent of the sample had used some contraceptive method prior to the most recent pregnancy; 72 percent had had prior pregnancies.

Several demographic factors differed significantly between first and repeat aborters as depicted in Table I. Repeat aborters were more likely to be in their early twenties, of lower socioeconomic status, and to have at least one living child. Education, marital status, and contraceptive method prior to abortion did not differ significantly between first and repeat abortion groups.

To assess emotional distress levels associated with abortion experience, study participants completed the Hopkins Symptom Checklist (HSCL-90) (Rickels, et al., 1976) at three time-points: (1) prior to abortion procedures; (2) two weeks post-abortion; and (3) one year later. The HSCL-90 is a self-report inventory of common feelings and behaviors that relate to nine emotional symptom dimensions (Derogatis, 1977). This 90-item version, developed by Derogatis, et al., incorporates the five empirically established and validated HSCL factors (somatization, obsessive-compulsive [performance difficulty], interpersonal sensitivity, depression, and anxiety) and four additional dimensions that stress feelings and behaviors in interpersonal relationships (hostility, phobic anxiety, paranoid ideation, and psychoticism [a scale of alienation]).

TABLE I: Percent Distribution for Selected Characteristics
of Women Receiving First or Repeat Abortions

Characteristic	Group 1*			
	First Abortion N= 125†	Repeat Abortion N= 65†	Total N= 190†	Significance
Age				
14-19	33	14	27	X^2 = 7.65,
20-24	34	45	38	2df p < .05
25-40	33	41	35	
Total	100	100	100	
Education				n. s.
< 12 years	21	23	22	
High school graduate	40	52	44	
> 12 years	39	25	34	
Total	100	100	100	
Race				X^2 = 11.39,
Black	70	92	78	1df p < .001
White	30	8	22	
Total	100	100	100	
Marital Status				n. s.
Never-married	71	69	71	
Div. , Sep. , Widowed	16	18	16	
Married	13	13	13	
Total	100	100	100	
No. of living children				X^2 = 17.95,
0	55	22	44	3df p < .001
1	27	45	33	
2	12	23	16	
> 3	6	10	7	
Total	100	100	100	
Most recent contra- ceptive before abortion				n. s.
Pill	33	38	35	
IUD	5	10	7	
Diaphragm	21	17	20	
Other**	16	15	15	
None	25	20	23	
Total	100	100	100	

*Comprises women who completed pre- and post-abortion assessments.
    Tests between first and repeat aborters using the total sample (N= 413)
    showed significant (p < .05) differences on the same variables.
**"Other" includes foam, condom, rhythm, withdrawal.
†N's vary slightly with missing data.

Source: Reprinted by permission of The American College of Obstetricians and
    Gynecologists from Obstet & Gynecol 55 (5):633, 1980.

Detailed data for the initial and follow-up findings reviewed here were reported previously (Freeman, et al. , 1980; Freeman, et al. , in press). Before abortion procedures, the highest emotional distress factor for the total sample was depression. Other high-distress factors were somatization, anxiety, hostility, obsessive-compulsive (performance difficulties), and interpersonal sensitivity. However, only the depression-factor scores were in ranges considered sufficient to warrant further clinical investigation (Winokur, et al. , 1979). Two weeks post-abortion, scores were significantly lower on all factors and depression was no longer in the clinically distressed range. The six factors with highest pre-abortion scores had the most significant decrease (p < .001). Further analyses of the direction of change in scores showed that nearly all patients decreased or maintained their scores at two weeks post-abortion.

Comparisons of first and repeat aborters in this sample showed that emotional distress levels of repeaters did not differ from first aborters before abortion procedures. Repeaters as a group were neither more nor less distressed than women with first abortion experience. However, two weeks after abortion, the scores of repeaters declined less than those of the first abortion group in dimensions of interpersonal sensitivity, anxiety, and hostility. Examples of items endorsed most frequently by these women were "being easily hurt," "others do not understand you," "most people cannot be trusted," "you should be punished for your sins," "the idea that something is seriously wrong with your body," and "thoughts about sex bother you a lot." Endorsement of these items in connection with abortion experiences suggested that emotional distress in part was related to problems or concerns about the disapproval of others or to feelings of disadvantage in interpersonal relationships. However, these self-report data collected pre- and post-abortion were not sufficient to determine cause of the difference in emotional distress between first and repeat aborters at two weeks post-abortion. We speculated that either emotional distress scores of repeaters declined more slowly than those of first aborters, perhaps from slower resolution of negative feelings associated with repeated unwanted pregnancies, or that the scores of repeat aborters were somewhat more stable and less affected by abortion experience.

An additional assessment of a sub-sample of first and repeat aborters was conducted one year following abortions. A repeated measures analysis (Bock, 1963) of the emotional

distress scores at three time-points showed significant changes
in depression (< .002), somatization (p < .002), and hostility (p < .05). Prior to abortion procedures, scores of first
and repeat aborters did not differ, as was found initially in
the total sample. Two weeks post-abortion, the scores of
the repeat group declined less than the first abortion group,
as was also found initially in the total sample. One year
later, the scores of first and repeat aborters in the sub-
sample no longer differed significantly. Scores of both groups
increased from scores at two weeks post-abortion (Time 2)
although they did not return to the still higher levels reported
pre-abortion (Time 1).

Since the pattern in this sub-sample was consistent
at Times 1 and 2 with the previously observed scores for the
total sample, we speculated that the response pattern at one
year was likewise similar for the total abortion sample. The
additional data at one year suggested that scores at two weeks
post-abortion (Time 2) were lower than the typical level of
functioning for these women. We inferred that these lower
scores reflected relief, with first aborters experiencing more
emotional relief than repeat aborters who were already familiar with the experience.

Further comparisons in this study between women having second abortions (N= 47) and women having third abortions
(N= 39) showed no significant differences in emotional distress
factors either before or two weeks after abortions (Freeman,
et al. , in press). It also appeared that, irrespective of the
number of abortions, unwanted pregnancies continued to be a
problem. During the follow-up year, one in three women who
continued in the family planning program had another pregnancy; three fourths of these pregnancies were terminated by
abortions. Finally, women who were most distressed prior
to abortion procedures, again irrespective of the number of
abortions, were less likely to return for the one year follow-
up. Further study is still needed to determine whether emotional distress factors affect repeated-abortion behavior.

Conclusion

Repeat abortion rates are within the expected range, given
the current contraceptive effectiveness rates. Repeat aborters are likely to have one or two children and are strongly
weighted toward the lower end of the socioeconomic scale.
These are historically the characteristics of women with unwanted fertility, which has long differed between the rich and

the poor. There is no evidence in clinical studies that repeaters prefer abortions to contraceptives; overall, prior
abortion is associated with greater acceptance of contraceptive methods. Also, repeat aborters appear to experience
the same emotional distress as first aborters prior to abortion procedures. Repeat abortions, like first abortions, represent one solution to unwanted births that are described by
social factors as well as by characteristics of the individuals
involved.

References

Bock, R. D. Multivariate Analysis of Variance of Repeated
Measurements: Problems in Measuring Change. Edited
by C. W. Harris. Madison: University of Wisconsin
Press, 1963.

Bracken, M. B.; Hachamovitch, M.; and Grossman, G. "Correlates of Repeat Induced Abortions." Obstetrics and Gynecology, 1972, 40: 816-825.

_____. "The Decision to Abort and Psychological Sequelae."
Journal of Nervous and Mental Disease, 1974, 158: 154-
162.

Brewer, C. "Third Time Unlucky: A Study of Women Who
Have Three or More Legal Abortions." Journal of Biosocial Science, 1977, 9: 99-105.

Cates, W., Jr.; Hogue, C. R.; and Tietze, C. "Repeat Induced Abortions: Do They Affect Future Childbearing?"
Presented at the 37th Annual Meeting of the American Fertility Society. Atlanta, Georgia, 1981.

Daily, E. F.; Nicholas, N.; Nelson, F.; and Parker, J.
"Repeat Abortion in New York City." Family Planning
Perspectives, 1973, 5: 89-93.

Daling, J. R., and Emanuel, I. "Induced Abortion and Subsequent Outcome of Pregnancy in a Series of American
Women." New England Journal of Medicine, 1977, 297:
1241-1245.

Derogatis, L. R. The SCL-90 Manual I. Baltimore: Johns
Hopkins University School of Medicine, Clinical Psychome-
trics Unit, 1977.

Freeman, E. W. "Abortion: Subjective Attitudes and Feelings." Family Planning Perspectives, 1978, 10: 150-155.

_____; Rickels, K.; Huggins, G. R.; Garcia, C-R.; and Polin, J. "Emotional Distress Patterns Among Women Having First or Repeat Abortions." Obstetrics and Gynecology, 1980, 55: 630-636.

Friedman, C. M.; Greenspan, R.; and Mittleman, F. "The Decision Making Process and Outcome of Therapeutic Abortion." American Journal of Psychiatry, 1974, 131: 1333-1337.

Fylling, R., and Svendsby, T. "Contraceptive Practice Before and After Therapeutic Abortion." Fertility and Sterility, 1979, 9: 99-105.

Harlap, S., and Davies, A. M. "Late Sequelae of Induced Abortion: Complications and Outcome of Pregnancy and Labor." American Journal of Epidemiology, 1975, 102: 217-224.

Henshaw, S.; Forrest, J. D.; Sullivan, E.; and Tietze, C. "Abortion in the United States." Family Planning Perspectives, 1981, 13: 6-18.

Hogue, C. J. "Low Birth Weight Subsequent to Induced Abortion." American Journal of Obstetrics and Gynecology, 1975, 123: 657-689.

Howe, B.; Kaplan, H. R.; and English, C. "Repeat Abortions: Blaming the Victims." American Journal of Public Health, 1979, 69: 1242-1246.

Institute of Medicine: Legalized Abortion and the Public Health. Washington, D. C.: National Academy of Science, 1975.

Jacobs, D.; Garcia, C-R.; Rickels, K.; and Precuel, R. W. "A Prospective Study on the Psychological Effects of Therapeutic Abortion." Comprehensive Psychiatry, 1974, 14: 423-434.

Jacobsson, L.; Von Schoultz, B.; and Solheim, F. "Repeat Aborters--First Aborters, a Social-Psychiatric Comparison." Social Psychiatry, 1976, 11: 75-85.

Leach, J. "The Repeat Abortion Patient." Family Planning Perspectives, 1977, 9: 37-39.

Maine, D. "Does Abortion Affect Later Pregnancies?" Family Planning Perspectives, 1979, 11: 98-101.

Miller, E.; McFarland, V.; Burnhill, M. S.; and Armstead, J. W. "Impact of the Abortion Experience on Contraceptive Acceptance." Advances in Planned Parenthood, 1977, 12: 15-28.

Nathanson, C. A., and Becker, M. H. "Obstetricians' Attitudes and Hospital Abortion Services." Family Planning Perspectives, 1980, 12: 26-32.

Oronsaye, A. U. "The Outcome of Pregnancies Subsequent to Induced Abortion." American Journal of Obstetrics and Gynecology, 1979, 12: 274-277.

Osofsky, H. and Osofsky, J., eds. The Abortion Experience. Hagerstown, Md.: Harper & Row, 1973.

Payne, E. C.; Kravitz, A. R.; Notman, M. T.; and Anderson, J. A. "Outcome Following Therapeutic Abortion." Archives of General Psychiatry, 1976, 33: 725-733.

Rader, G. E.; Bekker, L. D.; Brown, L.; and Richardt, C. "Psychological Correlates of Unwanted Pregnancy." Journal of Abnormal Psychology, 1978, 87: 373-376.

Richardson, J. A., and Dixon, G. "Effects of Legal Termination on Subsequent Pregnancy." British Medical Journal, 1976, 1: 1303-1304.

Rickels, K.; Garcia, C-R.; Lipman, L.; Derogatis, L. R.; and Fisher, E. L. "The Hopkins Symptom Chicklist: Assessing Emotional Distress in Obstetrics-Gynecologic Practice." Primary Care, 1976, 3: 751-764.

Rovinsky, J. J. "Abortion Recidivism, a Problem in Preventive Medicine." Obstetrics and Gynecology, 1972, 39: 649-659.

Seims, S. "Abortion Availability in the United States." Family Planning Perspectives, 1980, 12: 88-101.

Schneider, S. M., and Thompson, D. S. "Repeat Aborters."

American Journal of Obstetrics and Gynecology, 1976, 126: 316-320.

Shepard, M. J., and Bracken, M. B. "Contraceptive Practice and Repeat Induced Abortion: An Epidemiological Investigation." Journal of Biosocial Science, 1979, 11: 289-302.

Steinhoff, P. G.; Smith, R. G.; Palmore, J. A.; Diamond, M.; and Chung, C. S. "Women Who Obtain Repeat Abortions: A Study Based on Record-Linkage." Family Planning Perspectives, 1979, 11: 30-38.

Teitze, C. "Repeat Abortions--Why More?" Family Planning Perspectives, 1978, 6: 286-288.

_____, and Jain, A. K. "The Mathematics of Repeat Abortion: Explaining the Increase." Studies in Family Planning, 1978, 9: 294-299.

Trussell, J.; Menken, J.; Lindheim, N. L.; and Vaughn, B. "The Impact of Restricting Medical Financing for Abortion." Family Planning Perspectives, 1980, 12: 120-130.

U. S. Department of Health and Human Services. Abortion Surveillance, 1978. Atlanta, Ga.: Centers for Disease Control, 1980.

World Health Organization Task Force on Sequelae of Abortion. "Gestation, Birth-Weight, and Spontaneous Abortion in Pregnancy After Induced Abortions." The Lancet, 1979, 1: 142-145.

Winokur, A.; Rickels, K.; Garcia, C-R.; Huggins, G.; and Guthrie, M. B. "Emotional Distress in Family Planning Patients." Advances in Planned Parenthood, 1979, 14: 33-40.

PART III:

ATTITUDE TOWARD ABORTION

ABORTION ATTITUDES IN THE UNITED STATES: CONTINUITIES AND DISCONTINUITIES

By Helen Rose Fuchs Ebaugh and C. Allen Haney

Introduction

Nearly a decade before the 1973 United States Supreme Court decision of Roe vs. Wade, which forced a revision of abortion laws, the topic of abortion was being hotly debated in the popular press. Several researchers began studying public attitudes toward abortion in an attempt to discern how much support existed for allowing termination of pregnancy under certain conditions. Westoff, Moore, and Ryder (1969), in their now-classic National Fertility Study (NFS), conducted in 1965, included seven questions on abortion. They asked how the respondent would feel about a woman who had a doctor interrupt pregnancy. They then specified six conditions for the abortion and asked how the person would feel. The conditions were: pregnancy endangering the woman's health, woman not married, woman could not afford another child, couple didn't want any more children, possible deformed child, and woman had been raped.

Data for the NFS were made up of responses of a national probability sample of some 5,600 currently married females under 55 years of age. In general, the study found that the women were overwhelmingly in favor of abortion if the mother's health was threatened; they were about evenly divided in the case of deformity or rape; they were overwhelmingly opposed if the woman was not married, could not afford another child, or simply did not want any more children. More favorable attitudes toward abortion were held by older women who had completed childbearing. As expected, Catholic women were most opposed to abortion, Jewish women least opposed, and Protestant women from fundamentalist sects were more opposed than those from more liberal denominations. Education also affected attitudes toward abortion in that the more highly educated tended to be more favorable (Westoff, Moore, & Ryder, 1969, p. 33).

A research endeavor which overlapped with the NFS is the series of Gallup polls (GP) undertaken from 1962 through 1969 that included questions on abortion. Judith Blake (1971) analyzed the abortion items. The first four polls asked about three of the six conditions included in the NFS (mother's health endangered, child deformed, and poverty). In 1969, "parents not wanting any more children" was added. For these conditions, therefore, we have comparative data from the decades of the 1960s and 1970s, although the lead questions differ somewhat, with the Gallup polls emphasizing legality of abortion and the NFS asking if abortion would be "alright."

In the 1960s, as could be expected, mother's health (already a legal ground in many states) was more acceptable as a reason for abortion than economic grounds. Also, Catholics disapproved more than non-Catholics except that fundamentalist non-Catholics were on a par with Catholics in terms of level of disapproval.

The major unexpected findings had to do with the unanticipated high level of disapproval among lower-class non-Catholics; the relatively higher level of disapproval of women than men; of women for the "soft reasons"; and the generally more favorable attitude toward abortion among the older respondents.

Finally the firmly held opinion that the most disadvantaged women would be the most supportive of abortion was not supported (Rossi, 1967; Mannes, 1967; Harden, 1967; and Rosen, 1967). In fact, the data indicated that approval is highest among male, well-educated, non-Catholic, "establishment-type" individuals. It is also evident that a clear distinction existed in Americans' minds between "hard" and "soft" reasons for permitting an abortion. The "hard" reason over which a woman has little control, such as danger to her health and defect in her child, elicited more favorable responses than "soft" reasons such as financial plight and not wanting more children (Blake, 1971).

The National Opinion Research Center's (NORC) General Social Survey, conducted from 1972 to 1980, provided the type of data needed to extend Blake's study, for it included items on abortion attitudes as well as pertinent demographic data. The first survey of this decade was conducted in March 1972, approximately ten months before the Supreme Court decision in January 1973 that abortion in the first tri- mester of pregnancy is a decision between the mother and her physician and cannot be barred by state regulations. The second survey was done two months after the decision. The surveys thus provide data that allow before-after comparisons. In addition, the identical items on abortion were repeated in 1974, 1975, 1976, 1977, 1978, and 1980, thereby allowing the examination of attitudinal patterns over an eight-year span. Arney and Trescher (1976) used NORC abortion items in their analyses of attitudes toward the legalization issue; however, they include only 1972-1975 data. They also use only Catholic- Protestant differences, with no denominational breakdowns and excluding Jews and nonbelievers.

The sampling design for the NORC data consists of a cross section of persons 18 years of age or over living in noninstitutional arrangements within the United States. The item on abortion was worded as follow: "Please tell me whether or not you think it should be possible for a preg- nant woman to obtain a legal abortion if . . .

- there is a strong chance of serious defect in the baby
- she is married and does not want any more chil- dren
- the woman's own health is seriously endangered by the pregnancy
- the family has a very low income and cannot af- ford any more children
- she became pregnant as a result of rape
- she is not married and does not want to marry the man. "

The question utilized the same six conditions first used in the National Fertility Study, even though the exact wordings dif- fered. The issue of the legalization of abortion was also clearly stated rather than ethical considerations.

Findings on abortion during the 1970s have uniformly verified the importance of differentiating conditions under which abortion might occur. Our results using the NORC, 1972-1980 data, confirm the necessity of specifying conditions for abortion since attitudes vary greatly depending on the sit- uation. Three fourths or more of the respondents favor abor- tion for the three hard reasons while less than one half are favorable when soft reasons exist.

Previous studies have consistently shown that endangering the mother's health elicits the most favorable attitudes toward abortion. This finding holds true for all eight years of NORC data as well as for earlier studies. The chance of serious defect in the baby and rape also arouse strong feelings that an abortion should be allowed: however, slightly fewer people are willing to condone an abortion in these instances than if the woman's life is threatened. Reasons for this difference are, no doubt, the fact that by 1973 the mother's health was a legal ground for abortion in many states and the fact that many religious groups have traditionally taught that abortion is permitted only when a mother's life is seriously endangered by a normal pregnancy.

Of the "soft" reasons, poverty elicited the most favorable attitude. Approximately five percent more respondents favor legalized abortion when a family cannot afford more children than for either of the other two "soft" reasons. The condition of an unmarried woman wanting an abortion received slightly more favorable responses for all eight years than a married woman who is pregnant but does not want more children.

Even though attitudes vary greatly depending upon circumstances, in every instance over the eight-year period at least one third of the resondents favor legalized abortion. Given the long standing anti-abortion laws in this country plus the stringent religious restrictions on abortion, it is surprising that attitudes are as liberal as they are. By the time the Supreme Court made its ruling, there was strong public support behind the legalization of abortion.

General Trends

Some of the most interesting findings from our analyses are the changes in attitudes over the eight-year period. A dramatic increase in favorable attitudes appeared between 1972 and 1973. Six to eight percent more respondents favored abortion on all six items in 1973 than in 1972. In addition, the number of "don't know" responses decreased in 1973, which may indicate a crystallization of opinions regarding legalized abortion after the 1973 Supreme Court decision. Our data, therefore, support the position that the law not only reflects public sentiment but can be effective in influencing attitudes and moral decisions.

Attitudes seemed to stabilize after the Supreme Court

decision with very little change in attitudes between 1973 and
1974.   However, between 1974 and 1975, there was a consistent decrease in attitudes favoring abortion and an increase
in the number opposing it.   The 1975 changes in attitudes
were not as dramatic as the 1973 changes; however, the pattern existed for all six reasons, ranging from one to three
percentage point change.   One explanation for the 1975 change
in attitude is the influence of the pro-life movement which
gained widespread public attention in late 1974 and early 1975.
The 1976 data consistently showed a very slight increase in
favorable attitudes; however, the change was not statistically
significant nor did it in any instance reach the 1973 peak.

There was little shift in attitudes between 1976 and
1977.   However, in 1978 there was a definite trend toward
greater opposition to legalized abortions for "soft" reasons.
Six percent more people opposed abortion for poverty reasons;
eight percent more when the woman is unmarried; and seven
percent more when the woman is married but does not want
any more children.   The conservative shift occurred only in
regard to "soft" reasons.   By 1978, the pro-life movement
had gained considerable strength and was influential in several
court decisions regarding rights of the unborn fetus.

Despite the 1978 conservative trend, the 1980 data
show that attitudes regarding abortion were significantly more
liberal than in 1978 and, in some cases, more so than in
the two or three preceding years.   It is clear that 1978 was
a unique year and not part of a longer trend toward greater
opposition to legalized abortion.   What in fact seems to be
the case is that attitudes toward abortion have gradually become more favorable throughout the 1970s with the exception
of 1978.

The conservatism noted in 1978 has been documented
by several researchers in the field (Davis, 1980; Granberg &
Granberg, 1980).   However, no one has been able to explain
why attitudes were more conservative in that one year.   One
possibility is that specific national events could have occurred
just prior to the administration of the survey in early 1978.
However, a perusal of three major newspapers, between September 1977, and January 1978, did not result in the discovery
of any major events that might have explained the shift in attitudes.   The National Opinion Research Center reports no
systematic sample biases that could have altered responses.
So far, all we can do is report the shift and await further
explanations for its occurrence.

In an attempt to simplify our data and make cross-tabular analysis more feasible, we submitted them six times to Guttman scale analysis. For each year the coefficient of reproducibility was approximately .94 and the coefficient of scalability was .80 or above. The most significant changes in attitudes over the seven-year period occurred in three categories: 1) those who oppose abortion for all six reasons: 8 percent in 1972 to 6 percent in 1976, with the biggest decline in 1973; 2) those who favor abortion for the hard reasons and oppose it for the soft ones; 14 percent in 1972 to 20 percent in 1978, with a 3 percentage point increase in 1973; 3) those who favor abortion for all six reasons: 30 percent in 1972 to 38 percent in 1976, with an 8 percentage point increase in 1973, then a decline to 30 percent again in 1978.

Given the fact that the largest percentage of respondents (about two thirds) fall into one of the three patterns and that these three patterns demonstrate most clearly changes in attitudes toward abortion over the eight-year period, subsequent analyses were limited to these respondents.

Demographic Variables: Sex, Age, Education

Gallup polls conducted in the 1960s consistently showed a difference in the attitudes of men and women regarding abortion. Men tended to be slightly more liberal in their views than women, despite the fact that women suffer greater consequences in having an unwanted pregnancy (Blake, 1971).

Our data for the 1970s do not demonstrate such a clear-cut and consistent trend. In 1972, men were slightly more accepting of legalized abortion than women, although the difference was not statistically significant. In 1973, the difference shows up more sharply, but in 1974 there is a slight reverse in the trend with women equally as accepting of abortion as men. In 1975 and 1976 men again emerged as more liberal in their attitudes, but in 1977 and 1978 the sex differential disappeared. In 1980 men were again somewhat more liberal. What has happened in the eight years is that men have become consistently more pro-abortion (with the exception of the 1974 decrease), while increasing proportions of women favored abortion under all six conditions during 1972, 1973, and 1974 and then reversed the trend in 1975, 1976, and 1977. By 1978, fewer women favored abortion under all conditions than for any of the previous six years. Simultaneously, in 1977 and 1978, fewer men approved of abortion under all circumstances and the male-female differferences almost disappeared. While the women's liberation movement may well explain the greater liberalization of attitudes earlier in the decade, it seems to have lessened its impact in latter years. Perhaps this reflects the effects of a juxtaposition of two social movements, namely the women's movement and the pro-life movement.

Several studies in the 1960s presented evidence indicating that, contrary to what might be expected, younger people were more opposed to abortion than older people (Blake, 1971; Ryder & Westoff, 1971). It was suggested that one reason for this might be the greater pressure of control of fertility on the part of older women while younger cohorts are at earlier stages of childbearing. Blake indicates that by the end of the decade of the 1960s the age differential seemed to be weakening.

By 1972, however, the trend reversed itself, with younger people significantly more liberal in their attitudes than older groups. For all eight years, except 1977, the age differential was statistically significant with younger people more pro-abortion all years except 1980, when little difference existed between those under 18 and those in their mid-years. Beginning in 1974, however, an interesting change occurred. People under 30 appeared to be more conservative in their attitudes while increasing proportions of individuals aged 30 to 44 indicated more liberal attitudes than previously. By 1976 an equal percentage of individuals in both categories approved abortion under all conditions. However, in 1977 and 1978, both age groups were significantly less favorable toward abortion than in previous years. Simultaneously, people over 45 became more conservative after 1974 so that by 1976, only 3 percent more favored abortion for all six reasons than in 1972. In 1977, slightly more (5%) favored abortion under all conditions; however, by 1978, the decrease in favorable attitudes on the part of people over 45 was dramatic--48 percent compared to 60 percent in 1977.

A comparison of attitudes by age over the eight-year period shows that despite more liberal attitudes in 1973 and 1974, by 1975 and 1976 both the younger and older age groups had become somewhat more conservative than during previous years. This is especially evident among those over 45. In contrast, the middle age-group (30 to 44) showed a consistent trend (with the exception of 1978) toward greater liberalization of attitudes, with increasing proportions each year favoring abortion under all conditions.

In the 1960s data, education was consistently the best predictor of attitudes toward abortion; as education increased, so did pro-abortion attitudes. In the 1970s, the same relationship exists for all eights years (In each instance the statistical level of significance was less than .003). However, several interesting trends existed over the eight-year period, indicating changes in the impact of education on attitudes. Respondents with a grade-school education became more liberal in their attitudes while the college-educated and those with graduate degrees remained relatively constant in their attitudes among the less educated and a stabilization of attitudes among the educated.

Religion and Attitudes Toward Abortion

In addition to being a central social issue in the past decade, abortion has generated heated debates within many of the religious groups in the United States. The issue has traditionally been the concern of churches, and most theologies specifically address the ethical implications of abortion. It follows, then, that social scientists, and the popular press as well, have been interested in the ways that religious beliefs and affiliation have impacted upon attitudes toward abortion.

When attitudes toward abortion are considered for Protestants, Catholics, Jews, and those not affiliated with any church, a clear-cut pattern emerges for all eight years. Jews are most liberal in their attitudes, even more so than those not affiliated with any religious group. While Jewish attitudes remained rather constant over the eight years, those with no religious affiliation became less favorable toward abortion.

There is a significant difference in attitudes between both Jews and non-affiliates, on the one hand, and Protestants and Catholics on the other, with Protestants slightly more liberal than Catholics. However, the aggregation of Protestants into one category is misleading in many ways, since vast doctrinal as well as structural differences exist among Protestant denominations. Therefore, we disaggregated Protestants into the major denominations and compared attitudes across categories. As could be predicted, attitudes of those belonging to fundamentalist denominations (Baptist, Lutheran, Methodist) closely resemble Catholic attitudes, while Presbyterians and Episcopalians are significantly more liberal. In fact, for most years, the latter two Protestant groups do not differ greatly in their attitudes from respondents with no religious ties.

We predicted that respondents who attend "official" church services would be more conservative in their attitudes, because of greater exposure to church teaching and also a feeling of closer identification with the on-going activities of a church group. When considering the entire sample each year, we found a strong positive relationship between frequency of church attendance and attitudes toward abortion. Those who identify with a religious group but never attend services are much more liberal than any of the church-goers.

Although several researchers have noted the positive relationship between church attendance and attitudes toward abortion (Hertel, et al., 1974; Arney & Trescher, 1976; Granberg & Granberg, 1980), none had disaggregated on the basis of liberal-conservative churches. Yet, it seemed logical to assume that people attending services in liberal denominations would be exposed to different ideas and ethical positions than those attending services in conservative churches. We therefore analyzed the relationship between church attendance and attitudes toward abortion for both liberal and conservative churches (Ebaugh and Haney, 1978).

Roman Catholics were excluded from this analysis for several reasons: 1) the Catholic Church's stand on abortion has a unique history; 2) the obligation of attendance at Mass carries more serious consequences for Catholics than church attendance does for Protestants; 3) the previous studies on attendance and attitudes were limited to Protestants.

Designation of Protestant denominations as liberal or conservative was taken from Shortridge's classification (1976; 1977) based on his analysis of a national survey of churches conducted by the National Council of Churches. The liberal-conservative denominational classification is based upon measures of religious orthodoxy, church structure, and membership in selected cooperative associations.

When we disaggregated the data on the basis of conservative and liberal denominations, we found that the mean abortion score for respondents in conservative churches was 3.89 compared with a mean of 4.68 for those in liberal churches (F value = 1.42; significance = $p < .005$). This evidence indicates that real differences exist between the two groups. Analysis of the relationship between church attendance and attitudes toward abortion, controlling for conservative and liberal churches, demonstrated a relationship that is statistically significant for the conservative churches but not for the liberal churches.

Within conservative churches, frequency of attendance is positively associated with conservative attitudes, while in liberal churches frequency of attendance has no significant impact on attitudes toward abortion.   In fact, within liberal churches, those who attend services once a month are more liberal in their attitudes than any other group, including those who never attend.   In like manner, those who attend 2 to 3 times a month are most conservative in their attitudes.   It is impossible, therefore, to predict attitudes for liberal church-goers on the basis of how frequently respondents attend services.

What, then, might account for our finding that more frequent church attendance is related to greater disapproval of abortion among church-goers in conservative churches and the lack of relationship among respondents in liberal churches? We suggest the reason lies in the theological concerns that have historically characterized fundamentalist and liberal denominations.   In addition to positions on such issues as evolution and predestination, fundamentalist churches have consistently been concerned with issues of individual morality. Whether it be prohibition, homosexuality, birth control, or abortion, most fundamentalist churches have taken stands against the rights of the individual to decide such issues. Rather, the churches have issued official statements based on biblical interpretations.

In contrast, the history of the liberal churches in America derives from the Social Gospel movement and the concern to relate theology to political and social concerns of society.   In the area of personal ethics and morality, varying individual conditions and interpretations have been seen as mitigating circumstances when applying general moral principles.   In addition, the emphasis in liberal churches, as Johnson suggests (Johnson, 1967), is upon social and political issues rather than an overriding concern with individual morality.

Abortion Attitudes and Other Sociopolitical Attitudes of Americans

It is conventional wisdom today to proclaim that Americans have become more conservative during the past decade. Such phenomena as the election of Ronald Reagan, a Republican Senate majority, and the growing visibility and influence of the "moral majority," anti-ERA, and anti-abortion groups are cited in support of the conservative swing.

Data on attitudes toward abortion show that the U. S. public not only has not become more conservative on this issue but actually became more liberal in the middle of the decade and remained so through 1980 (with the exception of the unexplainable 1978). What was happening in terms of American attitudes toward other social and political issues?

Thirty-six items in NORC surveys, 1972 to 1980, reflect social and political views. These items were subjected to factor analysis (Chafetz & Ebaugh). Twenty-nine of them loaded on three factors across the entire time-span: 1) civil liberties (willingness to allow homosexuals, communists, and atheists to speak publicly, have their books in libraries, and teach at colleges); 2) abortion items; and 3) economics (public expenditures for human services, urban problems, racial equality, and the environment).

On two scales, it is clear that no conservative trend exists. Civil liberties attitudes fluctuated substantially and ended the decade about where they began in 1972. Abortion attitudes also fluctuated over time and by 1980 the mean was .13 lower than 1972. There is a decided conservative trend in the economic area, but this trend peaked in 1977 and has remained constant since then. Thus, even in this issue area it is not proper to speak of "growing conservatism in the U. S. ," which implies a continuation of a linear trend.

Two things are clear from these data. It is clear that Americans generally did not become "more conservative" in any global sense during the decade of the 1970s. It is equally clear that three specific problem areas which confronted the nation during that decade are reflected in significant attitude shifts: increasing crime, international problems that the nation was relatively powerless to control, and inflation. Americans clearly changed in their desire to spend more money on defense, retain more of their income by cutting human-services-oriented programs, and punish criminals more effectively. These issues formed the backbone of the Republican campaign and probably account for the Republican success in 1980. However, on most issues concerning civil liberties and personal morality, Americans became, if anything, slightly less conservative during this time period.

Discussion

Both the National Abortion Rights Action League (NARAL) and National Right-to-Life Committee (NRLC), as well as other special interest groups no doubt, gained momentum in the mid- to late-1970s, both in terms of the number of participants and visibility in the media. Given the stability of attitudes toward abortion on the part of the American public in the last half of the decade, however, it seems plausible to hypothesize that groups such as these served merely as points around which those individuals who already held firm positions on abortion could coalesce rather than as major attitude-change agents. There is solid evidence in the literature on social movements that predispositions are a primary factor in influencing recruits into specific movements (Greil, 1977; Brady & Tedin, 1976; Wilson, 1959; Lofland, 1965). It is highly probable, therefore, that those individuals who opposed abortion for a variety of reasons, including moral, religious, social, and political, were drawn into a movement that not only reflected their individual positions but was committed to effecting social policy built upon those convictions. The pro-life movement might well be another instance in which increased visibility, by means of a few highly publicized events, gives the impression of greater public support and influence than is, in fact, the case. Specific data on number and characteristics of participants in the movement are still being analyzed and only a few preliminary reports are available (Granberg & Granberg, 1980).

Historically, social movements have made their greatest impact in terms of bringing about specific legislative changes: the civil rights and women's movements are cases in point. It is evident from our data on abortion attitudes that the 1973 Supreme Court decision was influential in a liberal shift in attitudes toward legalization of abortion. If the pro-life movement is successful in effecting a constitutional amendment reversing or modifying the previous legislation, we might well see a shift in attitudes toward a more conservative direction. To effect such legislation, the number of members in the movement and general public attitudes may be less important than well-planned strategy and commitment of key members to effecting change.

As clearly articulated in Abortion Politics (Jaffe, Lindheim, & Lee, 1981) there is far from consensus among Americans regarding abortion. Only a minority of all American doctors, about half of the obstetricians/gynecologists who specialize in women's health care and only a few non-Catholic hospitals provide abortion services (Jaffe, et al., p. 32). Thus the priestly or apostolic function of the physician has not been available as a determiner of public perceptions and opinion regarding abortions. The ex-cathedra pronouncements so common from the medical profession where other issues are concerned have been largely absent regarding the abortion issue. When opinions have been voiced, the messages have been largely mixed. Similiarly, many public hospitals have taken a tacitly negative stand by banning most abortion procedures, and there is ample evidence that this stand has been taken for political and religious reasons. It should be noted that institutions do not make decisions--those who administer them do. All institutions have manifest and latent goals, and actions must be taken and decisions made that are designed to implement them. Chief among these goals is the institution's survival, for without it the institution can direct its efforts toward nothing else. Thus, with financial constraints and the need to be accountable to all manner of regulatory agencies, governmental offices, boards of directors, taxpayers, politicians, and the physicians who practice in them, it is not surprising that few hard-and-fast policy statements have been forthcoming regarding the abortion issue.

Another change agent, the federal government, has likewise not taken a firm stance. Governmental inactivity and inconsistency is not unique to the abortion issue, given the nature of the political system and the responsibility of its officials to a diverse electorate including special interest groups. Consider, for example, the nature of the conflicting pressures that allow at one and the same time the U.S. tobacco industry to be subsidized at taxpayer expense while simultaneously tax dollars are spent to discourage smoking, and detect and treat lung cancer.

Where abortion is concerned, the federal government has failed to establish directly clear guidelines regarding funding for abortion and the circumstances surrounding this form of medical care. Little more than an indirect de facto policy has been stated and this tends to center upon the financial provisions outlined in Medicaid legislation.

It cannot be determined with the data available whether public sentiment influences governmental policy and the stance of the American medical profession or whether it is informed by it. What is clear is that an organized leadership role has not been taken by those groups most deeply involved in the issue, and thus the level of approval expressed, in spite of counterarguments by voluntary organizations, rests upon deeply help values, beliefs, and attitudes.

176 / Perspectives on Abortion

References

Arney, William Ray and William H. Trescher. "Trends in Attitudes Toward Abortion, 1972-1975." Family Planning Perspective, 1976, 8: 117-124.

Blake, Judith. "Attitudes and Public Opinion: The 1960-1970 Decade." Science, 1971, 171: 540-549.

Brady, David and Kent Tedin. "Ladies in Pink: Religious and Political Ideology in the Anti-ERA Movement." Social Science Quarterly, 1976, 56: 564-575.

Chafetz, Janet and Helen Rose Ebaugh. "Growing Conservatism in the U.S.? An Examination of Trends in Political Opinion Between 1972-1980." Unpublished manuscript, n.d.

Davis, James A. "Conservative Weather in a Liberalizing Climate: Change in Selected NORC General Social Survey Items, 1972-78." Social Forces, 1980, 58: 1129-1156.

Ebaugh, Helen Rose Fuchs and C. Allen Haney. "Church Attendance and Attitudes Toward Abortion: Differentials in Liberal and Conservative Churches," Journal for the Scientific Study of Religion, 1978, 17(4): 407-413.

_____. "Shifts in Abortion Attitudes: 1972-1978." Journal of Marriage and the Family, 1980, 42(3): 491-499.

Granberg, Donald. "The Abortion Activists." Family Planning Perspectives, 1981, 13: 157-163.

_____ and Beth Willman Granberg. "Abortion Attitudes, 1965-1980: Trends and Determinants," Family Planning Perspectives, 1980, 12: 250-261.

Greil, Arthur L. "Previous Dispositions and Conversion to Perspectives of Social and Religious Movements." Sociological Analysis, 1977, 38: 115-125.

Harden, G. "Abortion and Human Dignity." In The Case for Legalized Abortion Now, A. F. Guttmacher, ed., Berkeley, Calif.: Diablo Press, 1967, pp. 69-86.

Hertel, Bradley; Gerry E. Hendershop; and James W. Grimm. "Religion and Attitudes Toward Abortion." Journal for the Scientific Study of Religion, 13: 23-24.

Jaffe, Frederick; Barbara L. Lindheim; and Philip R. Lee. Abortion Politics, New York: McGraw-Hill, 1981.

Johnson, Benton. "Theology and the Position of Pastors on Public Issues." American Sociological Review, 1967, 32: 433-442.

Lofland, John. Doomsday Cult: A Study of Conversion, Proselytization, and Maintenance of Faith. Englewood Cliffs, N. J. : Prentice-Hall, 1966.

Mannes, M. "A Woman Views Abortion." In The Case for Legalized Abortion Now, A. F. Guttmacher ed. , Berkeley, Calif. : Diablo Press, 1967, pp. 25-53.

Mileti, Dennis and Larry D. Barnett. "Nine Demographic Factors and Their Relationship to Attitudes Toward Abortion Legalization," Social Biology, 1972, 19: 43-50.

Rosen, H. Psychiatric Implications of Abortion: A Case Study in Social Hypocrisy." In Abortion and the Law, David Smith, ed. Cleveland, Ohio: Western Reserve University Press, 1967, pp. 72-106.

Ryder, Norman B. , and Charles F. Westoff. Reproduction in the United States. Princeton, N. J. : Princeton University Press, 1971.

Shortridge, James R. "A New Regionalization of American Religion." Journal for the Scientific Study of Religion, 1977, 16: 143-153.

Westoff, Charles F.; Emily C. Moore; and Norman B. Ryder. "The Structure of Attitudes Toward Abortion." Milbank Memorial Fund Quarterly, 1969, 47: 11-37.

Wilson, Bryan. "An Analysis of Sect Development." American Sociological Review, 1959, 24: 3-15.

CORRELATES OF ABORTION ATTITUDES AND IMPLICATIONS FOR CHANGE

By Barbara Agresti Finlay

Introduction

The study of attitudes toward abortion has usually focused on the rate and direction of change over time, and those studies that attempt to explain variation in such attitudes (e. g. , Blake, 1971; Westoff & Ryder, 1977) have usually been limited to the study of socioeconomic and demographic determinants. Previous studies have found, for example, that abortion approval is greater among those with higher educational attainment, among the less religious, among non-Catholics, and among residents of larger cities (see, for example, discussions by Granberg & Granberg, 1980; Westoff, et al. , 1969; Mileti & Barnett, 1972). The present study focuses on attitudinal correlates of abortion approval, while taking into account socioeconomic factors.

One of the problems in studying variation in attitudes on politically controversial issues is that of distinguishing between stereotypical rationalizations for opinions on issues and the "real," latent reasons for those opinions. If we ask for direct explanations for people's attitudes, we often get stereotyped answers derived from the rhetoric of current political debate, answers that may not represent the true reasons at all. For example, Rossi (1966) suggested that much of the opposition to abortion at the time reflected an "ambivalence" toward sexuality and a "punitiveness" toward women's sexuality. Yet, this anti-sexual attitude is not usually explicit in the rhetoric of anti-abortion groups, and few survey respondents would give it as their reason for opposing abortion. Instead, if we were to ask of an abortion opponent, "Why do you oppose legal elective abortion?" we would probably hear those socially acceptable and politically current arguments associated with the "right to life" of the unborn child.

The unreliability of direct explanations of abortion opinion makes it necessary to approach indirectly the problem of explaining its origins, by observing patterns of correlations between relevant attitudes. To continue the example given in the previous paragraph, even though people might not admit that their opposition to abortion is based on attitudes of anti-sexuality, if in fact that were the case, then independent measures of abortion attitude and sexual attitudes should be strongly correlated. The analysis presented in this chapter relies on such an indirect approach to the determination of some sociopsychological bases of abortion opinion.

Sociopsychological Correlates of Abortion Attitudes

Among the sociopsychological variables mentioned in the scholarly literature as having relevance for understanding abortion attitudes are attitude toward sexuality, attitude toward women's roles, political and social conservatism, religiosity, fertility values or the importance of children, and "prolife" attitudes (e. g. , Mauss, 1975; Rossi, 1966; Granberg, 1978; Singh & Leahy, 1978; Granberg & Granberg, 1980; Finlay, 1981). Expectations that these factors are related to abortion attitudes are based on the following rationales.

ATTITUDE TOWARD SEXUALITY

The more permissive or tolerant one is with respect to sexual behavior, the more one should accept abortion, partly because the need for abortion implies an active sexuality for the woman, which might be disapproved by those with strongly conventional attitudes, especially if the woman is unmarried. Mauss (1975) cites Rossi (1967) and Bell (1971) in suggesting that an important component of anti-abortion sentiment is a punitiveness toward female sexuality that finds expression in the denial to women of abortion.

ATTITUDE TOWARD WOMEN'S ROLES

Much of the support for liberalized abortion laws has come from groups that have been organized for the promotion of women's rights. Many arguments in support of abortion availability center around the rights of women to determine when and under what circumstances they will bear children, and abortion is seen as necessary for women's political and economic equality (e. g. , Bishop, 1979). Thus, we would expect that abortion is more readily acceptable among those with greater commitment to women's equality.

GENERAL POLITICAL AND SOCIAL CONSERVATISM

Political conservatives and those who are more conventional tend to oppose change and favor traditional mores. Since abortion is a relatively non-traditional method of birth control often associated with liberal political groups, it could be argued that anti-abortion attitudes represent more general conservative ideologies rather than issue-specific attitudes.

RELIGIOSITY

In general, the more religious one is, the more one is likely to oppose abortion, partly because most religions have been conservative on fertility and sex-related issues. This is especially true for Catholics and fundamentalist Protestants, but those are the groups usually gauged as "most religious" on the standard measures of religiosity. Religious attitudes are closely tied to right-to-life issues and sexual attitudes, and it seems logical that they would have an impact on abortion attitude as well.

FERTILITY VALUES AND IMPORTANCE OF CHILDREN

Many researchers have noted a negative relationship between fertility values (ideal family size, for example) and abortion acceptance. If one strongly values children, then abortion is likely to be defined as a limitation on a valued resource, and its justification would be more difficult.

PROLIFE ATTITUDES

The "right to life" is one of the most common rationales for anti-abortion stands in the current political debate. The key issue seems to be the question of when a fetus/child becomes a "person" whose rights must be recognized. While most people define human life as sacred, the specific definitions of the right to life vary in different circumstances (e.g., at conception, after "brain death," after committing heinous crimes). The question of when and if decisions can be made which affect the "right to life" is an important one in the abortion controversy, those taking an absolutist stand on these issues being among the most outspoken opponents of abortion.

Correlations

Empirical studies of the relationship of each of the above-mentioned sociopsychological variables to abortion attitudes have supported the expectation that abortion opposition is stronger among those with less permissive sexual attitudes (Singh & Leahy, 1978; Granberg, 1978; Granberg & Granberg, 1980); greater religiosity and orthodoxy (Clayton & Tolone 1973; Finner & Gamache, 1969; Granberg, 1978; Granberg & Granberg, 1980); and greater fertility ideals or expectations (Granberg, 1978; Singh & Leahy, 1978; Westoff, et al. , 1969; Finlay, 1981). Weaker support has been found for the notion that either sex-role attitude or political conservatism is an important factor in abortion attitude determination (Singh & Leahy, 1978; Granberg & Granberg, 1980).

Finally, Granberg and Granberg (1980) attempted to test the validity of the pro-life connection with abortion attitude. When dealing with such life-or-death issues as capital punishment and gun control, the researchers found almost no relation of abortion attitudes and the "prolife" position on these issues. However, they found strong correlations between acceptance of euthanasia and the right to suicide and pro-abortion attitudes, showing some support for a general pro-life attitude as a factor in abortion attitude.

In the present chapter, we look again at these factors in relation to abortion attitudes. Data are presented separately for males and females, to see if patterns of relationships differ by sex, since previous studies (Clayton & Tolone, 1973; Finlay, 1981) reported some differences between men and women in the correlates of abortion attitudes.

Methods and Data

Data were obtained from the NORC (National Opinion Research Center) 1977 General Social Survey (Davis, 1978), which contains information from 1,530 completed interviews with a probability sample for the adult population of the United States. For comparison, some data are presented for a 1978 college-student sample from a large southern state university (see Finlay, 1981, for detailed description of this sample).

The measure of abortion attitude for the NORC data was a scale consisting of a summation of acceptances/rejections of abortion in six different circumstances, ranging from "the pregnancy is the result of rape" to "the woman wants the abortion for any reason." For each item, the respondent was asked to say whether or not "it should be possible for pregnant woman to obtain a legal abortion" under the circumstance given. Higher scale scores indicate greater opposition to abortion (or opposition in more circumstances).

TABLE I:

Analysis of Correlates of Abortion Opposition, by Sex

A. MALE RESPONDENTS (N = 441)

Standardized Regression Coefficients and Significance of Background Variables

VARIABLE	BETA	SIGNIFICANCE
Education	-.167	.001
Marital status (married=1, unmarried=0)	.205	.000
Age	-.152	.002
Family income	-.144	.005

R-squared=.086

Partial Correlations of Social Psychological Variables, Controlling for Background Variables:

	Partial r	Significance
Sexual Permissiveness	-.422	.000
Sex Role Conventionality	.267	.000
Prolife orientation	.411	.000
Religiosity	.422	.000
Ideal no. children	.103	.031
Political conservatism	.150	.000

B. FEMALE RESPONDENTS (N = 514)

Standardized Regression Coefficients and Significance of Background Variables

VARIABLE	BETA	SIGNIFICANCE
Education	-.121	.010
Marital Status	.101	.029
Family income	-.195	.000
Size place of residence	-.124	.004
Race (0 = white, 1 = nonwhite)	.097	.028

R- squared=.091

Partial Correlations of Social Psychological Variables, Controlling for Background Variables:

	Partial r	Significance
Sexual permissiveness	-.387	.000
Sex Role Conventionality	.184	.000
Prolife Orientation	.431	.000
Religiosity	.390	.000
Ideal no. children	.236	.000
Political conservatism	.103	.021

Scales were also developed for sex role attitude (a higher score indicates a more traditional attitude); sexual permissiveness (a higher score indicates more acceptance of premarital, extramarital, and/or homosexual sexual relation); and prolife orientation (higher scores indicate opposition to euthanasia and suicide for the terminally ill). Religiosity was measured by "frequency of church attendance"; ideal number of children was asked as a direct question; and political conservatism was measured by a seven-point self-rating scale ranging from 1= "extremely liberal" to 7= "extremely conservative."

The analysis is based on examination of partial correlations of the attitudinal independent variables with the abortion scale score, controlling for significant demographic variables. In order to determine which demographic variables should be controlled, a multiple regression procedure was used, modeling abortion attitude as a function of the following seven independent variables: years of education, marital status (not married=0, married=1), race (white=0, nonwhite=1), age, family income, size of place of residence, and size of place of residence at age 16. Those demographic variables which were significant (p<.05) were used as controls in the partial correlation analysis. The analysis was done separately for males and females.

Analysis of Relationships

Table I shows the results of the regression and partial correlation analysis for men and women in the NORC sample. For men, those with more favorable attitudes toward abortion were those with greater education, greater income, the unmarried, and the older. For women, the five significant background variables were education, family income, size of place of residence, race, and marital status. Those women more favorable toward abortion were those with greater education and income, the unmarried, those from larger cities, and whites.

The partial correlations were obtained for the attitudinal variables and abortion score, controlling for the background variables. For men, sexual permissiveness and religiosity were the strongest predictors of abortion attitude. As permissiveness increased and as religiosity decreased, opposition to abortion decreased. Pro-life attitude was also fairly strongly related to abortion opposition. The partial coefficients for all three of these associations are of similar magnitude (approximately .4).

Sex role attitude was somewhat related to abortion attitude for men (partial $r = .267$), the more traditional men being more opposed to abortion. Political conservatism (partial $r = .150$) and ideal number of children (partial $r = .103$) were only weakly related to abortion attitude.

For women respondents, similar patterns emerged. As with the men, the three most important determinants of abortion attitude were pro-life orientation, religiosity, and sexual permissiveness. The magnitudes of the partial coefficients are all similar, and they are similar to those of the men. Thus, once demographic variables are controlled, these three variables seem to be the strongest attitudinal correlates of abortion attitudes.

Women's abortion attitudes were more strongly related to their fertility ideals than was the case for men, abortion opposition being greater for those with higher fertility ideals. Sex-role attitude and political conservatism were only weakly related to abortion attitude for both sexes.

The lack of important sex differences in abortion attitude correlates does not support findings of such differences reported in an earlier study based on a college-student sample (Finlay, 1981). It is possible that sex differences are stronger in the younger population, especially among the never-married, since most college students would be young and unmarried. As a test of this possibility, a further regression analysis was done, this time using only the never-married portion of the NORC sample. These summary data are presented in Table II, along with comparative data from the student sample mentioned above. Here one can see some support for the interpretation that sex differences in abortion correlates are important for the never-married, younger population, but that those differences disappear for the general population.

For both sexes in the younger samples, sexual permissiveness, church attendance, and "general conventionality," which contained church attendance as a component, were strongly related to abortion opposition, the first negatively and the others positively. For the variables "importance of children" and "death penalty opposition" (a substitute for "pro-life" sentiment, which was not measured in the student study), sex differences appear in both the student sample and the NORC never-married subsample. The data seem to show that, for young women, abortion opposition is tied not only to "conventional" sexual and religious/social attitudes but also to a

TABLE II: Comparison of Correlates of Abortion Opposition with Social Psychological Variables[a], by Sex: University Student Sample and NORC Never-Married Subsample. (Coefficients Are Partial Correlations, Controlling Significant Background Variables.)

	NORC Never-Married (N = 78)	University Student Sample (N = 132)		NORC Never-Married (N = 62)	University Student Sample (N = 130)	
	Abortion Scale	Abortion[b] Scale I	Abortion[b] Scale II	Abortion Scale	Abortion[b] Scale I	Abortion[b] Scale II
Sexual Permissiveness	-.531***	-.529***	-.557***	-.356**	-.389***	-.511***
Importance of children	.029	.001	.024	.283*	.311***	.218**
Sex Role conventionality	.214	.131	.057	.192	.187*	.507***
Church attendance	.514***	-----	-----	.384**	-----	-----
General conventionality	-----	.465***	.506***	.128	.466***	-----
Political conservatism	.244*	-----	-----	.087	-----	-----
Oppose death penalty	.035	-.032	-.014	.311*	-.017	.199*

Significance: *<.05; **<.01; ***<.001

(a) Measures of the variables for the University Student sample are different, but they were designed to measure the same concepts, and the comparisons are presented to illustrate similar patterns in sex differences. For complete descriptions of the variables and their measurements, as well as descriptions of the student samples, see Finlay, 1981.

(b) Two measures of abortion attitude were used in the student survey. Scale I was a cumulative scale, very similar to the one used in the NORC data analysis. Scale II was a simple rating of "Legal abortion," from "strongly favor" = 1 to "strongly oppose" = 5.

greater valuing of children and a more consistent opposition to life-taking than is the case for young men. Although these statements need further verification with other samples, the two independent samples do show interesting similarity. For young never-married adults, those for whom abortion is more likely to become a personal issue, differences between male and female attitude correlates seem to show more recognition of the complexity of the issue for females. This difference could possibly pose problems for young unmarried women with unwanted pregnancies who seek support and/or understanding from young unmarried men. However, it appears that married and older adults show no such differences by sex, owing perhaps to women's influence on husbands' attitudes, to greater empathy with women on the part of married men, or to some cohort effect that we have not yet recognized. At any rate, for purposes of understanding political opinions of the voting population, one may probably ignore sex differences, since voters come from the general adult population.

Political Implications of Findings

We have seen that, for both sexes, sexual permissiveness, pro-life attitude, and religiosity are stronger predictors of abortion attitudes than background factors or other attitudinal variables, such as sex-role attitudes. The implications of these findings are important, not only from a purely academic view but from a political standpoint as well.

Politically, if one is interested in increasing support for elective abortion, efforts that center around sex-role considerations (women's rights over their bodies, their need for equal participation in social and political life, for example) are probably not the most effective arguments possible, since sex-role attitude is not strongly related to abortion attitude. For the same reason, improvements in women's status and in people's commitments to women's equality may not necessarily increase the support for abortion availability.

On the other hand, since attitude toward sexuality is a much stronger predictor of abortion attitude, changing attitudes toward sexuality may have important latent impact on abortion attitudes. In view of the findings presented herein, one is led to surmise that much of the increase in support for abortion in the 1960s was an outgrowth not of changes in attitudes toward women but of changes in attitudes toward sexuality itself. The more tolerant society becomes toward nonmarital sex, the more openness we can expect toward the idea of abortion.

Another strong component of abortion opposition seems to derive from "prolife" concerns, at least in a narrowly defined sense in which the life to be ended cannot be defined to be "deserving" of death (i. e. , in such cases as euthanasia for the terminally ill, but not for capital punishment or military questions). In a rapidly changing society with capabilities for genetic engineering, test-tube fertilizations, and mechanical life-support systems, the question of the limits to the life-process and our right to control those limits must be addressed. If one wants to influence the opinions of those who seriously oppose abortion on this kind of ethical ground, one must take the argument seriously and deal with the ethical issue of the sacred nature of life.

Religiosity is a strong predictor of abortion attitude, and this factor must also be taken into account by those who would influence the status of abortion laws. If conservative religion increases in popularity in the next decade, then we will probably see a concomitant rise in anti-abortion sentiment, just as pro-abortion sentiment increased in the 1960s, when traditional religion was under pressure to become more "relevant."

Finally, the increasing political conservatism of recent years, by itself, may have little effect on abortion support, since political ideology per se does not appear to be strongly related to abortion attitude. And the decline in ideal family size, if it remains stable, probably will have some slight positive influence on abortion availability.

The present analysis has attempted to identify some of the primary socio-psychological correlates of abortion attitude variation. In view of the findings, there appear to be contradictory forces that will affect abortion support differentially. Increased religious conservatism may portend declining support for abortion, but continued relaxation of sexual standards and declining family-size ideals may work in the opposite direction. It is also probably true that if a more "rational" attitude is taken toward life-taking situations, then abortion would become more easily available. We can hope that as the sacred value of life is preserved, more meaningful definitions of its "true" beginning and end will be developed.

References

Bell, Robert R. Social Deviance. Homewood, Ill. : Dorsey 1971.

Bishop, Nadean. "Abortion: The Controversial Choice." In Jo Freeman, ed. Women: A Feminist Perspective, 2nd ed., Palo Alto, Calif: Mayfield Publishing, 1979, pp. 64-80.

Blake, Judith. "Abortion and Public Opinion: The 1960-1970 Decade." Science, 1971, 171: 540-549.

Clayton, Richard R. and William L. Tolone. "Religiosity and Attitudes Toward Induced Abortion: An Elaboration of the Relationship." Sociological Analysis, 1973, 34: 26-39.

Davis, James A. General Social Surveys, 1972-1978: Cumulative Data. Chicago: National Opinion Research Center, 1978.

Finlay, Barbara Agresti. "Sex Differences in Correlates of Abortion Attitudes Among College Students." Journal of Marriage and the Family, 1981, 43: 571-582.

Finner, Stephen L. and Jerome D. Gamache. "The Relation Between Religious Commitment and Attitudes Toward Induced Abortion." Sociological Analysis, 1969, 30: 1-12.

Granberg, Donald. "Pro-life or Reflection of Conservative Ideology? An Analysis of Opposition to Legalized Abortion." Sociology and Social Research, 1978, 62: 414-429.

_____ and Beth Wellman Granberg. "Abortion Attitudes, 1965-1980: Trends and Determinants." Family Planning Perspectives, 1980, 12: 250-261.

Jones, E. F. and C. F. Westoff. "Attitudes Toward Abortion in the United States in 1970 and the Trend Since 1965." In Research Reports, Vol. 1, Demographic and Social Aspects of Population Growth, C. F. Westoff and R. Parke eds. Washington, D. C.: Commission on Population Growth and the American Future, 1972, pp. 569-578.

Mauss, Armand L. "Abortion." In Social Problems as Social Movements, A. L. Mauss ed., Philadelphia: Lippincott, 1975, pp. 442-474.

Mileti, D. and L. Barnett. "Nine Demographic Factors and Their Relationship to Attitudes Toward Abortion Legalization." Social Biology, 1972, 19: 43-50.

Peterson, Larry R. and Armand L. Mauss. "Religion and

the 'Right to Life': Correlates of Opposition to Abortion." _Sociological Analysis_, 1976, 37 (3): 243-254.

Rossi, Alice S. "Abortion Laws and Their Victims." _Trans-Action_, 1966, 3: 7-12.

_____. "Public Views on Abortion." In _The Case for Legalized Abortion Now_, A. F. Guttmacher, ed. Berkeley, Calif.: Diablo Press, 1967, pp. 26-53.

Singh, B. K. and P. J. Leahy. "Contextual and Ideological Dimensions of Attitudes Toward Abortion." _Demography_, 1978, 15: 381-388.

Westoff, C. F.; C. Moore; and N. B. Ryder. "The Structure of Attitudes Toward Abortion." _Milbank Memorial Fund Quarterly_, 1969, 47: 11-37.

Westoff, Charles F. and Norman B. Ryder. _The Contraceptive Revolution_. Princeton, N. J.: Princeton University Press, 1977, pp. 163-178.

SOCIAL BASES OF SUPPORT AND OPPOSITION TO LEGALIZED ABORTION

By Donald Granberg and Beth Wellman Granberg

What will historians in the year 2030 write about abortion? By then, it may look like a minor conflict long since resolved. But possibly abortion will be viewed, in retrospect, as one of those issues, like slavery, suffrage, unionization, prohibition, civil rights, and the Vietnam War, that have periodically rocked this nation and shaken its foundation. If so, social historians and historical sociologists trying to illuminate our meanderings may appreciate a set of objective facts and generalizations concerning the social bases of support and opposition to legalized abortion.

In order to lay such groundwork, we have analyzed the abortion controversy as it has developed in the United States, focusing on 1965 to 1980. We analyzed existing time-series data on the attitudes of adults in the United States in representative sample surveys: nine surveys of the National Opinion Research Center (NORC), three National Fertility Surveys (NFS), and three surveys done by the Center for Political Studies (CPS).

Our society witnessed the emergence (late 1960s) and development (1970s) of a pro-legalization of abortion, or "pro-choice" social movement. In response, there emerged an equally involved anti-abortion countermovement, the "pro-life" movement. In 1980, we did two surveys of pro- and anti-abortion activists. The first was a state survey of the members of pro- and anti-abortion organizations (N = 524), the Abortion Rights Alliance (ARA) of Missouri and the Missouri Citizens for Life (MCL). The second (N = 898) surveyed members of the National Abortion Rights Action League (NARAL) and the National Right to Life Committee (NRLC).

191

We summarize here our analyses of the public and of the social-movement organizations. Details of our analyses are available elsewhere (Granberg, 1978, 1981 [a, b, c], 1982 [d, e, f, g]; Granberg & Denney, 1982; Granberg & Granberg, 1980, 1981. We also take into account analyses of the public reported by others (e. g. , Arney & Trescher, 1976; Blake, 1971, 1977; Jones & Westoff, 1978; Mileti & Barnett, 1972; Rossi, 1966; Singh & Leahy, 1978; Westoff, Moore & Ryder, 1969) and of activists (Leahy, 1975; Mitchell, McCarthy & Pearce, 1979; Kelly, 1981).

General Trend in Abortion Attitudes Over Time

Because abortion is a complex issue, there is no one item or set of items to describe adequately an individual's attitude toward abortion. However, when a set of questions, comprising a reliable scale, is asked, in the same order, of comparable samples of the same population at different times, we can examine the trend across time. The NORC and NFS used the same six circumstances, with NORC focusing on the matter of legal availability while NFS asked whether it would be "alright" if the woman got an abortion under various circumstances. The NFS surveys used only women respondents in the childbearing years, while NORC surveyed U. S. adults 18 years and older, so the results of the NORC and NFS surveys are not directly comparable. The NORC has no abortion data between 1965 and 1972, so the NFS 1970 data point is important. In 1972, 1976, and 1980, the CPS asked the same abortion questions of representative samples of U. S. adults. Because the questions used by these three polling organizations are different, one would not expect results to be identical. However, if the results across time are traced, the lines for the organizations should run parallel. Figure 1 summarizes the results for the NORC, NFS, and CPS surveys between 1965 and 1980. The lines do not depart significantly from running parallel. Overall, these observations can be made:

A.   1965 to 1975

Between 1965 and 1975, there was a substantial increase in approval of legalized abortion in the United States. The NFS data suggest that more change actually took place between 1965 and 1970 than between 1970 and 1975. This is not because there was more room for change between 1965 and 1970. If we calculate the actual amount of change relative to the maximum possible amount of change, it still appears that there was a larger shift between 1965 and 1970 than between 1970 and 1975.

B.   1975 to 1980

Between 1975 and 1980, there was virtually no change in approval of abortion.   In 1978, there was a slight but significant dip in approval, but by 1980 approval rebounded to the earlier plateau.   The most recent data, from NORC's 1982 survey, indicate that approval may have increased slightly between 1980 and 1982.

C.   SUPREME COURT DECISION, 1973

The Supreme Court's key decision in Roe vs. Wade (1973) had little or no effect on public opinion.   Thus public opinion was not determined by public policy.   Legalization did not necessarily confer legitimacy in the minds of the citizenry. If one looks only at the 1972 and 1974 NORC data, the years immediately surrounding the Supreme Court decision, there was a small but significant increase in approval.   However, if one plots a line between 1965 and 1975, the amount of change occurring between 1972 and 1974 does not deviate from the broader trend.   Also, the NFS data suggest that most of the changes that took place between 1965 and 1975 actually occurred prior to 1970, well in advance of, rather than after, Roe vs. Wade.   Overall, the public in 1972 perferred a more permissive situation than that which prevailed in most states at that time.   But the Supreme Court "leap-frogged" public opinion by creating a more permissive situation than preferred by the public--and the public has not yet "caught up" with the situation created by the Supreme Court.

D.   PUBLIC CONSENSUS

Most citizens in the United States avoid extremes on the abortion issue.   In the 1970s, a majority favored something between the highly permissive situation favored by pro-choice forces and the highly restrictive situation advocated by the pro-life forces.   Exactly where the public falls between the two social movements is more difficult to say.   On the "hard" or physical reasons for abortion (woman's health, rape, or a probably serious defect), the public is much closer to the pro-choice position.   On the "soft" or discretionary reasons for abortion (being single, economic duress, and not wanting more children), the public may be slightly closer to the pro-life position.   Actually the public is split almost down the mid-

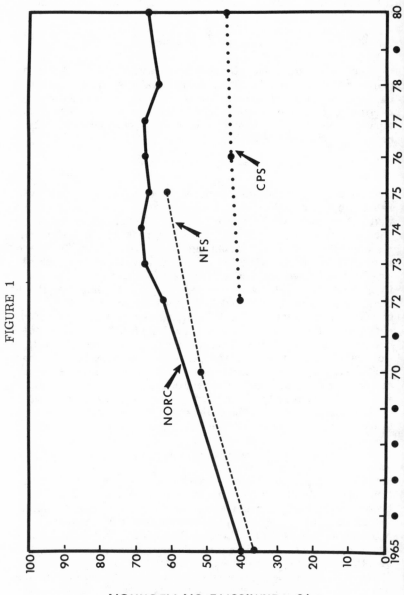

FIGURE 1

dle on the soft items, about halfway between the pro-choice
and pro-life groups. Also, recent experiments have demonstrated that the order of questioning used by the NORC (al-
ternating hard-soft-hard-soft-hard-soft) has led to an underestimation of the amount of public support for legalized abortion under the soft reasons (Schuman, Presser & Ludwig,
1981). If a highly restrictive anti-abortion situation were to
be created at the national level, it is unambiguously clear
that this would run counter to the preferences of the public
on the hard reasons, nor is there strong consensus in support of prohibiting abortions for the soft reasons.

Demographic and Social Status Characteristics

Among the public, there has been little difference between
the attitudes of men and women on abortion. (When a difference does appear, men may be ever so slightly more permissive.) Nor does gender interact significantly with education or religiosity in determining abortion attitudes. Women
are disproportionately present in both pro-choice and pro-life
groups, but more so in the pro-choice groups (78% women
in NARAL, 77% in ARA, 62% in MCL and 63% in NRLC).
Members of the advisory board listed on the letterhead of a
pro-choice group were predominantly women, while for the
pro-life group, they were predominantly men. Compared to
pro-choice members, pro-life members tend to be more likely
to be married, in the late childbearing years of 31 to 45,
to be homemakers, to have been raised in larger families,
and to have more children themselves.

People in New England and the Far West are more
likely to be pro-choice. Those living in an urban setting
are more likely to be pro-choice in their abortion attitudes
than people living in a rural area. The direction of the rural-
urban difference also appeared among activists, although about
half of the pro-life activists live in a metropolitan area.

As socioeconomic status increases among the public,
approval of legalized abortion increases. Of various status
indicators, education is the best predictor of abortion attitudes among the public. Results for occupational prestige,
income, and subjective social class are in the same direction
but the trend is not as strong as for education. The strongest relationship between education and approval of abortion
was in 1972, the year prior to the pivotal Supreme Court decision. Across years, this relationship has averaged about
+.23, significant but not strong enough to warrant the label
of class polarization as used by Skerry (1978).

The differences between the activist groups are in the same direction, with pro-choice members having somewhat higher income, education, and subjective social class than pro-life members. About 84 percent of NARAL members are college graduates, compared to 62 percent of NRLC members. The pro-life groups have somewhat more working-class participation, and the pro-choice groups more upper-class members. However, both the pro-choice and the pro-life groups are predominantly middle or upper-middle class.

Among the public, blacks are distinctively opposed to legalized abortion. Although not huge, the difference along racial lines remains significant when other factors, such as education, gender, age, income, and rurality are controlled. The activist groups are overwhelmingly Caucasian (over 98%) with no substantial minority-group participation in either the pro-choice or the pro-life groups.

The Religious Factor

There is no doubt that there is a most significant religious factor in attitudes toward abortion. Religious affiliation groups differ significantly in this regard: From most to least approving, the major groups would be 1) Jews, 2) those with no affiliation, 3) Protestants, and 4) Catholics. The big difference is not between groups 3) and 4), however, but between 3) and 4) on the one hand, and 1) and 2) on the other. There is more variation among Protestant denominations than between Protestants as a group and Catholics. Baptists and Catholics do not differ significantly on abortion attitudes in most comparisons. The tendency of Jews to be distinctively pro-choice remains significant when one controls for region, urbanism, political liberalism, and education.

As religious involvement (measured by attendance at religious services or intensity of one's subjective commitment) increases, approval of legalized abortion decreases; this relationship is stronger among Catholics than Protestants. We have examined other religiosity variables also. Among Catholics, having a child attending parochial school, having attended a Catholic college, feeling closest or close to Catholics as a reference group are all inversely correlated with approval of abortion. But attendance at religious services is still the indicator of religiosity that is most strongly linked to abortion attitudes. Panel data were used to try to unravel the causal flow between religious involvement and abortion attitudes. Among Catholics, the correlation between attendance

at Mass in 1972 and permissiveness on abortion in 1976 was
-.40, which was not significantly larger than the correlation
between permissiveness in 1972 and attendance in 1976 (-.38).
Thus, although it is clear that the two are significantly related, the direction of the causal flow remains clouded (Kenny,
1975).

The positive correlation between education and approval
of abortion occurs only among Protestants, not among Catholics. Among Catholics, if one excludes those who attended a
Catholic college, the relationship between education and approval of abortion more closely resembles the relationship
among Protestants. Among Protestants, approval of abortion
is positively correlated with condoning interracial marriage
(saying it should not be illegal) and with drinking alcoholic
beverages (not being a total abstainer). This supports the
thesis that the Protestant base of opposition to abortion has
its locus in the fundamentalist sectors that promoted prohibition of alcohol and opposed racial desegregation.

For the activist groups, the picture on religiosity is
quite similar. Religion is subjectively much more important
to pro-life activists, and they attend religious services much
more frequently than do pro-choice activists. Also, 44 percent of the MCL agreed that "a couple should have as many
children as God wills" to only 1 percent of their ARA counterparts. When activists in Missouri were asked to rank the
18 terminal values identified by Rokeach (1973), MCL members, on average, tended to rank salvation as most important, while it tended to be ranked as least important by ARA
members.

The large majority of pro-life activists are Catholics:
77 percent of the MCL and 70 percent of the NRLC, compared to only 2 percent of ARA and 4 percent of NARAL members and about 25 percent of U.S. adults. On the other side,
Jews, agnostics, and atheists are substantially overrepresented
among pro-choice activists, in comparison to their percentage
of the population.

Political Dimensions

Among the public, there is only a slight relationship between
political party identification, political ideology, and attitudes
toward abortion. Conservative-Democrats tend to be least
approving, while Liberal-Independents tend to be most approving of legalized abortion being available. Self-designated ide-

ology seems to be a better predictor of abortion attitudes than party identification. In the 1980 U. S. presidential election, it appears that Reagan voters did not differ from Carter voters in their attitudes toward abortion. The candidates were relatively distinct on abortion, but the voter groups were not polarized on this issue (King, 1978).

In the Missouri activist survey, MCL and ARA members did not differ significantly on party preference, but MCL members were much more likely to be conservative than were ARA members (56% to 7%). In the national survey, NARAL members were more likely to indicate Democrat affiliation than NRLC members (48% to 23%) and less likely to indicate Republican (14% to 41%). The difference on ideology was similar to the state survey, with 68 percent of NARAL members checking "liberal," compared to only 7 percent for NRLC members.

Perhaps the most interesting finding in this area was in relation to the matter of single-issue voting. NRLC members were much more likely than NARAL members (84% to 47%) to agree that "The matter of abortion is so important that I would refuse to support a candidate whose position on abortion was unacceptable to me, regardless of any other reasons there might be for supporting that candidate." This may be the most direct evidence available of single-issue voting inclinations within social movement organizations. When one group is much more inclined single-issue voting than the other, it presents an intriguing strategic dilemma.

Women's Liberation

As support for the Women's liberation movement increases, approval of legalized abortion increases. This is not an especially strong relationship, however, and it occurs more strongly among Protestants than among Catholics. A major goal for the women's liberation movement in the United States in the 1970s was ratification of the Equal Rights Amendment (ERA) to the U. S. Constitution. The abortion activist groups are sharply divided over this issue. Within NARAL, 93 percent favored the ERA compared to only 9 percent for the NRLC. The results for the Missouri activists were similar, with 91 percent of ARA, compared to 16 percent of MCL members, approving the ERA. The 1980 CPS data indicated that 61 percent of U. S. adults supported the ERA.

One should not infer from this that pro-life activists

are opposed to everything that the women's liberation movement has advocated. On other items pertaining to women's
liberation, the pro-life members were less supportive than
the pro-choice members, but pro-life members tend to be
more supportive than U. S. adults generally. For instance,
98 percent of NARAL members approve of "a married woman
earning money in business or industry if she has a husband
capable of supporting her," compared to 83 percent for NRLC
members and 73 percent of U. S. adults.

Commitment to Civil Liberties

As commitment to civil liberties increases, approval of abortion increases. This would seem to be empirical support for
the pro-choice definition of abortion. NARAL features the
State of Liberty on its letterhead, and the American Civil
Liberties Union has supported a woman's right to a legal abortion in numerous court cases. The relationship, although not
a strong one, does remain significant when one controls for
education and religiosity, variables known to predict both civil
liberty and abortion attitudes. This is another relationship
that occurs more strongly among Protestants than among Catholics.

Among the activists, results tended to be in the same
direction. Pro-choice ARA members were more likely to
indicate that a social deviant (atheist, militarist, racist, com-
munist, or homosexual) should be allowed to speak in the community than were pro-life MCL members. For the 5 free-
speech items, the average level of tolerance was 94 percent
for ARA and 66 percent for MCL members. At the national
level, for 15 civil-liberty items, NARAL averaged 92 percent
taking the pro-civil liberties position compared to 72 percent
for the NRLC members. This is a significant difference,
but it should be noted that when these same 15 questions were
posed to U. S. adults in the 1980 NORC General Social Survey, the comparable average was only 57 percent. So NARAL
members were significantly more supportive of civil liberties
than members of the NRLC, but the NRLC members are significantly more supportive than U. S. adults generally. Thus,
aside from abortion, it would be incorrect to argue that NRLC
members are distinctively prone toward a willingness to sup-
press civil liberties, at least relative to U. S. adults.

Other Matters of Life and Death

Only the comparisons involving attitudes toward suicide

and euthanasia support the pro-life thesis that opposition to abortion reflects a more general pro-life commitment. As opposition to suicide and euthanasia increases, opposition to abortion increases. That relationship occurs at a rather strong level among the public. There are also pronounced differences between pro-life and pro-choice activists on these items. Among NARAL members only 11 percent say that a doctor should not be allowed to end a patient's life, if the patient has an incurable disease and if the patient and the family request it, compared to 97 percent of NRLC members. Of NRLC members 94 percent say that one does not have the right to commit suicide if one has an incurable disease, compared to only 6 percent of NARAL members. On these questions, the U. S. public is split rather evenly, being somewhat closer to NARAL members on the euthanasia question but somewhat closer to NRLC members on the suicide issue.

The activist groups tend not to differ significantly on the question of capital punishment, although both pro-choice and pro-life activists tend to be more opposed to capital punishment than U. S. adults. Among adults in the United States, the relationship between abortion and capital punishment attitudes has generally been insignificant. A rather curious interaction in the 1980 NORC survey of U. S. adults indicated that, among people with less than a high-school education, opposition to abortion and opposition to capital punishment were positively correlated to a significant degree. Among college graduates, the relationship was in the opposite direction, though not as strong.

The public shows no significant relationship between attitudes toward gun control and abortion. Among activists, there was a difference, with 90 percent of NARAL members favoring a gun control law to only 63 percent of NRLC members, but this is in the direction opposite from the pro-life thesis. On the matter of whether the 55-miles-per-hour-speed limit should be retained, the Missouri abortion activist groups, ARA and MCL, did not differ significantly. But at the national level, NARAL members were slightly more likely than NRLC members to favor retaining the 55 m. p. h. limit (86% to 77%).

There is no evidence that opposition to abortion is linked with opposition to war, militarism, or imperialism. Among the public, there has been a slight relationship in the opposite direction. Approval of legalized abortion is linked, to a small extent, with favoring a cut in military spending.

Among activists, pro-choice groups were much more likely than pro-life groups to favor a decrease in military spending. In the Missouri survey, 77 percent of pro-choice ARA members indicated they had opposed U. S. military intervention in Vietnam compared to only 35 percent of pro-life MCL members. Also, 50 percent of MCL members thought "the U. S. should be ready and willing to use military force, if necessary, to assure our continued access to important resources, such as oil," compared to 27 percent of ARA members. The results from the national survey on that item were in the same direction but not significant, with 21 percent of NARAL and 29 percent of NRLC members agreeing with this pre-interventionist position.

Traditionalism in Matters of Personal Morality

Finally, we consider an alternative that has received strong and consistent support in analyses both of the public and of abortion activists. The thesis is that opposition to abortion reflects a traditional or conservative approach to matters of personal morality (Granberg, 1978; Singh & Leahy, 1978). Conversely, support for legalized abortion reflects a departure from traditional morality in the direction of a more relativistic and secular orientation. This trend seems to cut across religious groups.

One of the elements of the traditional approach was to favor large families. There tends to be a fairly strong positive correlation between the size of one's ideal family and one's opposition to abortion. Across years, the relationship occurs to the same extent among Protestants and Catholics. The difference also appears in the comparison of pro- and anti-abortion activists. The average number of children considered ideal was 3. 7 for NRLC members, compared to 2. 0 for NARAL members and 2. 5 for U. S. adults.

Generally, opposition to abortion is closely linked with a number of other attitudes, comprising a pattern or syndrome. The other attitudes include rejection or disapproval of premarital sex, birth control information being made available, sex education, extramarital sex, lenient divorce laws, homosexuality, and pornography. Many anti-abortion activists are disturbed by what they regard as a breakdown in the standards for personal morality. They advocate reversion to a situation in which the family unit was more stable and salient, divorce was difficult to obtain and occurred less frequently, premarital, extramarital and homosexual relations were considered to be unambiguously wrong, sex education was not

taught in the schools, and effective birth-control information
and techniques were unknown and unavailable, especially to
teenagers, and erotic and sexually stimulating materials were
not available in the mass media.   In some sense, their orientation is to grab hold of history and make it conform. That,
as they realize, is a difficult feat.   By comparison, pro-
choice activists are much more accepting and approving of
trends in personal behavior in contemporary society.   They
have a relativistic orientation in which they try to sense the
broad trends of history, to make some adjustment and refine-
ments in those trends, and then to make an accommodation to
what is evolving in social relations.

*   *   *

This Chapter uses data from the National Opinion Research
Center of the University of Chicago, the National Fertility
Survey of Princeton University, and the Center for Political
Studies of the University of Michigan.   The authors are solely
responsible for the analyses and interpretation.   The surveys
of the activist organizations were funded by the Graduate Research Council of the University of Missouri-Columbia.   The
analyses were supported by NICHD Grant No. 1-82834.   The
authors wish to thank Donald Denney, Mary Harbourt, Lynn
Taylor, Sherry Kilgore, Barbara Breen, Janice Meiburger,
Terry Brown, and Patricia Shanks for their assistance.

References

Arney, W. , and Trescher, W.   "Trends in Attitudes Toward
   Abortion, 1972-1975."   Family Planning Perspectives,
   1976, 8:   117-124.

Blake, J.   "Abortion and Public Opinion: The 1960-1970
   Decade."   Science, 1971, 171:   540-549.

_____.   "The Abortion Decisions: Judicial Review and Pub-
   lic Opinion."   In Abortion: New directions for policy studies, E. Manier, W. Liu, and D. Soloman.   Notre Dame,
   Ind. : Notre Dame University Press, 1977, pp. 51-82.

Granberg, D.   (a) "The Abortion Activists."   Family Planning
   Perspectives, 1981, 13:   157-163.

_____.   (b) "Abortion Activists in Missouri."   Social Bi-
   ology, 1981, 28:   in press.

_____. (c) "The Abortion Controversy: An Overview." The Humanist, 1981, 41: 28-38, 66.

_____. (d) "Comparison of Pro-choice and Pro-life Activists: Their Values, Attitudes and Beliefs." Population and Environment, 1982, 5, (2): 75-94.

_____. (e) "Family Size Preferences and Sexual Permissiveness As Factors Differentiating Abortion Activists." Social Psychology Quarterly, 1982, 45: 15-23.

_____. "Pro-life or Reflection of Conservative Ideology? An Analysis of Opposition to Legalized Abortion." Sociology and Social Research, 1978, 62: 414-429.

_____. (f) "Pro-choice, Pro-life: More on Stereotypes." Commonweal, 1982, 78: 78-80.

_____. (g) "What Does it Mean to Be Pro-life?" Christian Century, 1982, May 12: 62-66.

_____, and Granberg, B. "Abortion Attitudes, 1965-1980: Trends and Determinants." Family Planning Perspectives, 1980, 12: 250-261.

_____. "Pro-life Versus Pro-choice: Another Look at the Abortion Controversy in the U.S." Sociology and Social Research, 1981, 65: 424-434.

Granberg, D., and Denney, D. "The Coathanger and the Rose: Comparison of Pro-choice and Pro-life Activists in Contemporary U.S." Transaction/Society, 1982, May 19: 39-46.

Jones, E., and Westoff, C. "How Attitudes Toward Abortion Are Changing." Journal of Population, 1978, 1: 5-21.

Kelly, J. "Beyond the Stereotypes: Interviews with Right-To-Life Pioneers." Commonweal, 1981, 21: 654-659.

Kenny, D. "Cross-lagged Panel Correlation: A Test for Spuriousness." Psychological Bulletin, 1975, 82: 887-903.

King, M. "Assimilation and Contrast of Presidential Candidates' Issue Positions, 1972." "Public Opinion Quarterly, 1978, 41: 515-522.

Leahy, P. "The Anti-Abortion Movement: Testing a Theory of the Rise and Fall of Social Movements." Doctoral dissertation, Syracuse University, Syracuse, New York, 1975. (n. p.)

Mileti, D. , and Barnett, L. "Nine Demographic Factors and Their Relationship to Attitudes Toward Abortion." Social Biology, 1972, 19: 43-50.

Mitchell, R.; McCarthy, J.; and Pearce, K. Report on a Membership Survey. Washington, D. C.: The National Abortion Rights Action League, 1979.

Rokeach, M. The Nature of Human Values. New York: Free Press, 1973.

Rossi, A. "Abortion Laws and Their Victims." Trans-action, 1966, 3: 7-12.

Schuman, H.; Presser, S.; and Ludwig, J. "Context Effects on Survey Responses to Questions About Abortion." Public Opinion Quarterly, 1981, 45: 216-223.

Singh, B. , and Leahy, P. "Contextual and Ideological Dimensions of Attitudes Toward Discretionary Abortion." Demography, 1978, 15: 381-388.

Skerry, P. "The Class Conflict Over Abortion." The Public Interest, 1978, 52: 69-84.

Traugott, M. , and Vinovskis, M. "Abortion and the 1978 Elections." Family Planning Perspectives, 1980, 12: 238-246.

Westoff, C.; Moore, E.; and Ryder, N. "The Structure of Attitudes Toward Abortion." The Milbank Memorial Fund Quarterly, 1969, 47: 11-37.

PHYSICIANS, HOSPITALS, AND ABORTION:
THE INFLUENCE OF ATTITUDES ON MEDICAL PRACTICE

By Constance A. Nathanson

Women's access to legal abortion depends, at the very least, on their ability to locate a licensed practitioner, almost always a physician, willing to undertake the procedure. Depending on abortion-law provisions, which vary widely even among countries where elective abortion is available on a legal basis, they also may be required to find a cooperative hospital and physicians who are prepared to approve their application to have an abortion performed (Tietze, 1979). As pointed out in a recent review, "legal authorization of elective abortion does not guarantee that abortion on request is actually available to all women who may want their pregnancies terminated" (Tietze, 1979). This statement is true because legal authorization, although permitting physicians and hospitals to perform abortions, does not require them to do so. Consequently, there is ample room for the exercise of professional and/or administrative discretion in the provision of abortion services even in the most permissive legal climate.

Detailed information on the manner in which discretion is exercised and on how women with different social, economic, and personal characteristics are affected by variations in the providers' behaviors is unavailable for most countries. The purpose here is to review that evidence which is available, based largely on studies done in the United States but including, where possible, comparative data from Canada and the United Kingdom. Although there appear to be many common elements in the experience of these three countries, it is important to emphasize that practitioners' responses to abortion will depend on legal, medical, and religious traditions that vary from one country to another as well as on professional attitudes and circumstances. For this reason, care

205

should be taken in generalizing specific research findings across national boundaries.

Physicians, Hospitals, and Abortion Services

The role that is legally assigned to physicians and hospitals in making and implementing the abortion decision varies considerably among the three countries under discussion; this role is most significant in Canada and least significant, from a strictly legal perspective, in the United States. Both Canadian and British law require all abortions to be performed in hospitals, and both countries involve more than a single physician in the decision-making process. In the United States, by contrast, there is no stipulation as to where abortions may be performed (although states may regulate second trimester abortions in the interest of maternal safety) and no administratively or legally required approval or referral mechanisms. Purely on procedural grounds, then, the influence of physician- and hospital-imposed constraints on the volume of abortion services would be expected to be of least importance in the United States. Even in the United States, however, this influence is considerable, as we shall see.

Uneven regional availability of abortion services has been documented in all three countries (Seims, 1980; COAL, 1977; Cartwright & Waite, 1972). In part, these variations may be due to uneven distribution of health resources (particularly in Canada, where hospitals must meet rather stringent requirements in order to offer abortion services at all). However, it is clear from available evidence that the geographical and institutional location of physicians who have personal and professional values favorable to abortion also plays a major role in abortion availability. Data collected by the Canadian Committee on the Operation of the Abortion Law (COAL) point strongly to the effects of physicians' attitudes on hospital abortion practices (COAL, 1977); these effects are further documented in two recently published studies of hospital abortions in the United States (Miller, 1979; Nathanson & Becker, 1980). Data from the second of these studies, carried out in Maryland in 1976, are shown in Table I. Information on obstetricians' attitudes toward abortion and related issues, as well as on their hospital affiliations, was obtained in a survey of all obstetrician-gynecologists in private practice in the state.[1] Twenty-one percent of the explained variation in the number of abortions performed annually in the state's 30 non-Catholic hospitals is accounted for by two dimensions of private obstetrical staff attitudes:

TABLE I:

Multiple Regression Analysis of Number of Abortions
Performed by Non-Catholic, Non-Federal Hospitals,
Maryland, 1976.

Number of Hospital Abortions Performed

Independent Variables	Stand. Coeff. (1)	Cum. Variance Explained (r^2) (2)
Abortion Need	-.04	.33
Hospital Size	.62*	.57
Number Medical Departments	.14	.58
Fertility Service Attitudes	.33*	.69
Disturbance by Abortion	-.25*	.73
TOTAL r^2		.73

*$p \leq .05$

approval of policies that would increase women's access to
abortion services, and frequency of emotional disturbance by
participation in the abortion procedure. (These attitudinal
dimensions will be further discussed in a later section of
this chapter.) Similar results were obtained by Miller, based
on data collected in New York State following reform of its
abortion law in 1970. Both studies found that need for abortion in the hospital's geographical catchment area was not
significantly associated with the volume of hospital abortions
when hospital characteristics and obstetricians' attitudes were
controlled, while physicians' attitudes "have a strong independent impact on hospital abortion services" (Miller, 1979,
p. 369).

Individual physicians (as well as hospitals) vary in
their responses to request for abortion or abortion referral,
so much so that two studies carried out in Scotland describe
women's success in obtaining an abortion as largely a matter
of luck, depending on the attitudes of the physicians they hap-
pen to see (Farmer, 1973; Macintyre, 1977). Of fundamental

importance is the fact that substantial proportions of obstetrician-gynecologists, the medical specialists most qualified
to provide this service, do no abortions at all. The COAL
report (1977) states that 48.9 percent of the obstetrician-
gynecologists in eight Canadian provinces did no abortions
during fiscal year 1974-75; a similar figure of 43 percent
was obtained in the Maryland study referred to above (Nathanson & Becker, 1977).

When, as in Canada and the United Kingdom, several
physicians must concur in the abortion decision, their gate-
keeping role is clearly substantial. An absence of professional consensus on how this role should be performed, marked
variation in how it is performed, and a profound influence of
moral values on performance are strikingly evident in studies
from these two countries (COAL, 1977; Farmer, 1973; Macintyre, 1977). Qualitative data from the investigations carried
out in Scotland support the hypothesis that variability in physicians' abortion policies and procedures is largely a consequence of the fact that decisions are made on the basis of
moral rather than medical considerations. A more detailed
analysis of the nature of these moral considerations follows.

Dimensions of Obstetricians' Attitudes Toward Abortion

Research on physicians' approval of abortion and willingness
to provide abortion services has uniformly found religion to
be the most important variable in accounting for conservative
attitudes (Lerner, Arnold, & Wassertheil, 1971; Kirchner &
Colombotos, 1970; Rosen, Werley, Ager & Shea, 1971; Pratt,
Koslowsky, & Wintrob, 1974; COAL, 1977; Nathanson & Becker,
1977). The practical effect of adherence to the Catholic religion is to remove a physician from the pool of abortion per-
formers. Data from the Maryland study show that only 15
percent of Catholic obstetricians performed abortions, compared with 77 percent of obstetricians belonging to other religious groups. However, once the decision has been made
to do any abortions, other factors come into play to influence
the obstetrician's level of commitment to abortion as a component of his or her obstetrical practice. The relative importance of religion in abortion performance and abortion
practice "commitment" is shown in Table II.

Practice "commitment" is a composite variable derived from information on three dimensions of obstetricians'
abortion practice: 1) the number of abortions performed per
month, 2) whether or not second-trimester abortions were

TABLE II: Religion and Attitude as Predictors of Abortion Performance and Abortion Practice Commitment, Maryland, 1976

Independent Variables	Abortion Performance		Independent Variables	Abortion Practice Commitment	
	Beta	Cum. Variance Explained		Beta	Cum. Variance Explained
Religion	.39**	.27	Fertility Service Attitudes	.24**	.06
Fertility Service Attitudes [1]	.26**	.34	Religion	.13*	.08
Sex Role Attitudes [2]	.05	.34	Obstetrician's Age	.03	.08
Bioethical Attitudes [3]	.05	.35	Bioethical Attitudes	.03	.09
Obstetrician's Age	.03	.35	Sex Role Attitudes	.02	.09
Total r^2		.35	Total r^2		.09
(N = 308)			(N = 161)		

* p ≤ .05
** p ≤ .01

1. The fertility services attitudes scale is described on p. 210.

2. The sex role attitude scale is made up of five statements about the roles of women in contemporary society. A liberal position on this scale reflects an expanded view of these roles, extending beyond the conventional focus on home, reproduction, and child care.

3. The bioethical attitudes scale is composed of eight statements pertaining to the right of the physician or the patient to make critical life or death decisions. The liberal physician could support this right, and would not insist on supporting life irrespective of circumstances.

performed, and 3) the frequency with which the obstetrician was named by colleagues as a possible referral for women seeking abortion. Examination of the data presented in Table 2 shows that 77 percent of the explained variance in abortion performance is attributable to religious preference; however, religion accounts for only 22 percent of the explained variance in practice commitment. Much more important is the obstetrician's liberalism or conservatism on specific issues of policy affecting women's access to abortion and contraceptive services. However, even this variable accounts for a relatively small percentage of the total variation in practice commitment, suggesting the need to explore other attitudinal or practice dimensions.

A rather consistent theme in research on the abortion attitudes of service providers is the split between ideologically based approval of increased access to abortion (pro-choice ideology) and psychological or "moral" disturbance by the abortion procedure (Nathanson & Becker, 1977; Joffe, 1978, 1979). In the work of Nathanson and Becker, the ideological component is measured by a "fertility services attitude scale" consisting of nine statements on issues of access to abortion and contraception: for example, "publicly supported hospitals should be required to provide abortion services"; "consent of the spouse should be legally required prior to sterilization." Responses to each statement are given in terms of a five-point scale ranging from "strongly agree" to "strongly disagree" and are summed to obtain the total scale score. "Disturbance" is indicated by response to a single question asked of all obstetricians who had ever performed an abortion: "How do you personally feel about your participation in this procedure? Are you often, sometimes, rarely, or never disturbed by it?" The Pearson Product Moment correlation between frequency of disturbance and position on the fertility services attitude scale is only .20, indicating that these two indices are, indeed, measuring different dimensions of abortion attitudes. Furthermore, among physicians who have ever performed an abortion, the disturbance variable makes almost as much contribution to current abortion performance as does position on the fertility services attitude scale (the "ideological" variable). And, as shown in Table III, disturbance is of major importance (equivalent to religion) in affecting willingness to perform abortion late in pregnancy.

Based on these analyses, it is reasonable to suggest that the "moral considerations" that have been held to account

TABLE III:

"Disturbance" as a Factor in Abortion Performance, Abortion Practice Commitment, and Late Abortion, Maryland, 1976

Abortion Performance			Abortion Practice Commitment			Late Abortion		
Independent Variables	Beta	Cum. Variance Explained	Independent Variables	Beta	Cum. Variance Explained	Independent Variables	Beta	Cum. Variance Explained
Religion	.26**	.09	Fertility Services Attitudes	.21**	.06	Disturbance	-.19**	.05
Fertility Services Attitudes	.13**	.11	Disturbance	-.12	.08	Religion	.20**	.10
Disturbance	-.11*	.12	Religion	.11	.09	Fertility Services Attitudes	.11	.11
TOTAL r²		.12	TOTAL r²		.09	TOTAL r²		.11
(N = 199)			(N = 141)			(N = 148)		

* p < .05
** p < .01

for much of the variability in physicians' abortion decisions
have at least three underlying components: 1) religion itself,
in which institutionally based moral authority is invoked a-
gainst abortion, 2) individually based ideological value positions, 3) individually based personal value positions. The
final step is to examine ways in which these attitudinal influences on abortion practice are modified by structural and
situational constraints.

Structural and Situational Determinants of Abortion Perform-
ance

In their reports on the consequences of abortion-law reform,
both Canadian and British investigators suggest that physicians
are influenced in their abortion policies and procedures by
the professional climate of opinion in their local practice area
(Cartwright & Waite, 1972; COAL, 1977). Direct evidence
that opinion climate has an influence on physicians' abortion
performances that is independent of their personal attitudes
was obtained in the 1976 Maryland study. In this latter investigation, two indices of opinion climate were constructed--
the first labeled "practice environment" and the second labeled
"hospital climate." The first index combines three aspects
of practice environment: 1) location of practice (urban vs.
rural), 2) type of practice (group vs. solo), and 3) level of
participation in local medical-society activities. Since the
largest percentages of obstetricians who themselves do abortions are found in urban settings, in group practice, and among
medical-society nonparticipants, physicians who share these
characteristics are, we infer, most likely to be exposed to
norms favoring abortion services. "Hospital climate" is a
measure of the average position on the fertility services attitudes index of obstetricians affiliated with a given hospital.
The more "liberal" the hospital climate, the more likely that
physicians who practice in that hospital will be exposed to
professional norms in favor of abortion. [2]

"Practice-environment" and "hospital-climate" effects
on the abortion performance of obstetricians with liberal and
conservative personal attitudes are shown in Table IV (overall abortion performance) and Table V (late abortion performance). Comparison of the "Liberal" and "Conservative" portions of each table, together with inspection of the two sets
of chi-squares, demonstrates quite clearly that professional
opinion climate has a marked effect on the abortion practice
of personally conservative obstetricians, but little or no effect
on the practice of personally liberal obstetricians. [3] Thus,

TABLE IV: Abortion Performance, Practice Environment and Fertility Services Attitudes

Fertility Services Attitudes and Abortion Performance	Practice Environment			
	Liberal		Conservative	
	No.	Percent	No.	Percent
Attitudes: Liberal[1]				
Performs	62	78.5	25	83.3
Does not Perform	17	21.5	5	16.7
Total	79	100.0	30	100.0
Attitudes: Conservative				
Performs	58	54.7	21	33.3
Does not Perform	48	45.3	42	66.7
Total	106	100.0	63	100.0

1. Chi-squares testing the effect of environment on performance are calculated separately for physicians with liberal and conservative attitudes. For liberal physicians, the chi-square value is .317 (not significant); for conservative physicians, it is 7.26 (p < .001).

TABLE V: Late Abortion, Hospital Climate, and Fertility Services Attitudes

Fertility Services Attitudes and	Hospital Climate			
	Liberal		Conservative	
Late Abortion Performance	No.	Percent	No.	Percent
Attitudes: Liberal[1]				
Performs	40	65.6	20	51.3
Does not Perform	21	34.4	19	48.7
Total	61	100.0	39	100.0
Attitudes: Conservative				
Performs	18	90.0	23	33.3
Does not Perform	2	10.0	46	66.7
Total	20	100.0	69	100.0

1. Chi-square for climate effects among liberal physicians is 2.02 (not significant); for conservative physicians it is 20.04 (p ≤ .001).

the majority of liberal obstetricians will offer abortion services even in a conservative environment; but more noteworthy is the fact that conservative obstetricians also will offer these services if they practice in an environment where abortion is supported by the prevailing professional norms.   We may speculate that in a supportive climate abortion is redefined from a medically and morally questionable procedure to a legitimate component of obstetrical-gynecological services.   Under the latter conditions, failure to offer abortion services comes into direct conflict with accepted standards of professional practice.   Once the issue is defined in these terms, the rewards for conformity are sufficient to outweigh preferences based on personal attitudes and beliefs.

Focus up to now has been entirely on physicians' attitudes toward abortion in the abstract, as if these attitudes alone influenced physician behavior, quite independent of the characteristics of individual women presenting themselves with abortion requests.   Clearly this is an oversimplification. Work done in the United Kingdom and in the United States indicates that providers' response to abortion clients are strongly influenced by the perceived attributes of women seeking abortion and by the ways in which these women present themselves (Macintyre, 1977; Joffe, 1978; Nathanson & Becker, 1978). The research of both Macintyre and Joffe suggests that abortion providers are highly sensitive to the moral characters they attribute to their clients.   Among the Scottish physicians interviewed by Macintyre (1977), it is the "bad, promiscuous girls" who are least likely to be recommended for pregnancy termination; the "nice girls who had made mistakes" are most successful in having their abortion requests approved.   Joffe (1978; p. 115) found that abortion counselors were most upset by the "supercool client" who rejected pre-abortion counseling, and that they welcomed some emotional discharge as a sign that abortion was regarded with appropriate seriousness.

In an attempt to measure directly the influence of obstetrical patient characteristics on obstetricians' decision making regarding abortion, Nathanson and Becker (1978) constructed a series of vignettes in which seven patient characteristics (whether or not the woman was previously known to the physician, her age, race, marital status, number of living children, weeks of gestation, and financial resources) were systematically varied.   One vignette was randomly assigned to each obstetrician included in this study, each being asked a series of question designed to measure the degree to which he or she would become personally involved in the care of this patient (as opposed to referring her elsewhere for care). The most significant results of this investigation are shown in Figures 1 and 2. The woman's financial resources and her age were the two most important predictors of "involvement." Obstetricians were least likely to become involved in the care of women described as having "no money" or "on medicaid" (a federally supported medical insurance program tied to income) and in the care of very young women. Furthermore, attributed patient characteristics account for a substantially higher proportion of variation in "involvement" with the vignette patient (19%) than do the physicians' own attitudes or practice characteristics (3%).

Conclusion

Few health professionals oppose abortion under all circumstances; however, the legalization of elective abortion has placed many physicians and other potential providers of abortion services in a situation of profound conflict between opposing sets of personal and professional values. Even a cursory review of the available literature on providers' responses to abortion should dispel the idea that their attitudes and behavior are a simple function of religious beliefs. Although the analyses presented in this chapter have focused more on the consequences of attitudes for behavior than on the sources of these attitudes, it is clear that the latter stem from a complex mixture of professional and moral, as well as religious, scruples. A rather surprising finding of the Maryland study was that age of the obstetrician was a relatively unimportant influence on abortion practice, suggesting that conservatism with respect to abortion is not simply a function of adherence to traditional ways of thinking but may persist in future cohorts of medical and other health professionals.

Any set of arrangements for the provision of abortion services is potentially highly vulnerable to the "conservative" or "liberal" attitudes of the established medical profession. The relative impact of these attitudes on actual provision of services depends, I suggest, on at least two factors: 1) the degree to which abortion acquires or is awarded legitimacy as an essential aspect of professional obstetrical practice; and 2) the degree to which structural arrangements for the provision of abortion services gives to the physician a primary gate-keeping role. The fact that the 1973 Supreme Court decision legalizing abortion in the United States made no stipulation as to where abortions should be performed and imposed no conditions on abortion, other than agreement be-

FIGURE 1

INFLUENCE OF ABORTION PATIENT'S FINANCIAL RESOURCES ON
LEVEL OF PRIVATE OBSTETRICIAN'S INVOLVEMENT IN PATIENT CARE (N=238)

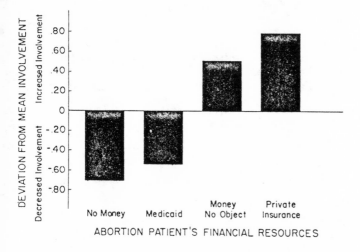

ABORTION PATIENT'S FINANCIAL RESOURCES

FIGURE 2

INFLUENCE OF ABORTION PATIENT'S AGE ON LEVEL OF PRIVATE
OBSTETRICIAN'S INVOLVEMENT IN PATIENT CARE (N=238)

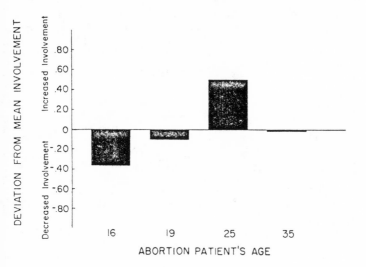

ABORTION PATIENT'S AGE

tween the woman and her physician, is probably a major reason for the relatively high abortion rates in the United States,
as compared with Canada or the United Kingdom--it is not
that U. S. physicians are more "liberal," but the wording of
the decision has made it easier to set up abortion services
outside of the traditional health-care system.

* * *

Preparation of this chapter was partially supported by Grant
No. RO1-09269 from the National Institute of Child Health
and Development, U. S. Department of Health and Human Resources.

Notes

1. The methodology of this study is described in detail in
   the following publication: Nathanson, C. A. and Becker
   M. H. , "The Influence of Physicians' Attitudes on
   Abortion Performance, Patient Management and Professional Fees." Family Planning Perspectives, 1977,
   9: 158-163; and Nathanson, C. A. and Becker, M. H. ,
   "Obstetricians' Attitudes and Hospital Abortion Services." Family Planning Perspectives 1980, 12: 26-
   32.
2. Further methodological details may be obtained directly
   from the author.
3. More detailed analyses of these data show: 1) that the
   interaction effects between climate and attitudes implied by the percentages shown in Tables 4 and 5 are
   highly significant; 2) that the effect of climate/attitude
   interaction on abortion practice is independent of obstetricians' ages or religious preferences.

References

Cartwright, Ann, and Waite, Marjorie. "General Practitioners
and Abortion." Journal of the Royal College of General
Practitioners, Supplement No. 1. 1972, 22: 1-24.

Committee on the Operation of the Abortion Law (COAL). Report of the Committee. Canada: Minister of Supply and
Services, 1977, p. 127.

Farmer, Colin. "Decision-Making in Therapeutic Abortion."

In Experience with Abortion, Gordon Horobin, ed. London: Cambridge University Press, 1973, pp. 333-357.

Joffe, Carole. "Abortion Work: Strains, Coping Strategies, Policy Implications." Social Work, 1979, 24: 485-490.

_____. "What Abortion Counselors Want from Their Clients." Social Problems, 1978, 26: 112-121.

Kirchner, Corinne, and Colombotos, John. "The Abortion Issue--Religious and Political Correlates of Physicians' Attitudes." Paper presented at the annual meeting of the American Sociological Association, New York, August, 1973.

Lerner, Raymond C.; Arnold, Charles, B.; and Wassertheil, Sylvia. "New York's Obstetricians Surveyed on Abortion." Family Planning Perspectives, 1971, 3: 56.

Macintyre, Sally. Single and Pregnant. New York: Prodist, 1977, p. 142.

Miller, Joanne. "Hospital Response to the Legalization of Abortion in New York State: An Analysis of Program Innovation." Journal of Health and Social Behavior, 1979, 20: 363-375.

Nathanson, Constance A., and Becker, Marshall H. "The Influence of Physicians' Attitudes on Abortion Performance, Patient Management and Professional Fees." Family Planning Perspectives, 1977, 9: 158-163.

_____. "Obstetricians' Attitudes and Hospital Abortion Services." Family Planning Perspectives, 1980, 12: 26-32.

_____. "Physician Behavior As a Determinant of Utilization Patterns: The Case of Abortion." American Journal of Public Health, 1978, 68: 1104-1114.

Pratt, Gail L.; Koslowsky, Meni; Wintrob, Ronald M. "Connecticut Physicians' Attitudes Toward Abortion." American Journal of Public Health, 1976, 66: 288-290.

Rosen, R. A. Hudson; Werley, H. H.; Ager, J. W.; and Shea, F. P. "Health Professionals' Attitudes Toward Abortion." Public Opinion Quarterly, 1974, 38: 159-173.

Seims, Sara. "Abortion Availability in the United States." Family Planning Perspectives, 1980, 12: 88-101.

Tietze, Christopher. Induced Abortion: 1979. New York: The Population Council, 1979, p. 7.

PART IV:

COUNSELING PROBLEM PREGNANCY

DOES COUNSELING REALLY HELP ABORTION PATIENTS?

By Mark Rutledge

Introduction

The state of the art of problem-pregnancy counseling is con-
spicuously lacking in controlled and methodologically rigorous
studies designed to answer the crucial question: Does counseling really help women who seek abortions? Other kinds
of reports abound. There are descriptive reports of pregnancy counseling programs (McCarthy & Brown, 1974; Canfield,
1974). There are also articles advocating a need for pre-
abortion counseling (West & Walsh, 1974). There are studies
of counseling effects on limited behavioral indices (Dauber,
et al. , 1972). Studies have also been done to show that counseling achieves therapeutic and personal growth effects (Friedman, 1974) and to demonstrate theological-moral perspectives
on pastoral counseling in situations of unwanted pregnancy
(Carmen & Moody, 1973). However, none of these reports,
which are representative of the literature, measured the effects of counseling on any particular personality dimension of
women who seek abortions.

Further, a survey of programs presented at a recent
Annual Meeting of the National Association of Abortion Facilities indicated that no abortion clinics reported experimental
studies of counseling effects (McNeely, 1976). Thus, the
omission in the literature of studies of counseling effects on
personality variables is serious because it is precisely those
factors which have been shown to be related to how women
respond to the abortion experience itself (Sachdev, 1975).

The author was the director of a controlled study conducted during 1977-1978 at a student health service at a large
midwestern university in the United States. The study was
designed to find out if counseling contributed, for women who

had undergone abortions, to decreased anxiety, to an increase in a sense of personal control over their own lives, and to a more positive self-concept.

Method

SAMPLE DESCRIPTION

Fifty-three women, who had received positive pregnancy tests and had requested referral to an abortion clinic, comprised the sample. Their participation was voluntary. They ranged in age from 16 to 30 with most clustering in the 18-to-22-year-old group. The mean age was 20. 6. In terms of religious preference, 22 women (41. 5%) were Protestant, 16 (30. 2%) were Catholic, and 3 (5. 7%) were Jewish, with 8 (16. 1%) reporting no religious affiliation. At intake, 44 women (88%) indicated that they had given some prior thought to what they would do if they became pregnant, and of these 31 (93. 9%) indicated that they had already been considering an abortion if pregnancy occurred.

SAMPLE SELECTION

Following experimentally controlled design, the 53 women were divided into four groups as follows: 1) 14 women were assigned randomly for brief counseling by the author; 2) 14 women were assigned randomly for extended counseling by the author; 3) 14 were assigned randomly to a female co-counselor for brief counseling; and 4) 11 were assigned randomly to the same female co-counselor for extended counseling.

TREATMENT CONDITIONS

Brief counseling was an attempt to approximate control conditions, and was defined as the minimum amount of counseling deemed necessary to help women make responsible decisions regarding their pregnancies. This was operationally defined as a limited cluster of items on Structured Counseling Interview Guides (SCIGs), which were designed for this study. Extended counseling was perceived as experimental conditions and was designed to encourage discussion of feelings, experiences, attitudes, and life events so that further exploration of self on the part of the client was facilitated. This was defined operationally as all items on the SCIGs. *

---

*Copies of these guides may be obtained by writing the author at 1801 Las Lomas NE, Albuquerque, NM 87106.

INSTRUMENTATION

We were looking for changes on three personality traits of dimensions: 1) anxiety, 2) locus of control, and 3) self-concept. We expected that counseling might result in less anxiety, a greater sense of personal control over life events (internal locus of control), and a more positive self-concept. In order to measure changes in these traits, three paper-and-pencil tests were selected: 1) the Affect Adjective Check List (AACL) (Zackerman, 1960) was used to measure anxiety; 2) the Internal-External Scale (I-E) (Levenson, 1974) was used to measure the degree to which clients believed they exercised control over their own lives, as opposed to the degree to which they perceived that their destinies were determined by chance or by other people; and 3) the Tennessee Self-Concept Scale (TSCS) Fitts, 1965) was used to measure self-concept. All three measures were administered before and after the counseling.

PROCEDURES

The women in the sample were seen four times during the course of the study.

(1) Upon entry to the health service to request a pregnancy test, they were asked to complete an intake questionnaire, which included the Affect Adjective Check List (AACL) as one of the items.

(2) When they returned the following day to obtain their pregnancy test results, they were asked to volunteer to participate in the study, by signing a consent form, and to complete two pre-tests, the Internal-External Scale (I-E) and the Tennessee Self-Concept Scale (TSCS). Women were then randomly assigned to either the male or the female counselor, who gave them their pregnancy test results and then randomly assigned those who requested abortion referral to either brief or extended counseling. At the conclusion of counseling they were asked to complete a second administration of the AACL.

(3) Two to four weeks following their abortions they were again counseled, according to their previous assignment to treatment conditions. At the conclusion of this counseling they were again asked to complete the AACL.

(4) Three to five weeks following the second counseling treatment, they returned to take the I-E and the TSCS post-test and complete a follow-up questionnaire.

ANALYSES OF THE DATA

Statistical analyses were conducted to assess 1) the significance of differences between groups on their pre- and post-test scores; 2) the differences within treatment groups on their pre- and post-test scores; 3) the differences between groups counseled by the male as compared to the female counselor; and 4) differences between groups on selected self-report items on the SCIGs. In order to determine the statistical significance of differences, t tests and Chi-square tests were conducted. All hypotheses were tested at p<.05 level of significance.

In addition, frequencies and percentages were reported for specific items on the SCIGs and the two questionnaires-- an intake and a follow-up. This method provided a great deal of descriptive information regarding the women's attitudes and perceptions.

Study Results

A major conclusion of the study was that women who received extended counseling did in fact show significant increases, pre- to post-test, in internal locus of control and in positive self-concept. On the other hand, women in the brief counseling groups did not show similar changes.

Brief counseling resulted in some changes in a positive direction, but not at statistically significant levels with regard to internal locus of control and self-concept. It was anticipated that some differences might occur within the "control" groups, because brief counseling was, in fact, perceived as a treatment. At the same time, it was expected that more differences would occur in the "experimental" groups, because extended counseling was designed to have a greater presumed effect. That counseling can be demonstrated to make such a significant difference to women should be valuable information for pregnancy and abortion counselors.

ABORTION EFFECT

Women in both the "experimental" and "control" groups showed significant decreases in anxiety at almost equal levels. Thus, one could not conclude that these observed decreases in anxiety following abortions are attributable to the effects of counseling. Rather, as suspected, they may be attributable simply to the effects of having had an abortion.

EFFECT ON NEGATIVE SEQUELAE

Another positive counseling outcome was observed with regard to short-term adverse sequelae to abortion. On the follow-up questionnaire women were asked whether or not they felt that their abortion experience had left them with any negative after-effects. Forty-one women (78.8%) reported that it had not, while 11 (21.2%) said that it had. But of those 11 women who reported negative after-effects, 81.8 percent were in the brief-counseling group while only 18.2 percent were in the extended-counseling group. This item approached statistical significance (P<.06). Thus, there was some support, though not statistically significant, that extended counseling was more effective in reducing perceived short-term negative sequelae to abortion than was brief counseling.

COUNSELING HELPFULNESS

In addition to "experimental" data supporting the helpfulness of counseling, descriptive data pointed to the same conclusion. On the follow-up questionnaire women were asked if the counseling had been helpful to them. Forty-six women (86.8%) reported that it had been helpful, while only seven (13.2%) said that it had not. A positive response rate to a similar question on the second SCIG was also noted, where 92 percent of the women indicated that such counseling had been helpful.

BIRTH CONTROL PROCESSES

In a tangential but important aspect of the study, some evidence was found to support Lindemann (1974) in the notion that abortion acts as a positive driving force, or transition, regarding on whom the women rely for birth-control information. Significant changes in ratings were evident, from pre- to post-test, indicating that women did in fact move through this process, from relying on self and peers to relying on professionals for contraceptive information. However, it could not be determined whether it was the abortion or the counseling that resulted in this change.

WOMEN/MEN COUNSELORS

Are women more effective than men as pregnancy counselors? No support for the hypothesis was found. There were no significant differences between those in either the extended- or brief-counseling groups assigned to a female counselor and

those assigned to a male counselor, except on one sub-scale
of the I-E, and that for the extended-counseling group only.
It was interesting to compare these results with women's self-
reported responses on the SCIGs as to perceived sex preference for counselor.   For example, women were asked, at the
conclusion of treatment, whether they would have preferred
a male or a female counselor.   Only 26. 5 percent reported
that they preferred a female, and all of these had in fact
been counseled by the female counselor.   It is suspected that
social stereotypes may have been operating in their responses.

COUNSELING EFFECTIVENESS

What kind of counseling makes a difference?   The use of the
SCIG had both advantages and disadvantages.   On the one hand,
it made it possible operationally to define counseling treatment procedures in great detail, which in turn might make
replication easier.   On the other hand, it is impossible to
know precisely which components of counseling contributed
to the differences.   All that can be concluded is that some
items on the SCIGs, or all items taken together, as guides
to the total counseling process, were the factors contributing
to the positive outcomes observed.   Finally, the use of the
SCIGs hopefully minimized idiosyncratic differences between
counselor approaches, which may add credibility to the overall study design.

DESCRIPTIVE FINDINGS

Another advantage of using the SCIGs was their usefulness in
collecting a great deal of descriptive data.   In the following
general areas, the findings of the descriptive aspect of the
study confirm selected findings reported in the existing literature but do not confirm others.

(1) Regarding the effects of abortion on women, this
study found that more than 86 percent of the subjects rated
their overall adjustment to be very good or good, while approximately 12 percent rated it fair.   This finding is contrary to reports of high rates of negative reactions, such as
the study by Zimmerman (1976) which indicated that one half
of the women having abortions report negative reactions.

The present study found that only 21. 2 percent reported
any negative effects following abortion.   However, it confirms
other reports finding that abortion can result in positive reactions, such as the conclusion by Monsour and Stewart (1972)

that many women experience an increase in positive views of themselves.   For example, 58. 8 percent of the women in this study responded that their experiences left them with positive effects, and 22 women out of 53 (42%) said that their self-perception had changed for the better.   This study's finding that 70 percent of the women felt relief following abortion is consistent with the report by Meikle (1973) that after abortion women experience a disappearance of psychological symptoms such as stress and anxiety.   It should be noted when considering such findings, however, that the abortion clinics to which this study referred women had been carefully selected to insure a high quality of health care.   It is impossible therefore, to determine if the same findings would result in a population receiving care in clinics that were, not so carefully screened for referral.

(2) Regarding women's use of contraceptives prior to pregnancy, this study does not support the findings of previous studies (Bracken, 1972; Ford, 1972; Kane & Lachenbruch, 1973) that a majority of women had not used birth control preceding the time they became pregnant.   For example, 71. 7 percent of our sample indicated that they had been using some form of contraceptive method prior to the time they became pregnant.

(3) There was some support for the findings of Kay (1975) that women receiving counseling used contraceptives with significantly higher frequency after their abortions than women not receiving counseling.   On the follow-up questionnaire 77. 4 percent of the study women indicated that they had made decisions to change previous methods of contraception, and 84. 9 percent indicated that their contraceptive behavior had changed since becoming pregnant.   Although no significant differences were found on these items between the control and experimental groups, both groups did receive counseling regarding birth-control information and use.

(4) These results did not confirm the findings by Sachdev (1975) that abortions had an adverse effect on the relationships of women with their male partners.   For example, 54. 7 percent of the sample women reported that their experience had strengthened relations with their male partner and 26. 4 percent indicated that there had been no change.   Only 13. 2 percent indicated that pregnancy and abortion had ended the relationship, and 5. 7 percent indicated that they had weakened it.   Most of our subjects indicated that their relationships with their male partners were important factors in overall adjustment to the abortion experience.

(5) Finally, there was some evidence to support the conclusion of Donovan, et al. (1973) that it is important for women to make their own decisions regarding pregnancy. Specifically, following their abortions, all of the women indicated that decision to abort was definitely the best thing they could have done under the circumstances. Further, 95.8 percent of the women reported that making the decision to abort was either "not difficult" or "mildly difficult," which is consistent with the finding by Shalaby (1975) that women quickly reach decisions to have abortions and generally without a great deal of difficulty.

Recommendations for Counseling Practice

These findings and clinical experience during the investigation form the basis for the following observations and recommendations for the practice of counseling women with unwanted pregnancies.

(1) Birth-control counseling that deals only with information about contraceptive methods and their availability will not be effective in preventing repeat incidents of problem pregnancies. Fifteen percent of our sample women had been pregnant at least once before. Counselors need to have some grounding in decision-making and contraceptive risk-taking theory, as well as in the psychological development of women, to focus the root issues involved in promoting the effective and consistent use of contraceptives.

(2) Counselors can help clients to extend the decision-making, coping, and problem-solving skills they employ in dealing with a problem pregnancy to other areas of their lives. For example, many of the women in this study made comments that indicated that having to make decisions and cope in this crisis situation helped them learn how to take personal charge of their lives in a larger sense.

(3) Highly emotionally charged issues relating to values, religious training and belief, and politically controversial aspects of abortion still abound in our society. Counselors need to be aware of their own views on these matters and to avoid imposing on clients negative and judgmental attitudes that they themselves may have, at a time when maximum support is needed. Doctors and nurses particularly need to be aware of this.

(4) It should be made clear to women, from the very

outset of counseling, that they do not need to demonstrate to the counselor that they "deserve" an abortion or must somehow "prove" its necessity in order to justify a referral. For this reason, it is important to get the referral information on the table immediately, to assure the client of help in implementing whatever decision she makes, and to establish the counselor as a nonjudgmental, concerned person. Thus the counselor should not coerce one alternative solution over others but, instead, should be ready to help women make their own decisions and assist in their implementation.

(5) Pregnancy counseling that is integrated into the total system of health-care delivery results in better service to clients than counseling that is incidental to that system. The fact that in this study counseling was offered by the student health service itself greatly facilitated the early establishment of helping relationships with our clients. For example, the counselor was the first person to present the results of pregnancy testing. This allowed for immediate establishment of a counseling relationship at a time of maximum anxiety, so that the client was not shuffled back and forth unnecessarily between personnel within the agency or among agencies, as is often the case. Thus, health-care services that do not function in such a holistic way may sacrifice the needs of women to the needs of the system.

(6) Counselors should also anticipate that many women will exhibit ambivalence. As previously noted, "mixed feelings" about having an abortion was a normal condition for many women. Helping them to be aware of any ambivalence they have may contribute to better decision-making and greater self-understanding, as well as to reduced incidents of negative reactions to abortion.

(7) Finally, counselors can learn much from the Lindemann notion (1974) of the birth-control process. In this context, abortion is a special case of growth and transition in which personal awareness is raised, self-concept is changed, sexual activity is disclosed, and contact is made with a professional. Women are more likely to be at a point of readiness to listen to what a counselor may have to offer and they may acquire experience and knowledge as they develop, going through the natural stages of relying on self, peers, and finally professionals for birth-control information. Counselors are privileged to be able to intervene at a critical point in this process, and if they do so wisely a crisis may be turned into a valuable opportunity.

Recommendations for Further Research

In view of the findings of this study, a number of recommendations for further research are offered.

(1) This study should be replicated with another sample of women requesting abortion, to enable generalizing beyond a population of university women. The effects of counseling on women at other institutions of higher education, as well as on those in the general population who seek medical care at abortion clinics, should be investigated.

(2) Future research should attempt to assess counseling effects on other psychological variables which have been shown to be related to women's responses to abortion, such as ambivalence, relationship dynamics with their male partners, and moral values.

(3) Attention should be given to those women who experience negative reactions to their abortion experience in order to learn more about the factors affecting negative responses to abortion, as well as appropriate counseling interventions in those cases.

(4) Further research should be conducted to assess the effects of counseling on attitudes and behaviors related to use of contraceptives. This is particularly relevant to the problem of repeat abortions. In this regard, the developmental theory of Lindemann (1974) warrants further investigation, as does that of Luker, the contraceptive risk-taking theory about decision-making Taking Chances: Abortion and the Decision Not to Contracept. Berkeley: University of California Press, 1975).

Conclusions

Under "controlled" study conditions, counseling can be demonstrated to result in outcomes of greater internal locus on control and positive self-concept of women seeking abortion. Counseling is also helpful in reducing perceived short-term negative sequelae to abortion, and women report that they personally find counseling helpful. Thus, the data of this study substantiate a positive evaluation of abortion counseling for women in this study.

On two counts, the study found evidence contrary to the conventional wisdom in our society. (1) It is traditionally

assumed that women who have abortions will automatically experience adverse reactions, such as guilt, anxiety, depression, and poor self-concept. This study found the opposite.
(2) In our society conventional wisdom holds the seemingly
paradoxical view that women who decide to have abortions do
so casually, with little thought or responsible reflection on
their actions. Again, just the opposite was found.

The author was impressed throughout the study with
reports by women about the excellent health care they received at the clinics to which they were referred, and the
positive influence they felt this had on the whole experience.
The present social and legal context in this country supports
the capabilities to make these kinds of referrals. Counselors
should consider the implications of current legislative efforts
to criminalize abortion once again. Based on this study it is
felt that if women were forced to seek abortions in a society
that labeled them criminals, incidents of negative sequelae
and psychological trauma would rise sharply, in spite of the
most efficient counseling.

References

Bracken, M. "Contraceptive Practice Among New York Abortion Patients." American Journal of Obstetrics and Gynecology, 1972, 114: 967-977.

Canfield, E. "Pregnancy and Birth Control Counseling."
Journal of Social Issues, 1974, 30 (1): 87-96.

Carmen, A., and Moody, H. Abortion Counseling and Social
Change. Valley Forge: Judson Press, 1973.

Dauber, B.; Zalar, M.; and Goldstein, P. "Abortion Counseling and Behavioral Change." Family Planning Perspectives, 1972, 4(2): 23-27.

Donovan, C.; Greenspan, R.; and Mittleman, F. "The Decision-Making Process and the Outcome of Therapeutic
Abortion." American Journal of Psychiatry, 1974, 131:
1332-1337.

Fitts, W. Manual: Tennessee Self-Concept Scale. Nashville:
Counselor Recordings and Tests, 1965.

Friedman, C. "Making Abortion Consultation Therapeutic."
American Journal of Psychiatry, 1973, 130(11): 1257-1261.

Kane, F. , and Lachenbruch, P. "Adolescent Pregnancy: A Study of Aborters and Non-Aborters." American Journal of Orthopsychiatry, 1973, 43(5): 796-803.

Kay, B. "An Evaluation of Long Range Aspects of Abortion Services in Chicago, Illinois: An Interdisciplinary Approach." Doctoral dissertation, Northwestern University, 1975. Dissertation Abstracts International, 1976, 36: 4807A-4808A. (University Microfilms No. 75-29, 673)

Levenson, H. "Activism and Powerful Others: Distinctions Within the Concept of Internal-External Control." Journal of Personality Assessment, 1974, 38: 377-383.

Lindemann, C. Birth Control and Unmarried Young Women. New York: Springer Publishing, 1974.

Luker, K. Taking Chances: Abortion and the Decision Not to Contracept. Berkeley: University of California Press, 1975.

McCarthy, B. and Brown, P. "Counseling College Women with Unwanted Pregnancies." Journal of College Student Personnel, 1974, 15: 442-446.

McNeely, J. Personal communication, November 15, 1976.

Meikle, S. "Therapeutic Abortion: A Prospective Study II." American Journal of Obstetrics and Gynecology, 1973, 115: 339-346.

Monsour, K. , and Stewart, B. "Abortion and Sexual Behavior in College Women." American Journal of Orthopsychiatry, 1973, 43(5): 804-824.

Sachdev, P. "Factors Relating to the Abortion Decision Among Premaritally Pregnant Females." Doctoral dissertation, University of Wisconsin at Madison, 1975. Dissertation Abstracts International, 1975, 36: 4027A-4028A. (University Microfilms No. 75-18, 194)

Shalaby, L. "How Women Feel About Abortion: Psychological, Attitudinal, and Physical Effects of Legal Abortion." Doctoral dissertation, University of Iowa, 1975. Dissertation Abstracts International, 1975, 36: 2035A. (University Microfilms No. 75-23, 083)

West, N. , and Walsh, M. "The Need for Pre-Abortion Coun-
    seling--Now More Than Ever." Nebraska Medical Journal,
    1974, 59: 34-36.

Zimmerman, M. "Passage Through Abortion: A Sociological
    Analysis." Doctoral dissertation, University of Minnesota,
    1976. Dissertation Abstracts International, 1977, 37: 7988A.

Zuckerman, M. "The Development of an Affect Adjective
    Check List for the Measurement of Anxiety." Journal of
    Consulting Psychology, 1960, 24: 457-462.

COUNSELING SINGLE ABORTION PATIENTS: A RESEARCH OVERVIEW AND PRACTICE IMPLICATIONS

by Paul Sachdev

When laws regarding access to safe and legal abortions were liberalized in some states in the late 1960s and were affirmed in 1973 as a constitutional right of women by the United States Supreme Court historic decisions in Roe vs. Wade and Doe vs. Bolton, there followed a rapid growth of medical abortion facilities. It also brought in its wake recognition by professionals that counseling, as a necessary adjunct to medical and legal services, plays a vital role in providing humane and dignified abortion services to women with problem pregnancies (Group for the Advancement of Psychiatry, 1969; American Public Health Association, 1970).

In Canada, following the amendment to the Criminal Code in August, 1969, the Department of Health and Welfare initiated a survey to assess the impact of legalized abortion on Canadian women, their fertility behavior, and family life. The report, _inter alia_, echoed the importance of pregnancy counseling as a means of ensuring women a "sympathetic handling of their problems" (National Health and Welfare, 1974, p. 25). Some went so far as to suggest that a medical practice that confines the parameters of its concerns to the female reproductive system represents an unsound and circumscribed abortion service and, more significantly, is not truly therapeutic (Whittington, 1960).

Despite its avowed emphasis, abortion counseling as a legitimate service area has been largely neglected. The relative lack of interest in counseling services has been due primarily to the fact that helping professions do not consider it an essential component because the woman requesting an abortion has pretty much made up her mind. Because physicians have traditionally viewed contraception and reproduction

236

as chiefly medical areas, they regard any information on this
subject as their unique responsibility. They have been slow
to recognize that these patients have emotional and psychological components that need to be dealt with by a counseling
and educational program. Also, they do not generally view
abortion counseling as a distinct entity requiring specialized
skills or training, and, therefore, believe that any member
of the medical team can render such advice and information.

Need for Abortion Counseling

There are women who may regard an abortion procedure as
a minor surgical interlude and thus may not find their decisions emotionally and morally stressful. Some women may
be irrevocably committed to seeking termination of pregnancy
the moment it is discovered and they may not experience personal dilemma. Some may have access to supportive milieu
to fill the need to discuss their decisions. Notwithstanding,
there is strong research evidence to indicate that, for a large
number of women, the decision to have an abortion presents
an acute emotional crisis and serious personal conflicts. Many
of these women live within a social network that is critically
deficient, which further restricts opportunities to share in
the decision-making and to seek objective, compassionate advice and support (Bacon, 1969; Fleck, 1970; Kerenyi, et al.,
1973; Martin, 1972; Niemela, et al., 1981; Osofsky & Osofsky,
1972; Sachdev, 1975; Ullman, 1972; Wallerstein, et al., 1972;
Young, et al., 1973). These studies observed that anywhere
between 48 and 95 percent* of the women in their samples
experienced moderate to considerable difficulty in making a
decision to seek pre-term termination. Theodore Lidz (1967)
believes that willful loss of the fetus constitutes a potential
major trauma because of its emotional significance for the
woman. Fleck (1970), too, considers abortion a special surgery not to be regarded merely as emptying the uterus, since
pregnancy involves the core of femininity, a woman's sexuality, her mothering capacities, and creativeness.

The need for active abortion counseling services for
young unmarried women is further demonstrated by the fact
that they account for the largest proportion among the abortion-
seekers in both the United States and Canada. In Canada, for

---

*The wide range in the findings is largely due to the discrepant
methods of evaluation and classification employed and the use of
mixed samples of married, ever-married, and single women.

instance, of all the abortions performed in 1981, about two thirds (65. 8%) occurred among unmarried women, with those under 20 constituting over one quarter (28. 3%) (Statistics Canada, 1981). The corresponding proportion for the single and ever-married women who sought an abortion in the United States in 1980 was about four fifths (79. 4%) with those under 20 constituting 29. 6 percent (Tietze, 1983).

Young single women are particularly vulnerable to intense emotional trauma upon unwanted pregnancy as they generally lack the needed emotional support and participation from the male partner involved in the pregnancy. Frequently, the pair-relationship terminates following pregnancy and abortion (Addleson, 1973; Greenglass, 1981; Hamilton, 1966; Lee, 1969, Mansour & Stewart, 1973; Martin, 1972; Smith, 1972). Studies have also shown that these women have little or no communication with their parents in the climacteric period, and most make their decisions without involving them (Fischman, 1977; Lee, 1969; Martin, 1972; Rosen, 1980; Smith, 1973). In a study involving 70 unmarried primigravids who underwent a first trimester abortion at a large hospital in metropolitan Toronto, Sachdev (1975) found that, of the sample women who confided in their male consorts, only one third received emotional or financial support from them; the rest of the males provided only perfunctory support or broke off the relationship. Parents were confided in the least--only 8. 6 percent--for sharing the pregnancy. Similarly, Bracken, et al. (1973) reported that one half of their 171 abortion patients, mostly single, found their male partners simply perfunctory in their support or completely unconcerned, and three fourths did not discuss the pregnancy with parents.

By contrast, married women seeking abortion usually have the benefit of a more stable relationship and the emotional support of spouse and family. Empirical evidence suggests that emotional support and assurance from significant others, especially the male partner or parents, greatly influence a woman's pre-abortion emotional status and psychological adjustments afterwards (Bracken, et al. , 1973; 1974; Greenglass, 1981; Sachdev, 1975). Open and honest communication between parents and adolescent women has also been shown to be a strong contributory factor in postponing sexual activity and in contraceptive-use effectiveness (Fox, 1979).

For many single women, the discovery of an unplanned pregnancy represents in itself a highly distressing experience because of social and psychological implications. The occurrence of an undesired pregnancy among married women does not present the same social penalties and emotional stress because of social acceptance and approval accorded the wedlock pregnancy. An undesired pregnancy can be especially overwhelming if it coincides with adolescence, a period characterized by sexual, physical, and emotional changes.

What Is Abortion Counseling?

Abortion counseling is a deliberate, planned activity involving diagnosis, interpretation, education, advice, and therapy. The abortion counselor uses the basic skills of the helping process with a specialized knowledge of the psychosocial determinants of sexual and contraceptive behavior, human reproduction, and the moral and ethical issues involved in abortion. The primary objective of counseling is to recognize and understand the nature of the woman's dilemma and help her reach the best decision possible by providing factual information. The counselor enables the woman to canvass each alternative with its attendant liabilities, keeping in view her psychosocial milieu and value system so that the choice made is deliberate, rational, and least undesirable. If an abortion is the choice of action, the counselor then diligently but assuringly unravels with her the basis of this decision. It is crucial that the woman be helped with her dilemma so that she can approach the abortion with the least doubts and anxiety. Feelings of ambivalence can be gauged by exploring her feelings about abortion itself and about the fetus. The possibility of fetal attachment can be expected if the woman shows positive feelings toward the man involved in the pregnancy and if the pregnancy was consciously or subconsciously desired to fulfill her underlying emotional and psychosocial needs.

The resolution of a woman's pre-abortion ambivalence is significant in light of research findings that indicate that adverse psychologic reactions of guilt and depression in the aftermath of abortion are highly likely to occur among those with unresolved feelings and negative emotions (Adler, 1975; Bracken, 1978; Osofsky & Osofsky, 1972). Younger women are more predisposed to these reactions than their older counterparts (Sachdev, 1975).

In fact, the resolution of the problem pregnancy is only a short-term goal of abortion counseling, which should also emphasize as its long-term objective the preventing of future undesired pregnancy and abortion. Given the heightened concern and health professionals' dismay and embarrassment over the burgeoning incidence of repeat abortions, particularly among young unmarried women,* contraceptive counseling constitutes another significant component in abortion services. The demand for an abortion generally represents a failure-- contraceptive, societal, or personal.

Several investigators have studied the contraceptive practice of aborting and premaritally pregnant women in North America and Europe. They are unanimous in observing that a large number of undesired pregnancies--from one third to as many as two thirds--result from failure to use regularly, or at all, any form of contraception, by either partner, rather than from contraceptive failure (Andolsek, 1974; Anderson, & Milsom, 1982; Barnes, et al. , 1971; Beard, et al. , 1974; Bawman, 1971; David, 1971; Diamond, et al. , 1973; Grauer, 1972; Greenglass, 1981; Herold & Goodwin, 1980; Hatcher, et al. , 1981; Kane, et al. , 1973; Lipper, et al. , 1973; Martin, 1972; Osofsky & Osofsky, 1972; Robins, 1976; Zelnik & Kanter, 1978). Younger and less educated women are found to be far less receptive to contraception (Bracken, et al. , 1972; Daily & Nicholas, 1972; Kantner & Zelnik, 1973; Mansour & Stewart, 1973; Poole, 1976; Russell & Schild, 1976; Nadelson, 1974; Siedlecky, 1982).

The most common reasons cited by single women for irregular or non-contraception use are "having a magical immunity against pregnancy"; that contraceptives are unromantic, calculated, and therefore unnatural; that their use signals advance preparedness, induces embarrassment and emotional ambivalence, and carries self-reputational implications. In a few cases, pregnancy results from a conscious or subconscious desire for impregnation and motherhood or genuine contraceptive failure or from society's structural barriers against availability of contraceptive means. It should be noted that a lack of knowledge about or access to birth-control methods, in most cases, is not related to the absence or minimal use of contraception. Research studies consistently report that anywhere from 75 to 94 percent of the women studied claimed familiarity with the modern methods of conception control, their use and source (Dauber, et al. , 1972; DeAmi-

---

*See, for instance, Charlene Berger, et al. , "Repeaters: Different or Unlucky?" in Abortion: Readings and Research, Paul Sachdev, ed. (Toronto: Butterworths, 1981), pp. 159-170; and Christopher Tietze, "Repeat Abortion" in this volume.

cis, et al. , 1981; Goldsmith, 1972; Mansour & Stewart, 1973;
Miller, et al. , 1977; Mallory, et al. , 1972; Nadelson, 1974;
Nadelson, et al. , 1980; Ryan & Sweeney, 1980; Sachdev, 1975;
Sullivan & Watt, 1975).   More recently, Rogel and Zuehlke
(1982) reviewed studies involving antecedent factors that influence adolescent contraceptive behavior and concluded that
"the problem is clearly more complicated than simply lack
of information" (p. 197).

      Considerable evidence also exists in the literature that
effective utilization of contraceptive methods depends to a
large degree on human, interpersonal, psychological, and
motivational factors (Anderson, et al. , 1978; Bogue, 1965;
Jorgensen, et al. , 1980; Rader, et al. , 1978; Reiss, et al. ,
1975; Whelpton & Kiser, 1954).   Studies also suggest that a
woman's commitment to contraception is greatly influenced by
her awareness of the need for fertility control and consequences of unprotected sex, norms disapproving out-of-wedlock
pregnancy in her referent groups, her ability to plan and regulate sexual activity, stable sexual relationship, open communication on sexual and contraceptive matters with her sex
partner, and mutual planning (Furstenberg, 1976; Luker, 1975;
Pick, 1980; Rainwater, 1960; Sachdev, 1981; Wallston, et al. ,
1976).

      Thus, obtaining and successfully using a contraceptive
method involves a complex set of variables and a counselor
should thoroughly evaluate the nature of relationship of the
woman with her sex partner, her attitudes toward contraception, the circumstances under which coital activity takes place,
and the psychosocial factors affecting her contraceptive practice.   Family planning is more than writing a prescription;
it involves discussion of various methods of conception control and assisting the woman to choose one best suited to her
age, religious scruples, sexual dossier, her ability to implement contraceptive responsibility, and her current sexual activity.

      For a woman whose sex life is less stable and un-
predictable, female-oriented contraceptive methods may be
appropriate.   However, in dealing with a couple in stable relationship it is important that consideration be given to the
cultural and emotional needs of both partners in helping them
make their contraceptive choice.   The method recommended
should offer the user satisfaction and confidence, factors identified as conducive to consistent and effective contraception
(Bachmann, 1981; DeAmicis, et al. , 1981; Niemela, et al. ,

1981). It may be emphasized that during assessment of the factors that underlie the woman's sexual and contraceptive behavior, the counselor should ascertain that there is agreement with the client in their mutual perception of the locus of responsibility for the undesired pregnancy. The woman, for instance, may impute societal forces for her failure to contracept, while the counselor may view the woman's carelessness, deliberateness, ignorance, and poor motivation as the source of personal responsibility for the act. The counselor may, therefore, encourage her toward greater self-control and self-concept and increased motivation. Clearly, counseling efforts based on divergent perceptions of responsibility will only prove to be misdirected and ineffectual (Gibb & Millard, 1982.)

Working with the Male Partner

As has been noted, effective contraception is a deliberate and cooperative act involving mutual planning and support. If a woman's partner is still in the picture, he should be involved in the decision-making process from the beginning. By encouraging his involvement, the counselor is emphasizing that reproductive responsibility is a mutual as coital activity. The counselor can also use this opportunity to effect a constructive and more meaningful relationship between the couple, which is crucial for emotional support for the woman during this potentially stressful period. This orientation is consistent with the emerging relationship-centered focus of family planning services (Figley & Scroggins, 1978). With the male's participation, the counselor is better able to assess the dyadic commitment, knowledge of which is useful for a more realistic plan of contraception. The male's active involvement and encouragement is particularly important if the couple chooses female-oriented contraception, a strong possibility in most cases. Studies show that most males do not take effective precautions against pregnancy and view contraception as the female responsibility (Finkel & Finkel, 1978). Studies have also shown that the male partner's support and encouragement significantly contribute to the initiation and maintenance of contraception among young females (Apkom, et al., 1976; Cvetkovich & Grote, 1982; Herold & Goodwin, 1980; Niemela, et al., 1981). Apkom, et al. (1976), for example, found in a family planning clinic that about three quarters (77%) of the single-women patients had the support of their boyfriends in regularly seeking contraceptive services. Rosen (1982) found in his sample of pregnant adolescents that the initiation of contraception was due mainly to the male partner's encouragement.

The male's involvement in counseling also serves the useful purpose of providing an opportunity for him to gain an appreciation of the emotional stress that a woman experiences. There is disagreement among investigators as to the male partner's reaction to the woman's experience with an abortion. A majority of women in Sachdev's study (1975) reported that their boyfriends considered abortion to be a woman's concern and were, therefore, indifferent to their experiences. However, Wade (1977), who has counseled many male partners of women who underwent abortions, observed that they usually feel upset and worried about the woman's situation and resent being excluded from the actual decision. It seems that the male consort's reactions depend, in large part, upon the nature of the dyadic relationship.

Research studies consistently report that for unmarried women the most common contraceptive methods employed are the condom and withdrawal, which puts the onus on the male to prevent pregnancy (Bauman, 1971; Bracken, et al., 1972; Goldsmith, et al., 1972; Hatcher, et al., 1981; Lambert, 1971; Meikle, 1975; Sachdev, 1975; Zelnik & Kantner, 1978). In such situations, a woman's vulnerability to pregnancy is linked to her ability to persuade the man to use protective devices and to his responsiveness to her persuasion, the process known as "negotiating" or "bargaining" (Furstenberg, 1971, p. 199). Thus, the counselor may teach the client assertiveness as a valuable social skill to enable her to exert a greater influence in sexual and contraceptive decisions. Fox (1977) found that women with a feminist orientation are more successful in obtaining compliance from their sex partners in contraceptive use than more conventional women. Jorgensen, et al. (1980) also observed in their sample of 150 clinic patients aged 12 to 17, that the female's active involvement in sexual decisions was directly related to the regularity of contraceptive use.

Since the act of contraception is intimately linked with sexuality, it is imperative that a counselor explore the woman's attitude toward sexuality, her sexual behavior, and how she views her responsibility. There are a variety of non-sexual needs that propel women toward sexual activity in addition to physical drive to release sexual tension or libidinal energy. These include a need to love and be loved, to seek emotional security, and to gain popularity and acceptance by peers. Some adolescent women may resort to sexual activity as an expression of rebelliousness and anger against parents or society. Some also use unprotected sex as a defense against loneliness and to fill a void by means of a baby seen as offering a love object and a strengthened sense of identity (Cobliner, et al. , 1973; Freeman, 1977; Mudd, et al. , 1978; Nadelson, et al. , 1980; Ryan & Sweeney, 1980; Russel & Schild, 1976). Such motives are usually masked as a lack of purposefulness and/or conscious acts of denial of consequences or impersonal acts of fate. The counselor needs the skill and training to understand the woman's underlying motives of sexual and reproductive behavior. Unless a woman's reproductive plans are uncovered and her defenses removed at the outset, her choice of action may further mask her pattern of behaviors.

There is compelling research evidence that women who have a positive attitude toward themselves and accept their sexuality and personal responsibility are more likely to prepare themselves contraceptively (Brandt, et al. , 1978; Cvetkovich, et al. , 1975; Dembo & Lundell, 1979; Fisher, 1978; Goldsmith, et al. , 1972; Lindemann, 1974; Miller, 1976; Nadelson, 1974; Notman, 1975). It stands to reason that women who view their sexual behavior as unacceptable are likely to feel guilty about it, since deliberate solicitation of contraceptive methods implies admission of their being sexually active. Such denial serves to prevent only contraception, not sex. Only by discussing with the woman the reasons and responsibility for her sexual behavior and helping her find more constructive ways of self-expression and dealing with interpersonal relationship can a counselor help the woman become sexually responsible and reproductively discriminating.

The service providers' positive attitude of acceptance of the unmarried woman and her behavior pattern is crucial in fostering her receptivity to contraceptive advice. In Sachdev's study (1975), it was found that many sample women resented the mechanical, perfunctory, and impersonal way in which the health-care professionals in some hospitals dispense contraceptive advice and supplies.

Abortion counseling does not end with the resolution of the pregnancy dilemma but continues even after a woman has made a decisive choice of carrying the pregnancy to term or ending it via abortion. In the former case, the counselor may refer the woman to a family and child welfare agency that provides follow-up and management of such cases with support, assistance, and guidance throughout the gestation period and following parturition. If the woman chooses the abortion option, it is vitally important that the counselor discuss the mechanics of the surgical procedure, its physical,

emotional, and sexual after-effects, the post-operative precautions, and the hospital protocols. Questions such as those
regarding physical pain and sterility should be fully discussed
prior to the procedure. It has been noted by some investigators that even the determined woman experiences nagging
doubts and eerie feelings regarding the abortion surgery, and
these essentially emanate from misinformation or a complete
absence of information about the technique (Kimball, 1970;
Osofsky & Osofsky, 1972). Sachdev (1975) found in his study
that the most common concern of the women related to the
possible damage to the reproductive system. This was reported by almost two thirds (62.5%) of the study women. Physical pain constituted another significant concern for more
than one third of the women. The significance of dealing with
surgery-related fears becomes abundantly clear when one considers the impersonal nature of the hospital environment and
the frequently not-very-supportive attitude of the health-care
personnel toward the premaritally pregnant women. Given
such circumstances, at times these women feel too threatened
to bring up their doubts with the health-care staff.

Post-Abortion Counseling

If the knowledge of what happens during abortion surgery is
important, it is equally important to know what to expect psychologically and emotionally following the surgery. The effect of an abortion on a woman's psychological health has
been the subject of intense controversy among professionals.
The research findings range from the suggestion that psychiatric complications are almost always the outcome of therapeutic abortions to their virtual absence (Anderson, 1966;
Dunbar, 1967; Malmfors, 1966; Smith, 1973; Todd, 1972;
Whittington, 1960; Walter, 1970). However, there is a growing consensus that while marked psychiatric disturbances are
very rare, many women do experience adverse psychological
sequelae, although these reactions are mild and limited (Greenglass, 1981; Sachdev, 1975; Zimmerman, 1981). This fact
is significant for those counselors who may not see the need
for post-abortal counseling. To be sure, follow-up counseling may not be required by some women, either because they
do not suffer from psychological reactions or because they
have a supportive psychosocial milieu. But for those women
having difficulty in assimilating their pregnancy and abortion
experience, post-abortion counseling can be of benefit, and
this group should be carefully identified and targeted for intervention. Research studies suggest that those women who
approach abortion with ambivalence, lack psychological strength

and a supportive system, identify with their pregnancy, have an unfavorable attitude toward abortion, are coerced into accepting an abortion, and whose pregnancy is terminated by saline procedure are highly susceptible to psychological trauma afterwards. These women make highly suitable candidates for follow-up counseling (Sachdev, 1975; Watters, 1976).

Psychologic disturbances are not the only basis for post-abortion counseling. Contraceptive and sex counseling can form an important component of follow-up with women who have undergone an abortion. In fact, once a woman is relieved from the anxiety brought about by her problem pregnancy, she is more likely to accept rationally contraceptive advice. During this phase, a counselor should also deal with a woman's attitude toward sex and men in general, as well as her self-concept, which may be adversely affected by guilt and depression as possible reactions of abortion. A few studies that examined the long-term effects of abortion report that it affects some women's ability to accept their femininity and sexuality. They may begin to distrust all men and to view sex as dangerous (Leiter, 1972; Sachdev, 1975).

It has been well documented that abortions performed in the first trimester are relatively safe, with minimal medical and psychologic risks. These risks progressively increase with the gestation period (Cates, et al., 1977; Wadhera, 1982). Obviously, for a woman to obtain an early abortion, she must initiate verification of her pregnancy and decide on the abortion option soon after interruption of the menstrual cycle. Research studies, however, show that it is generally the young, single, nulliparous, less educated, sporadic or non-users of contraceptives who seek late abortions (Bracken & Swigar, 1972; Cates, 1981; Kerenyi, et al., 1973; Mallory, 1972; Sachdev, 1975; Tietze, 1983). There are four factors contributing to this: (1) After pregnancy is suspected, a number of women resort to denial, hoping that some magical force will bring on their periods; (2) Some are, in fact, too inexperienced to recognize the symptoms of pregnancy; (3) Some may be unaware of services for pregnancy confirmation and termination; and 4) Most hospitals provide only limited abortion service because of its low priority and the unfavorable attitudes of many health-service providers toward premaritally pregnant women. As a result, sometimes women have to wait for weeks for an appointment. A study by Mallory, et al. (1972) found that of patients undergoing late abortions at the Hospital of the Albert Einstein College of Medicine in The Bronx, 25 percent were delayed for reasons related to the medical-care system.

On the basis of these findings, it would seem that one of the most effective ways of serving young unmarried women would be to affiliate counseling centers with well-advertised pregnancy test services (Raines, 1971). Three advantages would accrue from this: 1) Women who delay confirmation of pregnancy because they apprehend embarrassment or unpredictable reactions from the doctor or pharmacist are less likely to feel threatened in contacting a pregnancy test service; 2) The visit to the pregnancy test center will automatically bring the women in contact with a counselor at a much earlier stage of pregnancy, thus presenting an opportunity for initiation of the counseling process for those interested; 3) Women who receive negative pregnancy test can be offered contraceptive counseling for future prevention. Given our social and legal climate, providing contraceptive information and sex education to sexually inexperienced women often meets with serious moral objections. On the other hand, reaching women who have experienced a pregnancy scare would probably not be viewed with the same societal apprehension and condemnation. Care should be taken to staff these services with persons who have skills and knowledge about the problems of abortion and who are sensitive to the needs and problems of women seeking termination.

As noted earlier, women who present themselves for pregnancy termination in the second trimester run considerably higher emotional and medical risks than those who seek first-trimester abortion. They are particularly vulnerable to intense emotional trauma during the period between instillation of saline and the actual abortion, approximately 22 hours. This may be due to the fact that advanced gestation brings the woman closer to the reality of her pregnancy and to the experience of fetal quickening, which reinforces her awareness of bearing a child. She then goes through the experience of labor and childbirth without delivering a live child. These women need not only tremendous support and assurance during the complex and distressing saline procedure but also post-abortion counseling, as they are more vulnerable to remorse and depressive reactions than early aborters (Bracken, 1977; Leiter, 1972).

Counseling Effectiveness

Does counseling really help women to cope with their abortion experience and does it contribute to effective and sustained contraception after abortion? Studies that have attempted to evaluate abortion-counseling effectiveness are exceedingly limited, equivocal in their findings, and they lack methodological and theoretical rigor. For instance, Dauber, et al. (1972) exposed a group of 99 patients at San Francisco General Hospital to extensive counseling, prior to, during, and after the abortion surgery. In addition to emotional support and discussion of psychological and moral reactions to abortion, the counselor engaged the clients in extensive dialogue about contraceptive devices and their relative effectiveness. Another group of 99 women, used as a control group, was given a ten-minute lecture from a nurse on the family planning services of the hospital. Judging from the women's return rate to post-abortion checkups and the regularity of contraceptive practice after six months, the authors concluded that a far greater number of women in the counseled group "met the criteria" than the lectured women. Not only did more counseled women choose the most effective methods of birth control, they also made more frequent return visits for contraceptive supplies. The authors attributed the increase in return visits and the improved contraceptive dossier of the counseled women to the caring attitude and personal interest of the counselor.

However, a Vancouver study in Canada reported that, although the sample women in the counseled group indicated greater knowledge of contraception and reproduction than the non-counseled group, no significant difference was found in the incidence of repeat abortions in both groups at follow-up, 12 months after the first abortion (Marcus, et al., 1978). The authors further reported that, although the counseled group approached abortion surgery with less apprehension and anxiety than the non-counseled group, the difference in post-abortion depressive and guilt reactions of the women in both groups tended to have disappeared at 6 months. Their findings on the effects of counseling on contraception were supported by a more recent study at the Human Reproduction Unit of Obstetrics/Gynecology at the Ljubljana University in Yugoslavia. The investigators, Andolsek and Pretner (1982), hypothesized that women given contraceptive counseling and supplies at abortion, when motivations are high, are highly likely to show a sustained commitment to contraception. To test the hypothesis, the authors randomly assigned 1,030 women to counseling and non-counseling groups. Each group consisted of women who had had an abortion a month earlier and those who sought contraceptive devices. The counseled group was given detailed information on reproduction and contraception by a trained nurse. The women in the non-counseled group were given only brief information on contraception. At six-month follow-up, the authors found that there were as many women in the counseled group as there were in the non-counseled group who either adopted the most effective methods of birth control or discontinued their use.

A few studies attempted to compare the relative efficacy of individual versus group counseling procedures. Bracken, et al. (1973) randomly assigned 489 abortion patients to either individual counseling, group counseling, or group orientation in which women were given information without discussion. The contents that were uniformally discussed across the counseling groups related to abortion procedures, post-abortion precautions, contraceptive advice, psychosocial issues, women's attitudes toward abortion, and sexual and interpersonal relationships with their partners. Information was gathered from each woman following the abortion on physical and psychological reactions to the surgery, perception of the abortion's impact on relationships with key people, contraceptive knowledge and contraceptive plans for the future, and experience with the clinic. The authors found that, although women in individual counseling felt more comfortable with the counselor, those experiencing a group process approached the abortion surgery with fewer doubts and reacted more positively to the abortion, with minimum emotional disturbances and guilt reaction. In terms of age-specific differences, the study showed that for all types of counseling techniques, the older women (21 to 45 years) reacted more favorably to the abortion than did their younger counterparts. Another study by Burnell, et al. (1972) in Santa Clara, California, did not employ control groups but reached a similar conclusion based on their group-therapy sessions with 250 women, in groups of five each, held once or twice two weeks after abortion. The authors noted that "most women" felt a sense of relief from post-abortal depressive reactions (p. 221).

Corroborating earlier studies, Leiter (1972), too, found (although impressionistically) that group counseling proved significantly valuable in the resolution of conflicts and anxiety over abortion decision especially among young single women, at two New York hospitals. The authors further noted that these women were able, through group support, to gain a better understanding of their sexual and identity problems and their motivation for pregnancy.

Post-operative group counseling has also been reported to help reduce guilt feelings and enhance assimilation of the pregnancy and abortion experience for some women. Bern-

stein and Tinkham (1971) conducted short-term group sessions
with 20 women who underwent abortion at the Massachusetts
General Hospital and observed that the group discussions provided a helpful opportunity to seek support, share ideas, and
resolve the study of women's abortion-related conflicts. At
the Vancouver General Hospital in British Columbia, Canada,
Kaminsky and Sheckter (1979) instituted an abortion counseling
program in the early 1970s to provide emotional support and
assistance in the decision-making process as well as information on abortion procedures, reproduction, and contraception.
The authors administered questionnaires to counseled and non-
counseled women prior to their abortion surgery, at 5 weeks,
and at 6 months following the procedure, and concluded that
the counseling objectives had been met and that the women
felt that the counseling "service humanized the abortion experience" (p. 97). However, no differences were found between the two groups in their contraceptive utilization level
at 5 weeks following the abortion. The authors did not provide information on how the patients were selected, divided
into experimental and control groups nor how the information
was analyzed.

In a more intuitive than empirical sense, group approaches to counseling individuals and families in a variety
of problem situations have been viewed as useful in providing
members with corrective emotional experiences and psychologically safe atmospheres which are conducive to free expression
and open discussion. A group can provide safety in numbers
and makes it easier for members to accept a therapeutic relationship with the counselor and his suggestions for behavior
change. It also offers a unique opportunity for members to
share ideas and feelings and identify with one another. Notwithstanding these merits, some women may prefer individual
counseling because of its distinct features of privacy and in-
dividualization. Because the advantages of group counseling
are augmented if used in conjunction with individual counseling, many abortion service units offer both types of counseling to their clientele. In 1981 survey of the member clinics
and hospitals of the National Abortion Federation (NAF) (which
perform about half of the abortions in the United States) it
was found that more than one half of them provide both group
and individual counseling services "sometimes" or "nearly
always," and just 27 percent provide individual counseling only
(Landy & Lewit, 1982).

Research Dilemmas

The absence of a consensus among investigators on the effectiveness of counseling programs for abortion patients can be attributed to several methodological factors: 1) the discrepant conceptualization of parameters; 2) sampling criteria and procedures; 3) divergent measurement criteria; 4) study designs; 5) counseling contents; and 6) varying duration of follow-ups. Additionally, given the complex nature of successful contraceptive activity, it is not surprising that the research findings are inconsistent in reporting the impact of counseling on women's commitment to post-abortion contraceptive.

Some experts in the field suggest that it is not so much the counseling techniques and procedures that contribute to positive behavior change in clients as the personal attributes and suitability of the counselor (Bergin & Jasper, 1969; Rogers, 1957; Truax & Carkhuff, 1967; Fiedler, 1950, Strupp, 1955, Whitehorn, 1964). They contend that specific techniques and skills, while important, do not occur independent of the inherent qualities of the change agent. Truax and Mitchell (1977) reviewed a number of studies dealing with the effectiveness of counseling and psychotherapy, in addition to their own empirical research, and concluded that three core characteristics of a counselor--accurate empathy, nonpossessive warmth, and genuineness--are most significantly and positively related to both the therapeutic process and to behavioral and personality change. The authors' conviction as to the positive relationship between the counselor or therapist's interpersonal skills and beneficial client change is reflected in the statement: "We want to emphasize the therapist-as-person before the therapist-as-expert or therapist-as-technician" (p. 34). They further observe that the personal ingredients of the counselor, as aspects of therapeutic relationship, cut across all types of interventive modalities. Other investigators in the 1970s also lent support to the findings of the 1950s and 1960s that a conselor's theoretical allegiance is less important than his own personal expertise, style, attitudes toward the client, and type of relationship in influencing the counseling outcome (Kaminsky & Sheckter, 1979; Patterson, 1973; Shulman, 1979; Swensen, 1972).

Among counselors' personal traits, quality of relationship with the client has been noted by some investigators as the strongest determinant of positive outcome (Bergin and Lambert, 1978). Some psychoanalytic theorists (Langs, 1973; Menninger & Holtzman, 1973) also have identified the relationship between patient and therapist as a major therapeutic force. However, there are others who view clients' attributes, such as age, motivation, expectations from counseling, confidence in the counselor's ability, and the degree of distress, as the crucial factors associated with counseling outcome (Garfield, 1978). Some experts do not subscribe to any single theoretical system, favoring the therapist's attributes, or the client's characteristics, or a method of practice, but argue that positive counseling outcome is a function of the complex interaction between counselor variables, client characteristics, and techniques (Parloff, et al. , 1978).

Conclusion

The debate on the effectiveness of psychotherapy and counseling which was engendered by the publication of The Effects of Psychotherapy: An Evaluation by Hans Eysenck (1952), claiming that psychotherapy makes almost no difference, seems to have come full circle with the recent publication (May 1983) of Bernie Zilbergeld's book The Shrinking of America. After surveying the accumulating research studies and mass of literature on the subject, the American psychologist concluded that "consumers of psychotherapy usually feel better and treatment makes some changes in their lives, but the changes are modest and short-lived" (Time, May 23, 1983, p. 69). It seems that although Zilbergeld partially upholds the Eysenck claim, he reaffirms a belief in the value of counseling single pregnant women who are confronted with the difficult decision to seek pre-term termination but do not have supportive people to turn to for impassionate and well-reasoned advice. Zilbergeld argues that "the chief benefit of therapy seems to come from talking to a sympathetic listener.... It can be comforting and useful, even when one does not get what one asks for.... It can help us get things of our chests and clear our minds and make us feel more in control...." (Time May 23, 1983, p. 69).

Undoubtedly, the controversy remains unresolved and Zilbergeld's conclusions will spawn counterclaims, thus perpetuating the tide of research of many still-unexplored variables. However, until research delivers more conclusive findings on the effectiveness of abortion counseling, we have a body of knowledge and accumulating practice wisdom that should help foster our confidence in the value of counseling unmarried women faced with the problems of unwanted pregnancies.

References

Abernathy, Virginia. "Illegitimate Conception Among Teenagers." American Journal of Public Health, 1974, 64(7): 662-65.

Addelson, Frances. "Induced Abortion: Source of Guilt Or Growth?" American Journal of Orthopsychiatry, 1973, 43: 815-22.

Adler, N. E. "Emotional Response of Women Following Therapeutic Abortion." American Journal of Orthopsychiatry, 1975, 45: 446-54.

American Public Health Association. Recommended Standards for Abortion Services. Washington, D.C.: American Public Health Association, 1970.

Anderson, B., and Milsom, I. "Contraception and Pregnancy Among Young Women in an Urban Swedish Population." Contraception, 1982, 26(3): 211-19.

Anderson, E. W. "Psychiatric Indications for the Termination of Pregnancy." World Medical Journal, 1966, 13: 520-25.

Anderson, P.; McPherson, K.; Beeching, N.; Weinberg, J.; and Vessey, M. "Sexual Behavior and Contraceptive Practice of Undergraduates at Oxford University." Journal of Biosocial Science, 1978, 10: 277-86.

Andolsek, L. The Ljubljana Abortion Study. Yugoslavia: The NIH Center for Population Research, 1974.

Andolsek, Lidija and Pretner, Alenka. Influence of Counseling in Postabortal Contraception. Paper presented at the International Symposium on Reproductive Behavior, Maui, Hawaii, October 1982.

Apkom, C.; Amechi, K. L.; and Davis, D. "Prior Sexual Behavior of Teenagers Attending Rap Sessions for the First Time." Family Planning Perspectives, 1976, 8: 203-206.

Aug, R. G., and Bright, R. P. "A Study of Wed and Unwed Motherhood in Adolescents and Young Adults." Journal of American Academy of Child Psyciatry, 1970, 9: 577-94.

Bachmann, Gloria. "Contraceptive Failure in a College Population." Advances in Planned Parenthood, 1981, 15(1): 35-38.

Bacon, Hugh M. "Psychiatric Aspects of Therapeutic Abortion." Canadian Mental Health, 1969, 17: 18-21.

Barnes, Ann B.; Cohen, Elisabeth; Stoeckle, J. D.; and Mcguire, M. T. "Therapeutic Abortion: Medical and Social Sequels." Annals of Internal Medicine, 1971, 75: 881-86.

Bauman, Kar E. "Selected Aspects of the Contraceptive Practices of Unmarried University Students." Medical Aspects of Human Sexuality, 1971 (August), pp. 76-89.

Beard, W. W.; Belsey, E. M.; and Lal, S. "Contraceptive Practice Before and After Outpatient Termination of Pregnancy." British Medical Journal, 1974, 108: 418.

Bergin, Allen E., and Garfield, Sol L. Handbook of Psychotherapy and Behavior Change. New York: John Wiley & Sons, 1971.

Bergin, Allen E., and Jasper, L. G. "Correlates of Empathy in Psychotherapy: A Replication." Journal of Abnormal Psychology, 1969, 74: 447-81.

Bergin, Allen E., and Lambert, Michael J. "The Evaluation of Therapeutic Outcomes." In Handbook of Psychotherapy and Behavior Change, 2nd ed., Sol L. Garfield and Allen E. Bergin, eds. New York: John Wiley & Sons, 1978.

Bernstein, Norman R., and Tinkham, Caroline B. "Group Therapy Following Abortion." Nervous and Mental Disease, 1971, 152(5): 303-14.

Bogue, Donald, J. "Inventory, Explanation and Evaluation by Interview of Family Planning Motives--Attitudes, Knowledge, Behavior." International Conference on Family Planning Programs. Geneva: University of Chicago Press, 1965.

Bracken, Michael B. "A Causal Model of Psychosomatic Reactions to Vacuum Aspiration Abortion." Social Psychiatry, 1978, 13: 135-45.

_____. "Psychosomatic Aspects of Abortion: Implications for Counseling." The Journal of Reproductive Medicine, 1977, 19(5): 265-72.

Bracken, Michael B.; Grossman, G.; Hachamovitch, M.; Sussman, D.; and Schrieir, D. "Abortion Counseling: An

Experimental Study of Three Techniques." American Journal of Obstetrics and Gynecology, 1973, 117: 10-20.

Bracken, Michael B. , Hachamovitch M. , and Grossman, G. "The Decision to Abort and Psychological Sequelae." Journal of Nervous and Mental Disease, 1974, 158: 154-62.

Bracken, Michael B. , and Swigar, Mary E. "Factors Associated with Delay in Seeking Induced Abortions." American Journal of Obstetrics and Gynecology, 1972, 113: 301-309.

Brandt, Carol L.; Kane, Francis J.; and Moan, Charles A. "Pregnant Adolescents: Some Psychosocial Factors." Psychosomatics, 1978, 19: 790-93.

Burnell, George M.; Sworsky, William A.; and Harrington, Robert L. "Post-Abortion Group Therapy." American Journal of Psychiatry, 1972, 129(2): 220-23.

Canadian Facts. An Assessment of Mass Media Campaign for Family Planning, vols. 1-3. Toronto: Canadian Facts Co. , Ltd. , 1973.

Cates, W. , Jr.; Schulz, K. F.; Grimes, D. A.; and Tyler, C. W. , Jr. "The Effect of Delay and Choice of Method on the Risk of Abortion Morbidity." Family Planning Perspectives, 1977, 9: 266-73.

Cobliner, G. W.; Schulman, H.; and Romney, S. L. "The Termination of Adolescent Out-of-Wedlock Pregnancies and the Propsects for Their Primary Prevention." American Journal of Obstetrics and Gynecology, 1973, 115: 432-44.

Cvetkovich, G. , and Grote, B. In Pregnancy in Adolescence, Irving R. Stuart and Carl F. Wells, eds. New York: Van Nostrand Reinhold Company, 1982.

_____, Bjorseth, A. , and Sarkissian, J. "On the Psychology of Adolescents' Use of Contraceptives." The Journal of Sex Research, 1975, 11(3): 256-70.

Daily, Edwin F. , and Nicholas, Nick. "Use of Conception Control Methods Before Pregnancies Terminating in Birth or a Requested Abortion in New York City Municipal Hospitals." American Journal of Public Health, 1972, 62: 1544-45.

Dauber, B.; Zalar, M.; and Goldstein, Phillip J. "Abortion Counseling and Behavior Change." Family Planning Perspectives, 1972, 4(2): 23-27.

David, Henry P. "Mental Health and Family Planning." Family Planning Perspectives, 1971, 3: 20-23.

DeAmicis, Lyn A.; Klorman, R.; Hess, Wilson D.; and Mc-Anarnery, Elizabeth R. "A Comparison of Unwed Pregnant Teenagers and Nulligravid Sexually Active Adolescents Seeking Contraception." Adolescence, 1981, 16(61): 11-20.

Dembo, Myron H., and Lundell, Beverly. "Factors Affecting Adolescent Contraception Practice: Implications for Sex Education." Adolescence, 1979, 14: 657-64.

Diamond M.; Steinhoff, P. G.; Palmore, J. A.; and Smith, R. G. "Sexuality, Birth Control and Abortion: A Decision-Making Sequence." Journal of Biosocial Science, 1973, 5: 347-61.

Dunbar, Flanders. "Psychosomatic Approach to Abortion and the Abortion Habit." In Abortion in America, Harold Rosen, ed. Boston: Beacon Press, 1967.

Fiedler, F. E. "The Concept of an Ideal Therapeutic Relationship." Journal of Consulting Psychology, 1950, 14: 239-45.

Figley, Charles R., and Scroggins, Linda M. "Putting the 'Family' in Family Planning Services." Advances in Planned Parenthood, 1978, 13(3): 75-77.

Finkel, M. L. and Finkel, D. J. "Male Adolescent Contraceptive Utilization." Adolescence, 1978, 13: 443-451.

Fischman, S. H. "Delivery or Abortion in Inner-City Adolescents." American Journal of Orthopsychiatry, 1977, 47: 127-133.

Fisher, William A. "Affective, Attitudinal, and Normative Determinants of Contraceptive Behavior Among University Men." Unpublished doctoral dissertation, Purdue University, 1978.

Fleck, Stephen. "Some Psychiatric Aspects of Abortion." Journal of Nervous and Mental Disease, 1970, 151: 42-50.

Fox, G. L. "The Family's Influence on Adolescent Sexual Behavior." Children Today, 1979, 8: 21-36.

_____. "Sex Role Attitudes as Predictors of Contraceptive Use Among Unmarried University Students." Sex Roles, 1977, 3(3): 265-83.

Freeman, Ellen W. "Influence of Personality Attributes on Abortion Experiences." American Journal of Orthopsychiatry, 1977, 47: 503-13.

Furstenberg, Frank F. "Birth Control Experience Among Pregnant Adolescents: The Process of Unplanned Parenthood." Social Problems, 1971, 19: 192-203.

_____. Unplanned Parenthood. New York: The Free Press, 1976.

Garfield, Sol L. "Research on Client Variables in Psychotherapy." In Handbook of Psychotherapy and Behavior Change, 2nd ed., Sol L. Garfield and Allen E. Bergin, eds. New York: John Wiley & Sons, 1978.

_____, and Bergin, Allen., eds. Handbook of Psychotherapy and Behavior Change, 2nd ed. New York: John Wiley & Sons, 1978.

Gibb, Gerald D., and Millard, Richard. "Divergent Perspectives in Abortion Counseling." Psychological Reports, 1982, 50: 819-22.

Goldsmith, S.; Gabrielson, M.; Gabrielson, I.; Mathews, V.; and Potts, L. "Teenagers, Sex and Contraception." Family Planning Perspectives, 1972, 4(1): 32-38.

Grauer, H. "A Study of Contraception As Related to Unwanted Pregnancy." Canadian Medical Association Journal, 1972, 107: 739-41.

Greenglass, E. R. "A Canadian Study of Psychological Adjustment After Abortion." In Abortion: Readings and Research, Paul Sachdev, ed. Toronto: Butterworths, 1981.

Group for the Advancement of Psychiatry. The Right to Abortion: A Psychiatric View. New York: Charles Scribner's Sons, 1969.

Hamilton, V. C. In Nathan M. Simon and Aubrey G. Senturia's "Psychiatric Sequelae of Abortion: Review of the Literature." Archives of General Psychiatry, 1966, 15: 378-89.

Hatcher, Robert A.; Butterfield, Leslie M.; and Oakley, M. "Contraceptive Practices of 1,486 Women at the Time of First Act of Intercourse." Advances in Planned Parenthood, 1981, 16(3): 110-16.

Herold, Edward S., and Goodwin, Marilyn S. "A Comparison of Younger and Older Adolescent Females Attending Birth Control Clinics." Canadian Family Physician, 1980, 26: 687-94.

Jorgensen, S. R.; King, S. L.; and Terrey, B. A. "Dyadic and Network Influences on Adolescent Exposure to Pregnancy Risk." Journal of Marriage and the Family, 1980, 42(1): 141-55.

Kahn-Edrington, Marla. "Abortion Counseling." The Counseling Psychologist, 1979, 8: 37-38.

Kaminsky, Barbara A., and Sheckter, Lorraine A. "Abortion Counseling in a General Hospital." Health and Social Work, 1979, 4(2): 93-103.

Kane, F. J.; Lachenbruch, P. A.; Lockey, L.; Chafetz, N.; Auman, R.; Pocuis, L.; and Lipton, M. A. "Motivational Factors Affecting Contraceptive Use." American Journal of Obstetrics and Gynecology, 1971, 110: 1050-54.

Kantner, J. F., and Zelnik, Melvin. "Contraception and Pregnancy: Experience of Young Unmarried Women in the United States." Family Planning Perspectives, 1973, 5: 21-35.

Kerenyi, Thomas, D.; Glascock, E. L.; and Horowitz, Marjorie L. "Reasons for Delayed Abortion: Results of Four Hundred Interviews." American Journal of Obstetrics and Gynecology, 1973 117(3): 299-311.

Kimball, Chase Patterson. "Some Observations Regarding Unwanted Pregnancies and Therapeutic Abortions." Obstetrics and Gynecology, 1970, 35: 293-96.

Lambert, Joan. "Survey of 3,000 Unwanted Pregnancies." British Medical Journal, 1971, 4: 156-60.

Landy, U. , and Lewit, Sarah. "Administrative, Counseling and Medical Practices in National Abortion Federation Facilities." Family Planning Perspectives, 1982, 14(5): 257-63.

Langs, Robert. Technique of Psychoanalytic Psychotherapy. New York: Jason Aronson, 1973.

Lee, Nancy H. The Search for an Abortionist. Chicago: University of Chicago, 1969.

Leiter, Naomi. "Elective Abortion." New York State Journal of Medicine, 1972, 72: 2908-10.

Lidz, Theodore. "Reflections of a Psychiatrist." In Abortion in America, Harold Rosen, ed. Boston: Beacon Press, 1967.

Lindemann, C. Birth Control and Unmarried Young Women. New York: Springer, 1974.

Lipper, I.; Cvejic, H.; Benjamin, P.; and Kinch, R. A. "Abortion and the Pregnant Teenager." Canadian Medical Journal, 1973, 109: 852-56.

Luker, Kristin. Taking Chances: The Decision Not to Contracept. Berkeley: University of California Press, 1975.

Mallory, G. B.; Rubenstein, L. Z.; Drosness, D. L.; Kleiner, G. J.; and Sidel, V. W. "Factors Responsible for Delay in Obtaining Interruption of Pregnancy." Obstetrics and Gynecology, 1972, 40: 556-62.

Malmfors, K. Cited in Nathan M. Simon and Aubrey G. Senturia's "Psychiatric Sequelae of Abortion: Review of Literature, 1935-64." Archives of General Psychiatry, 1966, 15: 384.

Mansour, Karem J. , and Stewart, Barbara. "Abortion and Sexual Behavior in College Women." American Journal of Orthopsychiatry, 1973, 43: 804-14.

Marcus, Robert, J.; Brown, Barnie W. G.; and Reimer, L. E. "Abortion Counseling: An Outcome Study." Mimeographed report of the Vancouver General Hospital, Department of Social Service, 1978.

Martin, Cynthia D. "Psychological Problems of Abortion for

the Unwed Teenage Girl." Unpublished doctoral dissertation, United States International University, 1972.

Meikle, Stewart. "A Preliminary Analysis of Data Derived from the Calgary Birth Control Clinic." In Family Planning and Abortion Services and Family Life Education Program, vol. 5, Philip H. Hepworth, ed. Ottawa: The Canadian Council on Social Development, 1975.

Menninger, K. A., and Holtzman, P. S. Theory of Psychoanalytic Techniques, 2nd ed. New York: Basic Books, 1973.

Miller, E.; McFarland, V.; Burnhill, Michael S.; and Armstead, John W. "Impact of the Abortion Experience on Contraceptive Acceptance." Advances in Planned Parenthood, 1977, 12(1): 15-28.

Miller, Warren B. "Psychological Antecedents to Conception Among Abortion Seekers." The Western Journal of Medicine, 1975, 122: 12-19.

_____. "Sexual and Contraceptive Behavior in Young Unmarried Women." Health Care for Women, 1976, 3: 427-53.

_____. "Sexual and Contraceptive Behavior in Young Unmarried Women." Primary Care, 1970, 3(3): 427-57.

Mudd, E. H.; Dickens, H. O.; Garcia, C.; Rickel, K.; Freeman, E.; Hugging, G.; and Logan, J. "Adolescent Health Services and Contraceptive Use." American Journal of Orthopsychiatry, 1978, 48: 495-504.

Nadelson, Carol. "Abortion Counseling: Focus on Adolescent Pregnancy." Pediatrics, 1974, 54(6): 765-69.

_____; Notman, M.; and Gillon, Jean W. "Sexual Knowledge and Attitudes of Adolescents: Relationship to Contraceptive Use." Obstetrics and Gynecology, 1980, 55(3): 340-45.

National Health and Welfare. Pilot Survey of Hospital Therapeutic Abortion Committees, British Columbia 1971-72. Ottawa: Health Economics and Statistics Division, 1974.

Niemela, P.; Lehtinen, P.; Rauzamo, L.; Hermanssom, R.;

Karjalainen, R.; Maki, H.; and Stora, C. "The First Abortion--And the Last? A Study of the Personality Factors Underlying Repeated Failure of Contraception." International Journal of Gynecology and Obstetrics, 1981, 19: 193-200.

Notman, Malkak T. "Teenage Pregnancy: The Non-Use of Contraception." Psychiatric Opinion, 1975, 12: 23-27.

Osofsky, J. D., and Osofsky, H. J. "The Psychological Reaction of Patients to Legalized Abortion." American Journal of Orthopsychiatry, 1972, 42: 48-60.

Parloff, Morris B.; Waskow, Irene E.; and Wolfe, Barry E. "Research on Therapist Variables in Relations to Process and Outcome." In Handbook of Psychotherapy and Behavior Change, 2nd ed., Sol L. Garfield and Allen E. Bergin, eds. New York: John Wiley & Sons, 1978.

Patterson, C. Theories of Counseling and Psychotherapy. New York: Harper & Row, 1973.

Pick de Weiss, Susan. "Toward a Predictive Model of Family Planning." Revista Latinoamericana de Psicología, 1980, 12: 119-25.

Poma, Pedro A. "Contraceptive and Sexual Knowledge in Abortion Clients." Advances in Planned Parenthood, 1979, 14(3): 123-29.

Poole, Carol. "Contraception and the Adolescent Females." The Journal of School Health, 1976, 36(6): 475-79.

Rader, G. E.; Bekker, D. L.; Brown, L.; and Richardt, C. "Psychological Correlates of Unwanted Pregnancy." Journal of Abnormal Psychology, 1978, 87: 373-76.

Rains, Prudence Mors. Becoming an Unwed Mother: A Sociological Account. Aldine-Atherton, 1971.

Rainwater, Lee. And the Poor Get Children. Chicago: Quadrangle Books, 1960.

Reiss, Ira; Banwart, Albert; and Foreman, Harry. "Premarital Contraceptive Usage: A Study and Some Theoretical Explorations." Journal of Marriage and the Family, 1975 (August), pp. 619-30.

Robins, Joel. "Failure of Contraceptive Practice." New York State Journal of Medicine, 1976, 76: 361-65.

Rogel, Mary J., and Zuehlke, Martha E. "Adolescent Contraceptive Behavior: Influences and Implications." In Pregnancy in Adolescence, Irving R. Stuart and Carl F. Wells, eds. New York: Van Nostrand Reinhold, 1982.

Rogers, Carl R. "The Necessary and Sufficient Conditions of Therapeutic Change." Journal of Consulting Psychology, 1957, 21: 95-103.

Rosen, H. Personal Communication. In Kathryn A. Urberg's "A Theoretical Framework for Studying Adolescent Contraceptive Use." Adolescence, 1982, 17(67): 527-40.

Rosen, Raye H. "Adolescent Pregnancy Decision-Making: Are Parents Important?" Adolescence, 1980, 15(57): 43-54.

Russell, Betty, and Schild, Sylvia. "Pregnancy Counseling with College Women." Social Casework, 1976, 57(5): 324-29.

Ryan, George M., and Sweeny, Patrick J. "Attitudes of Adolescents Toward Pregnancy and Contraception." American Journal of Obstetrics and Gynecology, 1980, 137: 358-66.

Sachdev, Paul. "Factors Relating to the Abortion Decision Among Premaritally Pregnant Females." Unpublished doctoral dissertation, University of Wisconsin, Madison, 1975.

_____. "Problems of Fertility Control Among Canadian Women." In Abortion: Readings and Research, Paul Sachdev, ed. Toronto: Butterworths, 1981.

Shulman, Lawrence. The Skills of Helping. Itasca, Ill.: F. E. Peacock Publishers, 1979.

Siedlecky, Stefania. "Teenage Fertility in Australia." Paper presented at the International Symposium on Reproductive Behavior, Maui, Hawaii, October 1982.

Smith, Elizabeth M. "Counseling for Women Who Seek Abortion." Social Work, 1972 (March), pp. 62-68.

_____. "A Follow-Up Study of Women Who Request Abortion." American Journal of Orthopsychiatry, 1973, 43: 574-85.

Statistics Canada. Basic Facts on Therapeutic Abortion, Canada. Ottawa: Catalogue No. 82-215 Annual, 1981.

Strupp, H. "Psychotherapeutic Technique, Professional Affiliation and Experience Level." Journal of Consulting Psychology, 1955, 19: 97-102.

Sullivan, Gail, and Watt, Susan. "Legalised Abortion: Myth and Misconception." The Social Worker, 1975, 43: 78-86.

Swensen, C. H. "Commitment and the Personality of the Successful Therapist." Psychological Bulletin, 1972, 77: 400-404.

Tietze, Christopher. Induced Abortion: A World Review, 5th ed. New York: The Population Council, 1983.

Todd, N. A. "Follow-Up of Patients Recommended for Therapeutic Abortion." British Journal of Psychiatry, 1972, 120: 645-46.

Truax, C. B., and Carkhuff, R. R. Toward Effective Counseling and Psychotherapy: Training and Practice. Chicago: Aldine Press, 1967.

Truax, Charles B., and Mitchell, Kevin M. "Research on Certain Therapist Interpersonal Skills in Relation to Process and Outcome." In Handbook of Psychotherapy and Behavior Change, 2nd ed., Allen E. Bergin and Sol L. Garfield, eds. New York: John Wiley & Sons, 1971.

Ullman, Alice. "Social Work Service to Abortion Patients." Social Casework, 1972 (October), pp. 481-89.

Urberg, Kathryn A. "A Theoretical Framework for Studying Adolescent Contraceptive Use." Adolescence, 1982, 17: 528-40.

Wade, R. In Pregnancy in Adolescence, Irving R. Stuart and Carl F. Wells, eds. New York: Van Nostrand Reinhold, 1982, p. 280.

Wadhera, Surinder. "Early Complication Risks of Legal Abortions, Canada, 1975-1980." Canadian Journal of Public Health, 1982, 73: 396-400.

Wallerstein, J.; Kurtz, P.; and Bar-Din, M. "Psychosocial Sequelae of Therapeutic Abortion in Young Unmarried Women." Archives of General Psychiatry, 1972, 27: 828-32.

Wallston, K. A.; Maides, S.; and Wallston, B. S. "Health-Related Information Seeking as a Function of Health-Related Locus of Control and Health Value." Journal of Research in Personality, 1976, 10: 215-22.

Walter, G. S. "Psychologic and Emotional Consequences of Elective Abortion: A Review." Obstetrics and Gynecology, 1970, 36: 482-90.

Watters, Wendell W. Compulsory Parenthood. Toronto: McClelland and Stewart, 1976.

Whelpton, P. K., and Kiser, Clyde V. "Social and Psychological Factors Affecting Fertility," vol 4. New York: Milbank Memorial Fund, 1954.

Whitehorn, J. C. "Human Factors in Psychiatry." Bulletin of New York Academy of Medicine, 1964, 40: 451-66.

Whittington, H. G. "Evaluation of Therapeutic Abortion as an Element of Preventive Psychiatry." American Journal of Psychiatry, 1960, 126: 1224-29.

Wolf, J. R.; Nielson, P. E.; and Schiller, P. J. "Therapeutic Abortions: Attitudes of Medical Personnel Leading to Complications and Patient Care." American Journal of Obstetrics and Gynecology, 1971, 110: 730-35.

Young, Alma T.; Berkman, B.; and Rehr, H. "Women Who Seek Abortions: A Study." Social Work, 1973 (May), pp. 60-65.

Zelnik, M., and Kantner, J. F. "Contraceptive Patterns and Premarital Pregnancy Among Women Aged 15-19 in 1976." Family Planning Perspectives, 1978, 10(3): 135-44.

Zilbergeld, Bernie. The Shrinking of America. New York: Little, Brown, 1983.

Zimmerman, Mary K. "Psychosocial and Emotional Consequences of Elective Abortion: A Literature Review." In
Abortion: Readings and Research, Paul Sachdev, ed. Toronto: Butterworths, 1981.

EPILOGUE

PERSPECTIVE ON PERSPECTIVES

By Paul Sachdev and Michael J. Holosko

Abortion as a means of regulating fertility has been with mankind for centuries. Yet it continues to be an unsettling issue for legislatures, the general public, and professionals. Abortion, both as word and act, occasions a variety of reactions, as well as moral, ethical, and political controversies. Despite the availability of better and more effective contraceptive devices, demand for abortion, legal or illegal, continues to escalate, reviving traditional issues and generating provocative new concerns. A great deal is known about the problem of abortion, yet its complexity presents fresh justifications for exploring the issue from new perspectives.

We have consciously selected, from leading scholars in the field, papers that approach the subject with fresh orientations. The work of these contributors is based on empirical research, and the presentations avoid, as far as possible, subjectivity and emotionalism. The authors do not emphasize a particular position or engage in a prescriptive approach.

The contributors view abortion, for the most part, as a political and social issue; however, they do not eschew its moral basis, anchored in the "thou-shalt-not-kill" Judeo-Christian ethic. Historical evidence indicates that sexual and marital values, and family norms, by and large, shape the public opinion which influences abortion practices. Some readers, of course, may disagree with our view of causality.

Addressing a range of issues, the book, though far from being comprehensive is divided into four thematic sections. Part I establishes theoretical frameworks for understanding abortion in the western world. The five papers comprising this introductory section deal with the bases of the conflict over the place of abortion in American society. This conflict exists between two divergent factions--the pro-abortionists who essentially favor abortion on demand, and the anti-abortionists who seek to restrict its availability--and is discussed in terms of its historical origins, religious and sociopolitical contexts, and moral perspectives. The authors also suggest possibilities for a compromise solution, acceptable to the majority of members of the society.

The chapters in Part I generally provide a macro-orientation in a larger contextual framework, emerging in response to cultural forces, knowledge of human embryology, and Judeo-Christian values (Chapters 2 and 3). Information about the history of abortion, with reference to the resistance of the medical profession and their insensitivity to the needs of the women patients, is provided in Chapters 1 and 4. The legal and political context of the pro- and anti-abortion activism (Chapter 3), the relationship of this climate to public policy (Chapter 4), and new perspectives on the resolution of the policy dilemma in terms of social choice (Chapter 5) are systematically examined. All of these chapters confirm that this is not an easy issue to comprehend, bound as it is by numerous individual and societal complexities and contradictions. Implicit in these chapters is the belief that it is crucial to understand the contexts and theoretical bases of the issue over time, in order to better address its relevance in contemporary society.

Moving from the macro- to micro-level, Part II provides meaningful data about the women who seek abortions, addressing four fundamental questions: 1) Who are these women? 2) How are the decisions for abortion made? 3) What are the consequences of the decision? and 4) What can be speculated about the long-term effects on the abortion seekers?

Part II examines various aspects of legalized abortion, including which groups choose abortion to terminate unwanted pregnancies, the psychological and emotional effects of this choice, morbidity and mortality from different surgical procedures, and trends in repeat abortions. Several of the chapters discuss abortion in relation to contraceptive practices and suggest that the increase in abortion may, to some extent, be more apparent than real, since illegal avenues have been largely replaced by legal ones. From these perspectives, one begins to develop a comprehensive profile of the women who characteristically seek abortions.

Data from the United States (Chapters 6, 8, 9, 10, 11, 12), Canada (Chapter 7), Denmark (Chapter 8), and England and Wales (Chapter 11) provide much-needed information about women who obtain abortions. Two main observations emerge: 1) disparate methodologies used in sampling and instrumentation to obtain information for these studies seriously limit their generalizability, and 2) the issue of abortion involves multitudinal variables that make it extremely difficult to investigate.

Although advances have been made in methodology and excellent studies have been conducted on the aftereffects of abortion, these reports reveal that further empirical investigations are needed to fill the gaps in two major areas: 1) the long-term consequences of abortion on women's future fertility and 2) multi-disciplinary studies involving broad-based national populations across racial, ethnic, and geographic samples.

While technically legal abortion is permitted in the United States and Canada, its utilization depends to a significant degree on accessibility and the attitudes of both the users and the providers of abortion services. Part III deals with abortion attitudes, how they are shaped over time in sociopolitical contexts, and how they are expressed in the provision of abortion services. These papers correlate abortion attitudes with such important predictors as sex, age, education, race, socioeconomic status, religion, political orientation, commitment to civil liberties, and personal morality, in presentations that are well documented and analytical.

The final section, Part IV, addresses a neglected area of the abortion literature--namely, counseling problem pregnancy. Three general themes predominate: 1) the relative paucity of empirically based information in this area; 2) pre- and post-abortion counseling as an important component of abortion services; and 3) the difficulty of conducting research in this area.

As the title "Counseling Problem Pregnancy" appropriately suggests, Chapters 17 and 18 go beyond a discussion of counseling techniques specific to women who choose abortion; they also examine useful clinical information about teenage contraception, sexuality, and pregnancy; reproductive and contraception counseling; and types of counseling and their relative effectiveness. More specifically, Chapter 17 provides data on a controlled study that evaluates the effectiveness of abortion counseling from the perspectives of both the client and the therapist. Chapter 18 provides a comprehensive a-nalysis of both the nature and the process of abortion counsel-ing as it pertains to young single women, examining specific issues such as the decision-making process, the role of the male partner, and dynamics of sexual and contraceptive be-havior. It also identifies client-counselor variables conducive to effective counseling.

Conclusion

Western society has moved, over a long period of time, from condemnation-to-tolerance-to-acceptance of woman's sexuality and her right to choose her own sexual behavior and attitudes. But public opinion continues to be divided as to her right to decide, without outside interference, the outcome of the pos-sible consequence of such behavior--pregnancy. In 1973 the United States Supreme Court upheld the legality of abortion and the right of a woman to make this decision (Roe vs. Wade; Doe vs. Bolton). The Court later reaffirmed a woman's right to privacy and to make her own reproductive choices without third-party interference, in "Planned Parenthood of Central Missouri vs. Danforth" (1976) and in "Akron Clinic vs. The State of Ohio" (1983). Although the court established a wom-an's right to seek abortion, it could not guarantee the extent to which she is able to exercise this right, which is generally limited by the availability of and access to abortion services as well as the attitudes of physicians and their willingness to provide abortions. As conservatism sweeps across the countries in the western world, many hospitals and physicians are opting out of abortion services under pressure from anti-abortion activist groups.

If history is any indication, one thing stands clear: women will continue to need abortion, legal or illegal, ques-tions of morality notwithstanding. The only phenomenon that can usher in the era of true reproductive freedom for women is the breakthrough discovery of a female contraceptive de-vice that affords free choice on whether or not to get preg-nant and have children. For anti-abortionists and those op-posed to artificial pregnancy barriers, a volitional interven-tion that can forestall the occurrence of conception may offer a compromise solution to the abortion debate. Until then, however, and experts agree that the discovery of such a con-traceptive is years away, women must continue to depend on the cooperation of physicians, their professional autonomy, and personal judgment. And unwanted pregnancies will re-main a personal and societal dilemma.

As society continues to lack consensus on the issue, physicians themselves face painful contradictions between their traditional role as care-givers pledged to the needs of their patients and as citizens entitled to their personal values. The consideration by the United States Congress of a constitutional amendment to outlaw all abortions, except on exceptional medical grounds, raises the specter of a return to large-scale, illegal, "back alley" abortions, a serious threat to the health of women who refuse to accept unwanted pregnancies. Surely, if the pendulum swings back to the time prior to the U. S. Supreme Court 1973 landmark ruling on the legality of abortions, physicians may be relieved of the responsibility for making moral judgments on the desirability of abortion. But the abortion debate itself is not likely to be settled.

Nanch J. Binkin, M. D. , M. P. H.
Family Planning Evaluation Division, U. S. Department of
Health and Human Services, Center for Health Promotion
and Education, Centers for Disease Control, Atlanta,
Georgia.

Willard Cates, Jr. , M. D. , M. P. H.
Director, Division of Venereal Disease Control, U. S.
Department of Health and Human Services, Centers for
Disease Control, Atlanta, Georgia.

Henry P. David, Ph. D.
Director, Transnational Family Research Institute, Be-
thesda, Maryland.

Helen Rose Fuchs Ebaugh, Ph. D.
Associate Professor, Department of Sociology, University of Houston, Central Campus, Houston, Texas.

Nancy V. Ezzard, M. D.
Family Planning Evaluation Division, U. S. Department
of Health and Human Services, Center for Health Promotion and Education, Centers for Disease Control, Atlanta,
Georgia.

Barbara Agresti Findlay
Assistant Professor, Department of Sociology and Anthro-
pology, Texas A & M University, College Station, Texas.

Ellen W. Freeman, Ph. D.
Assistant Research Professor, Department of Obstetrics
and Gynecology, Hospital of the University of Pennsylvania, Philadelphia, Pennsylvania.

Beth Wellman Granberg
Research Service, Harry S. Truman Veterans Administration Hospital, University of Missouri. Columbia, Missouri.

Donald Granberg
    Professor, Center for Research in Social Behavior, University of Missouri, Columbia, Missouri.

David A. Grimes, M. D.
    Family Planning Evaluation Division, U. S. Department of Health and Human Services, Center for Health Promotion and Education, Centers for Disease Control, Atlanta, Georgia.

C. Allen Haney, Ph. D.
    Chairman, Department of Sociology, University of Houston, Central Campus, Houston, Texas.

Michael J. Holosko, Ph. D.
    Associate Professor, School of Social Work, Memorial University of Newfoundland, St. John's, Newfoundland.

Erik Holst
    Joint Center for Studies of Health Program, Institute of Social Medicine, University of Copenhagen.

Michael E. Kafrissen, M. D. , M. S. P. H.
    Family Planning Evaluation Division, U. S. Department of Health and Human Services, Center for Health Promotion and Education, Centers for Disease Control, Atlanta, Georgia.

Philip R. Lee, M. D.
    Professor of Social Medicine, Director, Institute for Health Policy Studies, School of Medicine, University of California, San Francisco, California.

Lauren B. LeRoy, C. Phil.
    Senior Research Associate, Assistant Director, Institute for Health Policy Studies, School of Medicine, University of California, San Francisco, California.

Stephen L. Markson, Ph. D.
    Assistant Professor, Department of Sociology, University of Hartford, West Hartford, Connecticut.

James C. Mohr
    Professor of History, University of Maryland and Stanford University, California.

C. N. Nair
    Chief, Institution Case Statistics, Health Division, Statistics Canada, Ottawa.

Constance A. Nathanson, Ph. D.
    Associate Professor, Department of Population Dynamics, The Johns Hopkins University, School of Hygiene and Public Health, Maryland.

Malcolm Potts, M. B. , B. Chir, Ph. D.
    Executive Director, International Fertility Research Program, North Carolina.

Niels Kr. Rasmussen
    Joint Center for Studies of Health Programs, Institute of Social Medicine, University of Copenhagen.

Mark Rutledge, M. Div. , Ed. D.
    Director, United Campus Ministry, University of New Mexico.

Paul Sachdev, Ph. D.
    Associate Professor, School of Social Work, Memorial University of Newfoundland, St. John's, Newfoundland.

Kenneth F. Schulz, M. B. A.
    Family Planning Evaluation Division, U. S. Department of Health and Human Services, Center for Health Promotion and Education, Centers for Disease Control, Atlanta, Georgia.

Patricia G. Steinhoff
    Professor of Sociology, University of Hawaii at Manoa, Honolulu.

L. W. Sumner
    Professor of Philosophy, University of Toronto, Ontario.

Christopher Tietze, M. D.
    Senior Consultant, The Population Council, New York City.

S. N. Wadhera
    Project Manager, Therapeutic Abortions Health Division, Statistics Canada, Ottawa.